On Television and Comedy

On Television and Comedy

Essays on Style, Theme, Performer and Writer

by
BARRY PUTTERMAN

McFarland & Company, Inc., Publishers
Jefferson, North Carolina, and London

British Library Cataloguing-in-Publication data are available

Library of Congress Cataloguing-in-Publication Data

Putterman, Barry.
    On television and comedy : essays on style, theme, performer and writer / by Barry Putterman.
      p.   cm.
    Includes index.
    ISBN 0-7864-0067-6 (sewn softcover : 50# alk. paper) ∞
    1. Television comedies—United States. I. Title.
PN1992.8.C66P88 1995
791.45'617—dc20
                                        94-44117
                                         CIP

Manufactured in the United States of America

McFarland & Company, Inc., Publishers
  Box 611, Jefferson, North Carolina 28640

It may be a kind of lunch-counter art, but then
art is so vague and lunch is so real.
                    —*Edwin Milton Royle*

Contents

Preface

One of the classic stories that emanated from those inevitable conferences of film academics had the romantic rebel of the avant-garde, P. Adams Sitney, giving a verbal presentation of a paper he had produced. After the presentation an audience member asked him how he would characterize the methodology used for his analysis. Sitney replied, "My methodology is called 'watching the films.'" I would like to think that my methodology in writing this book is firmly in the Sitney tradition. While I made frequent use of reference books, primarily Joel Eisner and David Krinsky's *Television Comedy Series* and Vincent Terrace's *Encyclopedia of Television*, I also made a conscious decision not to look at any of the previously written analytical books about television comedy while my work was in progress. Therefore, any similarity between my own critical conclusions and those of other writers on this subject, either living or dead, is purely coincidental.

Which is not to say that what you are about to read comes to you completely formed by my own individual consciousness. Every person's sensibility is a combination of that individual's perspective and the various influences that the surrounding society has had on them. I could not list all of the people who have made important contributions to the formation of my views on film, television, comedy, and life in general, but, I would like to single out three individuals for particular mention: Barry Gillam, Greg Ford, and Ronnie Scheib. And, beyond their general input to my thinking, I would like to thank each individually for the specific contributions they made to this book.

Through our ongoing partnership in sharing and trading videotapes, Barry Gillam made it possible for me to review many of the specific series episodes vital to the completion of my work. Without him, "watching the films" would have been a far less encompassing part of my methodology. Further, along with my sister Debbi Sambuco, Barry contributed significantly to making my physical manuscript actually look respectable.

Beyond his incisive comments on the work in progress, Greg Ford helped in the process of gathering the stills displayed in this book. He put me in contact with Virg Dzurinko and Eric Rachlis of Archive Photos who provided most of the hard-to-find pictures.

But mostly I want to thank Ronnie Scheib who constantly took time from her own writing projects to look through every chapter at each stage of development, tighten up the thinking, clarify the writing, and, in general, act as the necessary yin to my yang. Without Ronnie this book would never have been completed and I hope that someday I will be able to provide her with as much assistance as she provided me.

Introduction

Taking Comedy Seriously

This book is about exactly what it says it is about. It is about television: that vast wasteland, the idiot box, chewing gum for the mind. And it is about comedy: lightweight entertainment, frivolous escapism, fluffy trivia. How insignificant a subject can one find and still remain in the world of the arts?

In *Who Framed Roger Rabbit?*, the case is made that comedy in general and cartoons in particular exist exclusively to make us feel happy. They are the artistic equivalent of raindrops on roses and whiskers on kittens and we must honor and cherish the wonderment of it all for it would be a sin to kill a mockingbird.

This kind of condescension masquerading as glorification is typical of the suburban mall mentality of producer Steven Spielberg and his peers who have also managed to turn action/adventure, science fiction, and American history into their cinematic versions of theme parks. It would be nice to think that this view of comedy was the exclusive property of the world's collective Spielbergs, but it is really just the popular version of a classical refrain.

In his book about European directors in America during the 1920s, *Hollywood Destinies*, Graham Petrie spends a chaper analyzing the vision of F. W. Murnau. He describes Murnau's morality play ideology of country purity versus city corruption and concludes that Murnau's style of expressing thought visually was rejected by America as being too intellectually abstract.

In the next chapter Petrie describes the vision of Ernst Lubitsch. Here Petrie concludes that, since Lubitsch's ironic view of self-centered characters' reaching false conclusions through incomplete knowledge allows the characters to delude themselves into thinking that they have reached happy endings, Lubitsch has therefore compromised artistic integrity to conform to American mass taste. Then Petrie drags in a political manifesto drawn up by Betrand Russell and others calling for a wider social and sexual freedom with a particular emphasis on women's rights, and implies that Lubitsch is somehow remiss for not living up to these beliefs.

So why is it that Petrie feels it necessary to compare Lubitsch to an alien political standard when this same, but unmade, comparison would make Murnau look like a Muslim fundamentalist? Why is it that Lubitsch's "happy endings" secured only through the characters' smug self-delusions are seen as compromise while Murnau's fairy tale morality plays are badges of artistic integrity? Well, Lubitsch worked in comedy, so the audience is never forced to see what is being expressed beneath the surface lightness and hence that heretical compromise of allowing the audience to have a sinfully frivolous time.

My point here is not to judge the comparative merits of Murnau and Lubitsch but merely to indicate that comedy is a form with a history and tradition to match drama's, and the artists working within it are communicating ideas of equal profundity if in a different style of expression.

Both forms, comedy and drama, have certain built-in advantages, and artists of differing temperaments will find their styles fitting comfortably within one or the other. One of the major advantages that comedy has over drama, and that which dogmatists can claim is comedy's evasion of "reality," is the same advantage that painting has over photography and poetry has over prose: the innate capacity to express its viewpoint in a more stylized and figurative manner.

Unfortunately we live on a predominantly literal-minded planet and while the classical traditions of painting and poetry have all but caused them to build up a barrier to the point where they are now thought of as "intellectual arts," comedy has remained steadfastly plebeian. Most of the public and critical establishment are intimidated by the highfalutin reputations of painting and poetry and rather than trying to understand what these arts are expressing, many will simply mutter, "I know what I like." But everybody knows what is and isn't funny, and one thing funny isn't is profound. Or, to quote Caryn James about the film *Miracle Mile*, "the film is too funny and bizarre to be truly upsetting."

By and large only in its most blatantly social form, satire, is comedy ever given credit for meaning what it is saying. In terms of television this translates into a majority of honors going to such midcult gasbags as *All in the Family* and *M*A*S*H* which all but bracket off their little bromides in neon.

Aye, but television, there's the rub. Even among those hardy souls who take comedy seriously, few have any respect for the corporate, mass market medium of television. Like vaudeville, radio, movies, and pop records, television and its comedy suffer the slings and arrows both of the traditionalists who see it as a hamfisted vulgarization of *commedia dell'arte* and of the populists who see it as a homogenized commercialization of folk art. These approaches are essentially the same, the difference being whether you see mass culture as a betrayal of the few or of the many.

The majority of popular culture artists spend the prime of their careers being dismissed as shallow barbarians or cynical sellouts, only to be embalmed by the academy thirty years after the dangerousness of their immediacy has passed. Only now does it become safe (and indeed necessary) to construct a Rock-and-Roll Hall of Fame and pontificate about the artistic contributions of such former godless maniacs as Chuck Berry and Jerry Lee Lewis so that we can continue to seriously discuss censorship of present-day rockers.

And so it is that Jackie Gleason and Lucille Ball are similarly being bronzed and eulogized, while the recent vitality in television comedy can be found among the ignored (*The Comic Strip*), the patronized (*ALF*), and the ridiculed (*The Gorgeous Ladies of Wrestling*).

The essays that follow are not intended to form a rigorous history of television comedy, although a great deal of history needs to be recounted and put in perspective. By the same token, the topics of these essays are by no means the only subjects in television comedy worthy of discussion. A wide array of important and influential figures and programs, both fondly remembered (Nat Hiken, Sheldon Leonard et al.) and regrettably obscure (*Love on a Rooftop*, *Sledge Hammer*, etc.) deserve similar attention. The subjects of these essays are simply those which I find most remarkable.

I do not mean to imply that the history of television comedy is just one long round of artistic triumph. Much of what has passed before our eyes the past forty years is pretty much the theatrical realization of Groucho Marx's line about Chico in *Duck Soup*: "Gentlemen, Chicolini may talk like an idiot, and look like an idiot, but don't let that fool you. He really is an idiot." It is only because so little attention has previously been paid to the subject of television comedy that so much remains to be said.

PART I
Traditional

1
Defining Our
Television Heritage I
Traditional Television Values

"Preserving our television heritage" is the slogan of Nickelodeon, one of the cable networks. And, if haphazardly broadcasting a hodgepodge of chopped-up reruns were all there was to our television heritage, then we would indeed owe these businesspeople an enormous debt.

However, every one of the shows that they air, as well as all the shows that they do not air, belong to a vast interlocking complex of genre traditions, network decisions, artistic temperaments, and historical inevitabilities. While it is both aesthetically pleasurable and historically valuable to sit down and watch the shows that Nickelodeon broadcasts, it is a much more complicated task to understand their places within our television heritage.

The essays presented in this book attempt to define the people and programs that have influenced television comedy in terms of their positions within the complex of television history. The essays also describe how some individual artistic qualities both transcended and transformed that history.

Yet if you added up all of the historical placements of everything discussed in this book, you still would not have a coherent vision of our television heritage. Or, to put it in aphoristic terms, you would have a pretty fair-sized collection of trees but not a forest. It would take a book of much vaster proportions to present a satisfactorily well-rounded vision of television history, even if you limited it only to comedy.

This book is divided into two stylistic categories: traditional television comedy and modern television comedy. Traditional television comedy falls within the two basic traditional television forms—the variety show and the situation comedy. Situation comedy and variety formats existed and thrived in American performing arts before the invention of television, and the television versions of variety and sitcom adapted many elements from these earlier stage, radio, and motion picture incarnations. But in order to understand how the dynamics of the traditional situation comedy and variety show operated in this new medium, we must recreate their origins at the birth of network television itself.

Television has become such a matter-of-fact part of our daily lives that we hardly notice its subtle day-to-day changes, let alone remember what the medium looked like even a few short years ago. When the cable company A&E recently reran NBC's "as it was happening" coverage of President John F. Kennedy's assassination, it was shocking to encounter just how primitive that coverage had been in relation to the technological communication facilities we now take for granted. It was particularly astonishing for those of us who recall watching that coverage in 1963 but had since mentally transposed our memory of it into the mode of present-day news reporting. Resurrecting the television of our past is a bit like revisiting the house you grew up in: and to recreate the climate when network television first became firmly established in the late 1940s requires a leap of imagination beyond the most elaborate of historical explanations.

Much has been made of the motion picture industry's hostility towards television and its attempts to will the new medium into oblivion by refusing to produce any programming or provide any talent for it.

What has not been as thoroughly explored is how completely interdependent the film studios were with the radio networks. Cross plugging was common between movies and radio. Some very popular radio characters were transferred to the big screen, and many actors who began on radio went on to long careers in movies. But beyond this, the relatively slight need for rehearsal in radio (everybody simply stood around the microphone and read from their scripts) made it possible for well-known, studio contract film actors to also star in weekly radio series.

So while CBS, NBC, and even struggling ABC might have wanted to stock their new medium with established radio sitcoms, like *My Favorite Husband*, starring Lucille Ball and Richard Denning, *The Life of Riley* with William Bendix, or *Our Miss Brooks* with Eve Arden, they would have had to begun all over again with entirely new casts since none of these actors were prepared to give up their film careers for anything as risky as this new television. Neither were any of the highly popular radio variety show comedians, such as Jack Benny or Fred Allen, prepared to gamble that their established formats would transfer gracefully to a new medium.

As such, television simply had to forget about the established pools of nationally popular programs and actors in California. And, just as radio and the movies had done at the dawns of their histories, television began defining its identity from the ground up in New York and Chicago.

Another issue to consider was which corporations would be willing to take the risk of sponsoring television shows. The shocking revelation that corporations sponsor entertainment programs in order to further stimulate consumer buying is a wheel that is constantly being reinvented by television critics from Erik Barnouw to Mark Crispin Miller. From medicine shows to the renting of advertising space on vaudeville backdrop curtains to the current economics of dinner theater, in one form or another every artist in every medium has had to deal with the demands of commercial sponsorship.

Throughout the history of radio and on through the first decade of television, programming was pretty much controlled by the sponsoring companies. The companies bought a block of time on a given night and from year to year they would decide what kind of program featuring which artists would be presented. The program was calculated to appeal to the sponsor's market and the show's stars were often so closely identified with the sponsor's product that they appeared in its advertising both in and beyond the show itself.

The system was less monolithic in practice than it sounds in description. For example, *Martin Kane*, a 1950s television live-action adventure show, established a tobacco shop as a setting where the title character would frequently hang out. That setting was used to stage the final commercial with the show's actors beginning the spot in character and gradually turning to address the audience directly as the pitch progressed. In a filmed action-adventure show, the series' star would step out of character to introduce the teaser for the next week's episode; the end of the teaser would have the actor throwing in a final endorsement of the sponsor's product. In a filmed situation comedy, Lucille Ball and Desi Arnaz, for instance, might step out of character both at the beginning and end of each episode to make a pitch for the sponsor. Or, in a somewhat different mode, Phil Silvers and Maurice Gosfeld of *You'll Never Get Rich* might pose for a print ad for their sponsor as their Sergeant Bilko and Private Doberman characters.

In all of these cases, the commercials never became part of the storylines. In fact, the commercial presentations tended to underline the multiple roles of the actors as commercial spokespeople, fictional characters, and private citizens, thus ensuring a distanced and ambivalent message for the audience. The ways that commercial messages were structured into live variety shows not only varied in style, but were used by the performers as another strategy to define their relationship to the audience.

The level of sponsor interference with program content also varied. The entire system of single sponsoring a block of network time, however, was dealt a staggering blow when sponsor interference was so deeply implicated in the quiz show scandals of the late 1950s. A few years later, the system seemed to disappear completely because of the increasing costs of purchasing commercial television time. All that really happened, though, was yet another transmutation in the never-ending saga of commerce's marriage to the entertainment industry. For instance, instead of television programs, corporations now single sponsor major sporting events. And, while actors such as Candice Bergen and Angela Lansbury now sign up to be the commercial spokespeople for products like Sprint and Bufferin, the ads are written and performed as if the spokespeople were actually Murphy Brown and Jessica Fletcher.

Today, the series adventures of Murphy Brown and the commercial appearances of Candice Bergen appear as separate entities, but such was not the case for Bergen's father, who was one of radio's most popular variety show comedians. Many remember how phenomenally popular Edgar Bergen and his dummy Charlie McCarthy were on radio, but few recall that they were simply the mainstays of *The Chase and Sanborn Hour*. Similarly, Milton Berle, often referred to as television's first star, did not come to be known as Mr. Television on *The Milton Berle Show*, but as the host of *Texaco Star Theater*.

Since television was shut off from Hollywood's films and network radio shows, it was also shut off from their genre structures. New York's legitimate stage and nightclubs became the original forms and talent pools from which television operated. For example, *Texaco Star Theater* was fashioned along the lines of stage revues, like *Earl Carroll's Vanities* and *The Ziegfeld Follies*, featuring comedy sketches, musical production numbers, and solo singer spots.

In Berle's case live performance television on a theater stage gave him the opportunity to show a national audience what he did best. Berle was a veteran of the stage revues as well as the nightclub circuit for stand-up comedy. In a career dating back to the teens, Berle had also appeared in movies and on radio but had had limited success in the nationwide electronic media. His milieu was primarily performance in front of a live audience.

Berle's brand of broad stage farce was something that the television audience, which at the time was primarily in the eastern urban United States, could not get from movies or radio. *Texaco Star Theater* and Berle's enormous popularity are commonly credited with providing the consuming public with a compelling reason to buy a television set, and with providing television its first distinctly identifiable format.

Over the next few years, the revue variety format flourished on television. Shows such as *The Four Star Revue* (later called the *All-Star Revue*), *The Colgate Comedy Hour*, and *Cavalcade of Stars* gave veteran comedians, whose careers had been defined by success on the New York stage and sustained by popular success in radio (e.g., Eddie Cantor, George Jessell,

Ed Wynn, and Jimmy Durante), a natural setting to continue their nation-wide media careers. The revue variety format also propelled other per-formers, whose best medium was live performance but whose faces were even less familiar than Berle's, to national attention. Jackie Gleason first presented his wide array of characters while hosting *Cavalcade of Stars*; singer-monologist Danny Thomas was one of the four stars of *Four Star Revue*; and the only preservation of Dean Martin and Jerry Lewis' legend-ary stage work is from their many appearances on *The Colgate Comedy Hour*. One stage revue show, *Admiral Broadway Revue*, lasted only six months. The sponsor, Admiral television sets, found that once they began sponsoring this program, demand for their product was outstripping their manufacturing facilities. However, the core of that show, producer Max Liebman, writers Mel Tolkin and Lucille Kallen, and performers Sid Caesar, Imogene Coca, and Howard Morris, returned the following year to begin one of the longest lasting and most influential shows in this genre, *Your Show of Shows*.

The stage revue shows introduced all of the qualities of the New York theater performance style to a huge audience of people who had only known the nationwide media stylistics of movies and radio. While the ten-sion and energy generated by live performances from a parade of fresh, sophisticated acts provided a new sensation for the mass audience, these shows also transmitted formal qualities of theatrical presentation that were not as positive. The theater experience offers a much more distanced rela-tionship between the audience and the actors, emphasizing performance over personality. During the early stages of their histories, both movies and radio had also tried to maintain that theatrical distance but the mass audi-ence rebelled and defined their own more personal relationship with the performers which became known as "the star system." Star performers like Berle and Caesar emerged from the television stage revues just as stars had emerged from the previous Broadway revues, but the form always kept all of the performers working within an ensemble. The dramatic New York live television shows, such as *Armstrong Circle Theater* and *Philco Television Playhouse*, recreated the Broadway experience by becoming anthologies of different plays with different casts each week. *Texaco Star Theater* and *Your Show of Shows* recreated the Broadway experience by emphasizing the abundance of performers rather than the personal qualities of the stars. Broadway revue stars like Will Rogers and Eddie Cantor had to move on to movies and radio to further their careers. If the stage revue television shows were going to compete with movies and radio for a national au-dience, they too had to move on. The type of show with which they cross-bred also dates its history from the first years of network programming.

While the stars of the Hollywood radio comedy shows were un-available to television, other radio performers such as newsmen, disk jockeys, and talk show personalities, whose careers were not based in California, were very available. As radio performers, these people had already learned how to relate to a national audience. Further, within the genres that they worked, it was not so much a question of a more even balance between personality and performance. For them, personality all but was the performance. And just as the stage revues had Milton Berle, this mode of program had Arthur Godfrey.

Godfrey had come up through the South to join CBS's Washington, D.C. network station where he hosted news, talk, and entertainment programs. He brought with him a relaxed, informal style of speech marked by a conversational cadence and filled with personal, down-to-earth asides from the formal content of his shows which built on the work of daytime radio's Southern gentlewoman of convivial conversation, Mary Margaret McBride.

The appeal of a personality like Godfrey's was that he served as a kind of reassuring conduit between performer and audience. With his head in the world of news and show business but his heart with the folks in the audience, Godfrey translated entertainment and information into a form that was comfortable and familiar to the public. In *Arthur Godfrey's Talent Scouts*, one of Godfrey's *three* concurrently running television shows, established celebrities introduced aspiring show business newcomers to the viewing audience with Godfrey serving as convivial catalyst. His presence linked all of the participants together onto the same wavelength of comfort and respect.

Godfrey's counterpart in stage revue was Ed Sullivan, whose show, like Berle's and Godfrey's, began in 1948. Godfrey had come up through the American heartland doing human interest radio broadcasts. Sullivan was a born and bred New York celebrity newspaper columnist. Whereas Godfrey intermingled with and formed connections between everybody who appeared on his shows, Sullivan stood completely apart from the acts he presented.

Although Sullivan's was the only stage revue series to outlive its era and eventually became known as *The Ed Sullivan Show*, during the stage revue period, like every other show of its ilk, it did not have anybody's name in its title and was known as *Toast of the Town*. *Toast of the Town* was committed to presenting the very best, the most celebrated, most accomplished variety acts from around the world, secured for the audience through the auspices of that powerful New York writer—Ed Sullivan. It was *a really big show*.

Godfrey's main prime-time show, *Arthur Godfrey and His Friends*, like all of his shows, had his name in the title. This show did not present a new slate of top-flight acts every week, but featured a continuing cast of regular performers. Although some of his "friends" such as Julius La Rosa and

Dave Garroway and the stark, bare-staged intimacy of *Garroway at Large*.

The Chordettes went on to gain a measure of individual popular success,
the program was not designed to showcase exceptional performers. The
cast was presented as a "family" of performers who, like papa Godfrey,
staked their audience appeal as much on personal rapport as they did on
artistic talent.

Another area of contrast between Godfrey and the stage revue shows was in their approach to sponsorship. The sponsoring products often took the place of the star performer's name in the stage revue title and the star performer was never asked to participate in the sponsor's live on-air commercials. Just as the commercial backing of Broadway plays never intruded into the performances, the commercials within the stage revue shows (as well as the dramatic anthologies) were either filmed inserts dropped into the program or were handled live onstage by designated commercial spokespeople, such as Julia Meade on *Toast of the Town*, who appeared in no other part of the show. Godfrey not only handled his own commercial spots for Lipton soup and tea but treated them as particularly special moments during which he could share quality time with the audience. A performer who could actually pull off opening a show with a few minutes of aimless chit-chat about how difficult it had been to get to the studio through crosstown traffic, Godfrey would take the time during the demonstrations while the tea was brewing or the soup was heating to offer anecdotal evidence of how helpful and beneficial these products had been to himself and others.

Godfrey was a one-of-a-kind phenomenon but his highly personalized approach was not uncommon to performers who came from the South or Midwest. Chicago's Dave Garroway, for example, worked within the same format but with a totally different approach. During his disk jockey days, Garroway had bestowed the nickname "The Divine One" on Sarah Vaughan, but his own style was much closer in spirit to Peggy Lee. Deep-voiced and soft-spoken, Garroway's dry, subtle, clip-toned understated approach was the unaffected version of what would later become ritualized as the stock FM disk-jockey-style. His Chicago-based *Garroway at Large* reflected his personality and countered the New York theatrically distanced spectacular shows with a starkly intimate, regular cast performing on a bare stage. The show's stylized elements thus emphasized the camera's link between the performer and the viewer.

These two polarities—the frenetic New York stage revues and the easygoing heartland personality shows—were firmly in place when established Hollywood radio stars like Jack Benny and Red Skelton began switching over to television in the early 1950s. Thus, *The Jack Benny Program* and *The Red Skelton Show* were able to use elements from both structures to create the enduring star-driven variety show format. All the radio stars faced the task of translating their own particular established comedy style and series format from radio to television. The common denominator was that they all used a highly charged live stage performance featuring a continuing cast of audience-endearing personalities. For Benny, the cast consisted of his supporting players like Eddie "Rochester" Anderson and Don Wilson; for Skelton, it was sketches featuring his character creations like Clem Kadiddlehopper and Freddie the Freeloader.

The radio stars were also able to stake out a middle ground position in regards to sponsorship. On radio, they had been personally linked to the sponsor's product. As their personal rapport with the audience grew through the years, however, many stars become more important commodities than the products they represented. As such, they were able to integrate sponsoring messages into their programs and still keep an ironic distance from the process—a distance probably best summed up by Skelton's quip, "The longest word in the English language is the one that follows 'and now a word from our sponsor!'"

The successful establishment of the star-driven, family-friendly variety show by the radio stars also offered new opportunities to performers who had come up through the ranks of the two previous styles. Jackie Gleason left *Cavalcade of Stars* and began *The Jackie Gleason Show* which, like Skelton, featured continuing sketches with his character creations such as Joe the Bartender, Rudy the Repairman, and Ralph Kramden. And while Sid Caesar did not get a show with his name in the title until 1956, *Your Show of Shows* did develop continuous sketches for characters like the ever-arguing married couple Charlie and Doris Hickenlooper, and created a family out of the regular cast members Caesar, Coca, Morris, and Carl Reiner.

From the opposite style and in the Garroway tradition came George Gobel. Gobel had progressed through the midwest country and western circuit as a stand-up who offered quietly sardonic commentary through his wistful "little guy" persona. In the Godfrey tradition came Garry Moore. Moore, who had been Jimmy Durante's second banana in radio, offered a hipper collection of "friends," which included Carol Burnett.

At the same time radio's established variety comedians began moving over to television, many comic actors who dominated the radio sitcoms were also concluding that television was the wave of the future. First and foremost in this group was Lucille Ball. It was the comic approach and the stylistic format that she insisted on for *I Love Lucy* that not only established situation comedy on television, but also made it abundantly clear that TV was indeed the new center of popular culture art.

Although situation comedy existed on television prior to *I Love Lucy*, it was primarily in an awkwardly stage-bound form that would be unrecognizable today. When Ball agreed to take a chance on television, she insisted, over network objections, that her show needed the production values of film to capture the full range of her physical comedy plus the theatrical presence of an audience to duplicate the intensity of the revue variety shows. She and Desi Arnaz got Hollywood cinematographer Karl Freund to construct the three-camera set-up with studio audience format that freed television situation comedy from its stiff stage restraints. Thus, the filmed sitcom became the second traditional form of television comedy.

Beyond the formal qualities *I Love Lucy* was pioneering, Ball also established a tradition of female-dominated situation comedy that has survived in television to this day. The husband and wife comedy team was an established radio form which usually featured the husband as straight man for the wife's screwball verbal inversions of accepted normality. While George Burns and Gracie Allen are the pair that history has remembered, the *Easy Aces* (Goodman Ace and Jane Sherwood Ace) were equally popular on radio. Among many other such couples, Fred Allen interacted with his wife Portland Hoffa in much the same manner on his show. But by translating the relationship to an overtly physical form of comedy, *I Love Lucy* made the wife's creative imagination the dominant element of the show. Further, the manner in which Ball played the physical comedy established for television the continuation of a very short list of film comediennes (Mabel Normand, Constance Talmadge, Marion Davies, Carole Lombard, Ginger Rogers, occasionally Irene Dunne and Claudette Colbert) who could make the public accept the powerful image of a woman doing aggressively physical clowning while she still retained her sensual potency.

The astonishing popularity of *I Love Lucy* gave rise to a flood of female-dominated situation comedies. CBS opened its own production facilities in Hollywood in order to film radio-moveover *My Friend Irma* with Marie Wilson and *Meet Millie* with Elena Verdugo. Ball and Arnaz's own production comedy, Desilu, brought Eve Arden's *Our Miss Brooks* from radio and fashioned a sitcom for Spring Byington called *December Bride*. Ball's old radio sitcom *My Favorite Husband* was brought to television with Joan Caulfield now in the lead. Hal Roach studios attempted their own version of *I Love Lucy* with Gale Storm as *My Little Margie*. Motion picture stars Joan Davis and Ann Sothern entered television with *I Married Joan* and *Private Secretary*, respectively.

Just from the titles of these shows, it is evident that they wanted to be loved like Lucy. But *I Love Lucy* always remained the standard everyone else was measured against. Many of these shows and actresses matched Ball/Lucy in one comedic aspect or another, but none possessed Ball's particular combination of talents for such fast, fast comic relief.

Most closely approximating Ball's style of physical comedy were Joan Davis and Gale Storm.

My Little Margie was so clearly trying to associate itself with *I Love Lucy* that it even began its run as *Lucy*'s summer replacement. However, as the title indicates, Margie is actually the junior league version of Lucy. Indeed, as the daughter of a bachelor father, Margie is actually posited as the least sexually involved member of the family. Storm had spent the previous decade cultivating a minor film career, primarily as the peppy singing ingénue in Monogram musicals. Like Ball, Storm had the ability

Joan Davis demonstrates her dance with a chicken for housekeeper Hope Emerson in *I Married Joan*.

to pull comic faces while retaining the aura of sexual attractiveness. But physical clowning did not come naturally to Storm and her movements always seemed more mechanically directed than improvisationally inspired.

On the other hand, since the mid–1930s Joan Davis had been practicing a form of gracefully loose-limbed body gesture comedy that was almost musical in its cartoony intensity. In films, Davis always seemed to be living in the shadows of Martha Raye who had come to public attention about a year before she did. When *I Married Joan* debuted a year after

I Love Lucy, unfortunately it simply reinvented her situation on television vis-a-vis Ball. Further, like many male clowns, both Raye and Davis muted their sexuality by exaggerating the unconventional aspects of their physical appearances to fashion film images of self-deprecating plain Janes.

Ann Sothern and Eve Arden came from a more verbal tradition of film comedy. They were the wise-cracking, seen-it-all, done-it-all working women who heckled the nudniks within the plot and provided a running ironic analysis of both their own and everybody else's emotional status throughout the progressing story. Pictured as the most intellectually accomplished characters in the story, they would usually have to remain sexually isolated in order to allay societal fears both of intellectuality, in general, and intimidatingly analytical females, in particular. (Ball had often been among their ranks during her film career and she forged close connections with both women on television. Not only did Desilu produce *Our Miss Brooks* but, when she was not working with Vivian Vance, Ball often teamed with Ann Sothern.) On their respective television shows, English teacher Connie Brooks (Arden) and all-purpose office manager Susie McNamara (Sothern) ran rings around the hopelessly timid teaching colleague and ego-inflated employer with whom they were paired. But no matter how creatively they were able to swing the spotlight back over to these males, they were always left alone with their competence at episode's end.

The sharp-tongued working women and creative clown shows all possessed a level of energetic theatricality that roughly corresponded to the stage revue branch of the variety show. The quieter, simpler, personality as performance branch found its equivalent in the suburban family shows. The spiritual father to this mode of sitcom presentation was Ozzie Nelson.

During the swing era, Nelson led a popular dance band which featured vocalist Harriet Hilliard, who soon became his wife. In 1941, Ozzie, Harriet, and the band were featured on Red Skelton's radio show. On radio variety shows, many bandleaders, and often their vocalists, were characters within the shows themselves. Some of the bandleaders became more popular as comic characters than as musicians. The most popular comedian/band leader, Phil Harris from *The Jack Benny Program*, was spun off onto his own show, a situation comedy about his home life with his wife, singer Alice Faye. And, in 1944, Ozzie and Harriet were given their own radio sitcom with the same premise.

The show-business-couple-at-home theme, established by George Burns and Gracie Allen, was not uncommon in radio situation comedy. And, Burns and Allen took it along with them when they moved over to television. *I Love Lucy* belonged to the same genre to the extent that Desi Arnaz was a well-known bandleader and the public understood that

Lucille Ball was his wife. The fact that the Arnazes had fictional names on their show only heightened the level of theatricality they brought to television situation comedy.

When *The Adventures of Ozzie and Harriet* moved to television in 1952, it continued to chronicle the home life of the entire Nelson family. Neither during the media changeover nor at any other time during its long television run did the show reestablish its origins in the show-biz-family-at-home genre. Thus, many viewers who were unfamiliar with the show's origins did not know what Ozzie did for a living and could not understand why he was always at home. Downplaying the Nelsons' show business background, however, was part and parcel with Ozzie's interest in detheatricalizing the show and emphasizing comedy which grows out of the home life of a more universally identifiable family structure.

In the Nelson family, Ozzie was the comic center, the character prone to childish enthusiasms and irrational attachments. This was an unexpected reversal for audiences who were familiar with the original show-biz couple format as well as all the variations that *I Love Lucy* inspired. Television audiences were not used to seeing the man of the house behave this way. Many episodes were dominated by verbal interplay as Ozzie offered all kinds of justifications as to why, for instance, it was important for the family to get the new toy being offered on a television kids' show for the educational enlightenment of children David and Ricky Nelson. And it was the Nelsons' approach to dialogue, an extremely naturalistic, quietly conversational style full of hesitations and digressions in which the punchlines were spoken in the same off-handed tone as the small talk, that distinguished *The Adventures of Ozzie and Harriet* from the more theatrically charged sitcoms of the period.

The low-key casualness of the Nelsons' behavior tended to hide the many wacky elements of the show from its insistence on the word "adventures" in the title of this most placid of series to the almost mind-boggling reversals of the fictional and factual Nelsons during the introductions ("Here's Ozzie who plays the part of Ozzie Nelson. Here's Harriet who appears as Harriet Nelson" etc.). But it was the naturalistic tone and the suburban setting that later shows used to create the middle-class family sitcom genre. Ozzie's premise of the father figure as the most comically childish member of the family was also abandoned as the shows that became the touchstones in this genre, *Father Knows Best* and *Leave It to Beaver*, veered sharply towards moralistic patriarchy.

Indeed, the images of *Father Knows Best* and *Leave It to Beaver* have become so overwhelmingly dominant as representative of the era that Ozzie's original approach as well as later variations within the form have all but been lost to history. Just as the variations on *I Love Lucy* tended to mute the sexual image of the female comic center, so the variations on the

The entire Nelson family (from top to bottom), David, Ozzie, Harriet, and the irrepressible Ricky, in *The Adventures of Ozzie and Harriet.*

family in the suburbs would make the paternal figure more ambivalent by increasing his sexual availability in such shows as *The Bob Cummings Show* (a.k.a. *Love That Bob*) and *Bachelor Father*.

By the end of the 1950s, many of the basic structures of the traditional forms were firmly in place and functioning smoothly. The 1960s became a decade of experimentation—trying out variations on existing themes and recombinations of established elements.

In fact, the traditional variety show all but became extinct in the early 1960s. The gradual shift in production techniques from live shows broadcast from New York to videotaped shows from Hollywood drained much of the vitality from the format without substituting a new aesthetic that could take advantage of those changing conditions. Further, as rock-and-roll emerged as the now-dominant form of mainstream pop music, the established shows, which were steeped in the sound of big band music, could find no way to co-exist with the new rhythms. It was not until shows like *Shindig* and *The Monkees* established presentational modes for rock-and-roll that interest in variety shows began to revive. By the end of the 1960s, a new wave of variety shows like *Rowan and Martin's Laugh-In* and the second *Andy Williams Show* had developed new strategies for using videotape to their comedic advantage.

In terms of sitcoms, every possible variation on the family-in-the-suburbs show was attempted and a few of those attempts actually succeeded. There was the animated family (*The Flintstones*), the horror family (*The Addams Family, The Munsters*), the fantasy family (*Bewitched*), the country family goes to the city (*The Beverly Hillbillies*), the city family goes to the country (*Green Acres*) . . . the list goes on and on towards the vanishing horizon. The 1970s saw the last major aesthetic innovations within the traditional sitcom form. *The Mary Tyler Moore Show* redirected the female-dominated sitcom towards low-key naturalism, and *All in the Family* re-directed the family sitcom towards highly charged theatricality.

The traditional forms have been spinning their wheels since the mid–1970s. And, with few exceptions, all of the most vital and creative work in television comedy since then can be found outside of their parameters. This does not mean that the traditional forms cannot make a comeback. Nor can all of the remarkable accomplishments they have already established be negated.

2
Jack Benny and the
Surrealism of the Ordinary

As the star-spangled hype machine drones turgidly onward for the 1990s' latest comedy "genius" Garry Shandling, the continuing debate about the originality of *It's Garry Shandling's Show*'s format has at least helped to refocus attention on the most profoundly creative and influential of television comedy's originators, Jack Benny. For like the Griffiths and Stroheims of motion pictures' first generation of artists, Benny's status has now settled into that of a revered icon whose work, like a child being given a pat on the head, is routinely praised but rarely examined.

Perhaps one of the reasons why Benny and his work no longer draw attention, is that, unlike most of television comedy's pioneer innovators (e.g., Steve Allen, Lucille Ball, Ernie Kovacs), Benny and his format were not new to the audience when they were first viewed on television. Benny is more often cited as having been an innovative force in radio since he not only made the jump from radio to television, but also from vaudeville to radio—a jump considered by many to be even more difficult.

Vaudeville was always treated as the legitimate theater's working-class poor relation, even though the manner in which actors forged their relationship with the audience used the same set of dynamics in both forms. In the theater, a broad range of material and a wide variety of performance styles were permissible because each separate audience constituted a small group of people who had made the very conscious decision to see this one particular show. The advent of mass market electronic media (first movies, then records, finally radio) changed these dynamics.

Among the electronic mediums, radio most closely patterned itself on the structure of vaudeville. But the air waves were free (assuming you only wanted to listen to them), and performance styles had to be designed for an audience that was no longer a room full of consciously focused local people, but an entire nation of casually window-shopping listeners who had no specific idea of what they wanted to hear. In comedy, much of the more hard-edged material and many of the more exotic regional styles and attitudes had to be abandoned or at least modified in order to fit into what emerged as the two generalized styles (east coast urbanization and mid-west small town) that translated well on the national medium.

One style—the view of the outsider looking in, or, for the more politically oriented, looking from the bottom up—is often mistakenly stereotyped as New York and Jewish, but is actually more generally urban east coast and immigrant ethnic. Recent newcomers to an urban, cacophonous culture, these comic figures are constantly being reminded of their alien status. The comic personas from this camp usually fell into one of two types: the loud, aggressive puncturers of the established culture's pretensions and arrogance who are looking to push themselves by force onto the culture, or, poor innocent victims of said culture longing to be helped into the "family of America" by sympathetic onlookers. Groucho Marx might be considered the prototype of that first character; and, although he was not born in this country, Charlie Chaplin the prototype of the second.

The other dominant national style was small town and midwestern in origin and confidently within the societal power structure in perspective. The tone here is quiet and ironic, an all-inclusive self-deprecating look at our culture's foibles, blind spots, and excesses from one of its own valued members who has the added perspective of being able to interpret the view in the mirror. Like most Southerners who found it necessary to adapt to this style, Will Rogers mixed in a kind of down-home earthiness and created the mold that most others tried to fill.

There is considerable range within the two styles; an interesting midwestern sub-stratum of multiple impersonations of gothic folk types can be traced from Red Skelton through Jonathan Winters to Lily Tomlin for instance. But it was Jack Benny, the Jew from Waukegan, Illinois, who was able to combine the ethnic outsider with the comfortably native social figure to create a character of stunning complexity: both victimizing instigator and reactive victim, comic monster and audience surrogate, oppressor, and schlemiel.

Other seminal figures mixed elements of the two styles. For instance, Benny's longtime friend and closest comedy colleague George Burns developed a delivery for his New York street-smart irony that was as cool, dry, and quiet as any midwesterner. Burns made his material stylistically compatible by setting it in the one area of life where he was an insider, show business. Show business as metaphor for life served Burns brilliantly. But Benny's character and approach to the show business metaphor were even more universal in their flexibility of application because he tapped into something very deep in the national psyche: the insecure giant.

Rejecting a rigid, pre-ordained caste system, the promise of American life was that the value of every individual would be defined externally by how far he or she rose within the fluid competition of a diverse and pluralistic society. But this model, like all models, proved to produce more ambiguous results in practice. Rising within the society turned out to have as much to do with chance, luck, and chicanery as it did with achievement. This haphazard mixture of the personal and the impersonal left the individual with ambivalence and uncertainty about his or her individual redemption.

Benny's character captures all of this. He is the boss of *The Jack Benny Program* (everyone else in show business has a "show"; Jack Benny has a "program"), yet his every thought and action is designed to prove over and over again that he is an important enough person to exist in this world. He presides over a collection of eccentric, specialized subordinates all unambitiously satisfied in the narrow focus of their functions. For example, there is the enthusiastic and jovial announcer Don Wilson, the sardonic and subversive servant Rochester, and the optimistic and child-like singer Dennis Day. All of them are anxious to support Benny within the limits of their capabilities. But Benny continually sabotages them, and therefore himself, with his obsessive need to have his vanity and authority reassured. While he continually conspires to have all emotional and monetary gratification shower down on himself, he never realizes that it is impossible to filter out any of the antipathy that accompanies so much attention. Thus, he is constantly drowning in a downpour of abuse.

Further, his total self-absorption makes him completely unprepared for anybody outside of his immediate circle. He is continually surprised to find that there are people who are either offended by his megalomania (e.g., James and Gloria Stewart, who object to Jack double-dating with them on their wedding anniversary, or Andy Williams, who resents having his brief trip for groceries turn into a p.r. performance at Jack's supermarket opening), or who are just like him, obnoxiously guarding their own isolated patch of turf. This complete self-concentration leaves Benny in utter ignorance of the world around him and it is the almost child-like helplessness of his reactions that opens the door for audience sympathy when his over-inflated ego inevitably blows up.

All of this was already in place when television entered the scene. By the time it became inevitable that television would do to radio what motion pictures had done to vaudeville, it was assumed that Benny and all of radio comedy's stars would simply pack up their shows and move them over to the visual tube.

But television proved to be more than just radio with pictures. The dynamics of how the performer related to the audience changed in subtle and unpredictable ways. Television combined differing aspects of radio

Jack Benny with his offscreen wife and onscreen girlfriend Mary Livingstone, and Eddie Anderson who was so closely identified with his onscreen role as Benny's manservant that "Rochester" became his middle name.

and motion pictures, and transplanted radio shows had to find ways to make the adjustments.

Like most radio comedy stars, Benny had made intermittent forays into movies. But neither he nor his colleagues, with the exceptions of that singular phenomenon Bob Hope and, to a lesser extent, Red Skelton, had had much success. Indeed, these futile attempts to take performers whose popularity is based on playing the same character in the same setting every week and thrust them onto the public in completely new and undefined feature film roles continues to the present. In retrospect, it might have made more sense for radio comedians to have tried their hands at the continuous series two-reelers, à la The Three Stooges, since this was the motion picture format that television would most closely come to resemble.

Two-reelers were dominated by the contrasting philosophies of the field's two major rival forces: Mack Sennett and Hal Roach. Sennett's films featured emblematic caricatures being driven at high speed into death-struggle competition for the satisfaction of elemental appetites and urges. Roach presented highly individuated and eccentric characters meticulously failing at small, ordinary tasks and sharing their frustrations with the audience.

It was Roach's model, particularly as practiced by Laurel and Hardy, that became the motion picture foundation of television comedy. In many ways all of television comedy comes out of Laurel and Hardy. Both as individuals and as a team, their styles can be seen as major influences on comedians as disparate as Jackie Gleason and Tom Smothers. But it is the way in which they developed their rapport with the audience that became the key to how weekly television comedy would work. And, of all of the originators of television comedy, Benny most intelligently applied the Roach/Laurel and Hardy approach to series television.

Benny's relaxed, conversational delivery was already in place when he entered television. Thus, the development of a slow-paced visual style dependent on medium two-shots and with close-ups that could become so jarringly frequent that they almost destroyed basic narrative rhythm, were a natural extension of his verbal style. And, it was Benny's appeal for audience sympathy with his stricken disbelief in these close-ups, like Laurel's bewildered incomprehension or Hardy's contemplative exasperation in theirs, that bonded the performer to the audience as the mutual victims of the surrounding mayhem. In truth, Benny's character was petty and mean-spirited, just as Laurel and Hardy's were perverse and sadistic, and the characters and events which plagued him were the natural extensions of his own shortcomings. But this strategy of forming a very direct bond with the audience threw everything into double reflecting, making Benny the rational exception to a grotesque world.

This long, direct contact between performer and audience not only melted the emotional distance between them, but also called into question any kind of philosophic or psychological distance as well. Laurel and Hardy, and most of the television comedians that followed them, rarely acknowledged this temptation to what has come to be called "break the fourth wall." In radio, where it was assumed that the home audience was creating its own artificial reality based on what it was hearing, comedians continually referred to the artifice of their studio setting, particularly in variety shows. But when that artifice became literalized by television photography, the situation reversed itself and it was the comedians who found it necessary to suspend their disbelief in order to maintain the audience's illusion of reality. Years later audiences were prepared to accept television formats that examined their own artifice, but during the 1950s it was considered destructive to the "come into my parlor" relationship developing between performer and audience.

Nonetheless, Benny, whose basis was the merging of opposites, was able to use his audience rapport to posit a format where the elements of his onstage, backstage, and home lives merged into one extended, consistent space. This space was filled with all of the same characters moving at will from one aspect of one world to another and carrying their exact same personas everywhere they went. Like the merging of east coast and midwest styles and the dual role of monster antagonist and audience surrogate, the blending of these normally distinct spaces was presented in such a seamless, matter-of-fact way that the normality of this surrealistic world view never became an issue for the audience.

Yet as striking as Benny's normality of surrealism was, even more stunning was the way his show turned normality into surrealism through that other pillar of weekly programming, repetition.

For most people, the flow of daily life through work with colleagues at the job site and home with family and friends is a constant circle of the same activities with the same people. To help keep these familiar situations comfortable and friendly, most people develop internal jokes, phrases, and gestures in order to put an individual spin on their own little slice of monotony. The introduction of the weekly radio, and then television, show provided many the opportunity to expand and dramatize their individualized monotony and also to glamorize it by linking it to the magic of show business by tuning in regularly and making medium part of their "family."

For example, many aspects of Benny's show, such as his cheapness, his bad violin playing, his vanity about the blueness of his eyes, his constant age of 39, and his catch phrases as "Well," and "Now cut that out!" fulfilled the audience's desire for the repeating motifs that would make it as familiar and friendly as the rest of the viewer's life. But on another level, Benny was using repetition to undermine the entire concept of familiarity. On one hand he would use repetition to link completely disparate ideas which formed chains of thought that sounded familiar but actually made no sense whatsoever. On the other hand he would use repetition so insistently that it would progress from being comfortably familiar into a fanatic nightmare of frustrating stalemate.

A simple example of the former concept can be seen in an episode where Dan Duryea guest stars. As was his wont, Dennis Day came out on stage to interrupt Benny's monologue. During the course of their exchange, Benny got off a joke about how Day's mother had thrown Duryea out of his dressing room. Then, during the ensuing gangster movie sketch, after the dressing room joke had long been disgarded, Duryea made reference to his tough guy scar. Day piped in that Duryea got the scar when his mother threw him out of the dressing room. Because Benny had gotten the audience to accept that there is a continuity between backstage and onstage life, his viewers accepted that the same joke could continue from one space to the other. But the repetition out of logical context still induced surprise for the audience and frustration for Benny who reacted with the expected, "Now cut that out!" as his authority was once again undermined.

A complex example of the second concept is the way in which the Benny show employed its semi-official recurring presences such as Frank Nelson and Mel Blanc. The function of semi-regulars in comedy shows is somewhat akin to that of star soloists in musical groups. Spots are picked within the flow of events for everything to stop and allow these people to get up, express their own idiosyncratic interpretation of the narrative, and then sit down again to let the flow continue. Like good musical soloists their voices, approaches, and individual mannerisms are immediately recognizable, and part of the pleasure of their turn is to once again fall under the spell of their very particular and familiar view of the world.

On a sitcom this spot will be taken by a continuing character such as William Sanderson as Larry on *Newhart*. On a variety show it will be one of the members of the troupe who will pop up in different guises along the route, such as Tim Conway on *The Carol Burnett Show* or Carol Burnett on *The Garry Moore Show*. *The Jack Benny Program* blended sitcom with variety show and so created a blended function for these comics where they would appear over and over again in different roles, but playing the same character.

The use of Nelson in this manner was particularly effective. No matter what kind of service Benny would need in any given episode, up would pop Nelson with his elongated "Yeees." And, Benny would give a stunned "You again" reaction. Once Nelson turned up as Benny's waiter asking him whether he wants male or female oysters. Benny wanted to know how Nelson could tell their sex. Nelson answered, "Easy, we check their drivers' licenses." This version of condescension and humiliation masquerading as humble service gave not only the pleasure of its familiarity but also became its reverse: the repeating nightmare of a boogeyman you run away from over and over again but who always seems to find you wherever you go.

Many of these major motifs can be seen at work in the episode about Benny's impending train trip to meet with his sponsor in New York. The episode opens with Benny and Rochester packing for the trip and discussing Benny's New York accommodations at the Acme Plaza Hotel, where he will get the basement penthouse "underlooking the park." After a few more "fleabag hotel" gags Benny defends all of the improvements that the Acme Plaza has made, such as no longer having to stand in line to take a bath because they have now installed a bench. Then Benny gets a seemingly unrelated phone call from plump, loud, semi-hysterical Muriel Landers, giving an unending string of instructions to her fiancé Chuck while a stunned Benny listens mutely, unable to tell her that he isn't Chuck.

Jack and Rochester resume packing and hear loud banging on the pipes from the upstairs wash basin where the plumber is working. When Benny goes up to ask him to muffle the noise, the audience finds Mel Blanc playing one of the bitter and sarcastic workmen that always seem to plague Benny. The plumber suggests that Benny put his head between the hammer and the pipe to muffle the noise, and offers a few other choice observations before Benny retreats to the lower level to take another monologue phone call of instructions for Chuck—this time with Landers detailing their elopement plans. When the plumber finally finishes his work, Benny asks him to send the bill to the Acme Plaza Hotel. Here viewers get the first instance of Benny's surreal idea linkage from disconnected spaces as the plumber mentions that he has done work for the Acme Plaza Hotel—not plumbing but installing a bench.

The scene then shifts to the railroad station. Vaudeville performers spent a lot of time in railroad stations during their careers, and throughout his radio and television work, Benny was able to use the seemingly random convergences of people and off-space public address announcements at the railroad station as the focus of some of his best material.

This sequence opens with the announcement of Benny's classic train for Anaheim, Azusa, and Cucamunga, which in this instance is being held indefinitely (Definitely being situated two miles east of Cucamunga), and then asks that the holder of a particular baggage check report to the ticket agent to pick up the turkey he has just won.

Since information is clearly not the strong point of this station, it is inevitable that Benny encounters another of his semi-regular tormentors behind the information counter. Here it is Benny Rubin, who answers every question Jack puts to him with "I don't know." Every question, that is, except why is he so stupid, which produces a long complicated medical explanation to which Benny asks, "Is there a cure?" and Rubin answers, "I don't know."

This stream of public information announcements is interrupted by a personal information announcement: Landers tells Chuck that she has arrived at the station and is waiting for him with the ten thousand dollars for their honeymoon. This, of course, momentarily convinces Benny that he is Chuck. But Chuck turns out to be the plumber, who explains that he was delayed in getting to the station "by some jerk who had a leaky water basin."

Benny is now ready to board the train but at the last minute is told that somebody else is already in his compartment. He must quickly get this straightened out with the ticket agent, who is the *coup de grace*—Frank Nelson. Amidst the insults, Nelson has given Benny's compartment away to somebody named Chuck who is eloping with Nelson's daughter.

Benny finally persuades Nelson to give him another compartment. When Benny asks if he will have to later change trains, Nelson replies, "Oh, indubitably. Dubitably is two miles east of Definitely." This naturally brings on a "Now cut that out!" from Benny.

Finally, as Benny struggles to pull away from the counter to catch his train, Nelson asks to see his baggage ticket in order to move his luggage to the new compartment. Nelson finds that Benny has the winning ticket, hands him a live turkey, and Benny dashes off, turkey in hand, to catch up with the most logical linkage of a chaotic train of thought you will ever see.

The influence of Benny's strategies and structures on the history of television comedy has been enormous both in the traditionalist sense of creating a more complex character by blending styles, and in the modernist sense of creating a surreal normality by blending spaces and repeating ideas in unexpected ways.

Jackie Gleason, the most prolific and influential of television's first generation of traditionalist east coast comedians, created many memorable characters who were either aggressive outsiders (Charlie Bratten, Rudy the Repairman) or pathetic societal victims (Fenwick Babbitt, The Poor Soul). But it was only when Gleason was able to blend the two tendencies that he was able to create a character of lasting complexity in Ralph Kramden. Through Kramden the mold for the east coast sitcom *The Honeymooners* was set, a mold that has been carboned *ad infinitum* by such "originals" as *The Flintstones* and *All in the Family.*

As for the current "original" modernist, that favorite of the yuppie-schluppie television reviewers, Garry Shandling, on closer inspection turns out to have more in common with fellow Arizonian Steven Spielberg than with Jack Benny. Like Spielberg, Shandling seizes the popular forms of earlier eras claiming to celebrate them but actually to use them as a cover for resurrecting the discredited social values and attitudes from their time periods. Whereas Benny worked against his natural niceness to create a character that nakedly exposed and examined so much that is childlishly insecure and selfish in our culture, Shandling affects a "gosh gee wiz" innocence to mask his fear and loathing of women.

Shandling used the 1950s Benny Burns stylistics to trot out the kind of stereotypical female images that were accepted in that era. His parade of "comic" gargoyles was led by Jennifer Tilly, doing her dopey, innocent child-woman schtick in a two-parter, but also included the sweet young thing who turns into a bon-bon munching slovenly shrew as soon as she marries Shandling, the "unladylike" rebelliously aggressive date who tries to devour the chaperone, the dumb-as-dirt blonde whose greatest pleasure is watching reruns of *Gilligan's Island,* and on into the horrific night. Shandling even managed to literally recreate that misogynist milestone of the late 1960s, *The Graduate.* To paraphrase Secretary of the Treasury Lloyd Bentsen, Garry Shandling is no Jack Benny.

Benny's list of achievements is staggering and his influence is being felt even more strongly today than it was ten or fifteen years ago. In the early 1950s, Benny continued doing his radio show during the first few years of his television career. He opened one of these early television shows by coming out on stage and apologizing for being a bit late: "But I was backstage listening to my radio show and, gee, I was so *good*." It was Benny's genius for understanding and examining the reasons why his character felt the need to say that which made him so *good*.

3
The Boys
of Benny and Burns

Dobie Gillis, Green Acres,
The Bob Newhart Show, *and* Newhart

Jack Benny and George Burns—their names have become so intertwined that those of short or casual memory may even think that at one time they had been a comedy team. Stylistically they had more in common than other names which have become similarly meshed (e.g., John Ford and Howard Hawks, The Beatles and The Rolling Stones). But the reason why their names became linked is that within their art forms they defined an approach, an attitude, an era during which each member of the duo became the alternative stylistic poles of excellence.

Beyond the brilliance of their own work, Benny and Burns laid a foundation of structural and intellectual ideas which came to be adopted by some of the most creative shows in television comedy history. Among those innovative shows are: *Dobie Gillis* from the late 1950s through the early sixties, *Green Acres* from the mid–1960s to the early 1970s, and Bob Newhart's *The Bob Newhart Show* and *Newhart* from the early 1970s to the present.

Both Benny and Burns came to television from the world of radio comedy. While many of their colleagues were unable to find their footing in the transition to television, Benny and Burns not only survived but continued to flourish in the new medium. In television they found that the off-the-cuff, format-busting flights of fancy allowable in the "mind's eye" world of radio had to be abandoned due to the visually concrete limits the television camera placed on the viewer's imagination. In an odd way the confinement that these comedians found in the supposedly "opened up" visual world of television paralleled the constrictions silent movie directors found at the dawn of the talking pictures era.

In television Benny and Burns found their format selection limited to the rigidly regularized choices of the sketch-song and monologue variety show, or the same character in the same setting situation comedy. Both Benny and Burns circumvented the deadlock by creating shows that blended various aspects of both formats.

Through the subtle application of film techniques and the force of his own physical presence, Benny was able to translate his radio format to television. He blended his home life (situation comedy), his onstage life (variety show), and his backstage life (a no-man's-land between them) into a single, integrated world with the same characters, situations, and jokes wandering back and forth between the spaces.

Burns, and his inseparable, irreplaceable wife/partner Gracie Allen, could not literally translate their vaudeville-based comedy routines into a television format. They had to work from the ground up to reinvent the wheel. They did this by starting out with a Lucille Ball–styled sitcom which was pretty much *The Adventures of Gracie Allen* as Gracie dragged a cast of mildly neurotic or helplessly sane characters through her wonderland of Chico Marxian logic. Then, weaving in and out of this came *Commentary with George Burns*, featuring George in stand-up monologue, by turns serving as fatalistic philosopher, show-biz historian, and television critic. This combination created an ironic, deconstructive counter-current to the conventions of television sitcoms.

Benny and Burns were working the opposite ends of the same ideas. By concentrating on the blending of forms, Benny's model was more subtle, appearing to be exceedingly normal and matter-of-fact with the complexity of its surrealism only becoming apparent when you stopped to reflect on it. By concentrating on the parallel splits between forms, Burns' model was more modernist, drawing attention to the artifice in the theatrical presentation of normality. They were both setting up a structure in which they were, at the same time, both the center of their show's attention, and the behavioral exception to the way the rest of the cast interacted with each other. As such, the worlds of the Benny and Burns shows came to resemble a wheel with them as the isolated figures in the center, the hubs that defined the spokes' movement by their own stasis.

Benny and Burns define a comic approach for television just as Lucille Ball and Desi Arnaz defined the three-camera setup physical comedy sitcom, Jackie Gleason defined the working-class family sitcom, and Ernie Kovacs defined the TV version of free-associative conceptual modernist comedy. To a great extent, everything that followed has been a variation on these four themes, adapting them to the relevant circumstances of the times and the specific interests of the particular artists involved.

All four of these structures were in place by the end of television's first epoch—dated from the medium's inception to its first turning point in 1958, the year, not coincidentally, of Gracie Allen's retirement.

In 1958, Blake Edwards' *Peter Gunn* and, to a lesser extent, Roy Huggins' *77 Sunset Strip* brought elements of cool, white, west coast jazz into the private-eye genre. These shows changed the stylistics of the entire medium and made television safe for the inception the following year of its first "hip" sitcom, *The Many Loves of Dobie Gillis*.

Dobie's literary father was Max Shulman, who, like Jack Benny, was a Jew from the midwest, specifically Minneapolis. And, like fellow Minnesotan Sinclair Lewis, Shulman sardonically depicted an America of shallow, materialistic values divided between the many conformists who are half-consciously suffering from a spiritual impoverishment that they can't define, and the few well-intentioned but pretentious and half-educated rebels who are freezing in social isolation.

Shulman's Dobie Gillis stories already had lives on stage and screen before they came to television, but in neither case was the stinging, cartoony social satire of Shulman's writing retained. However, in the unlikely medium of television, as producer/director Rod Amateau structured the series along Benny/Burns principles, the most authentic and consistently satisfying version of Shulman's vision was produced.

Amateau had scored a major success directing *The Bob Cummings Show* during the mid–1950s. It featured Cummings as a libidinous fashion photographer who was forever falling into tickle-and-tease sexual complications with his shapely models while his teenage cousin Chuck (Dwayne Hickman) looked on admiringly. Amateau went on to direct the final seasons of *Burns and Allen* where he instituted the show's *coup de grace* of surrealism, the Tex Avery time warp structure in which George keep abreast of the ongoing plot developments by watching the progressing episode on his upstairs television set between his own appearances in the plot.

On becoming the producer/director of *The Many Loves of Dobie Gillis*, Amateau combined elements of both *Burns and Allen* and *The Jack Benny Program* to create a radically unique structure for an ensemble cast situation comedy. As Dobie, Dwayne Hickman played a version of Chuck stripped of *The Bob Cummings Show*'s smarmy illusions of easy access to beautiful women. Dobie speaks to the audience directly while at his favorite spot in the town park next to the statue of Rodin's The Thinker a la George Burns. But he speaks not with the Burnsian conspiratorial detached amusement at how the conformist world attempts to pacify his wife's wild whims, but rather in tones both furiously exasperated and whiningly pleading with his only potential allies in a world conspiring to frustrate his ambitions.

Dobie's problem, as he explains continuously, is that he loves girls but to get girls you need money and to get money you have to work. In his own way Dobie has discovered the Iron Triangle of the American Dream: power=money=sex. In a culture consumed with commerce, love has become the ultimate status possession and "Dobie has to have a girl to call his own." But for Dobie, the son of a working-class grocer, power is not given and since he is not particularly bright or ambitious, his alternative is to become selfish, sneaky, underhanded and cunning, in short, the young American go-getter, the embryonic Jack Benny.

Towards this end, Hickman as Dobie picks up many of Benny's mannerisms: the arms folded in both guarded repose and waspish resolve or wildly flailing in moments of exasperation, the little head nod with smirky self-satisfied smile and widened eyes after getting off a good line, the contemplative "hmmmmm" while being apprised of his present situation, and, of course, the ever-popular "Now cut that out!" when the conversation careens wildly out of his control.

The conversation often speeds beyond Dobie's power since one of the show's most aggressive innovations was its fast-paced, almost sing-songy speech pattern somewhat reminiscent of Preston Sturges. This stylization of speech, often underscored by soundtrack musical dots and dashes, is one of the main approaches by which the society in *Dobie Gillis* affirms its collective belief in the sex, money, power triumvirate and also each member's individually immobile place within the society's hierarchy.

Throughout the show's first and probably best season Dobie was hopelessly stuck on one girl, Thalia Menninger. Thalia, played by Tuesday Weld, is a kooky, self-raptured logical and sociopathical mercenary. Like all of the characters Dobie encounters, Thalia has a fixed, clear-cut, and completely self-serving concept of who she is and what she wants out of life. She only recognizes other people in relation to how they fit into her plans. No matter what track Dobie would take to woo Thalia, he would inevitably run up against her declaration of self-definition which she incanted like a litany and which he would begin muttering along with her in dejection and frustration:

> Because if there's one thing I intend to have it's a rich husband. But it's not for myself you understand. You see, my father is sixty years old and has a kidney condition and my mother isn't getting any younger either. Also, I've got a sister who's married to a loafer, and my brother, he shows every indication of becoming a public charge. So it's up to me. You see, I've got an obligation to my family.

Practically every character had such a speech or phrase which they repeated endlessly to affirm their righteous isolation. For instance, Dobie's father Herbert T. Gillis, played with Irish irony and dancer's grace by Frank Faylen, cynically bitter and defeated, rants about the injustices

inflicted on a "veteran *with* a Good Conduct Medal." The senior Gillis
pushes to lower Dobie's level of romantic and financial hopes to that of his
own harsh experience.

Another character, Chatsworth Osborne, Jr., played by Steve Franken,
is Dobie's childishly smug, rich kid rival. Osborne constantly reminds the
audience of his... "two hundred acre estate on the top of the hill with
twenty-eight rooms, eight bathrooms, and surrounded by a twenty foot
fence with glass embedded in the top."

And it is Chatsworth with his petulantly condescending "Gillis baby"
and "Dobie doo's" who surfaces over and over again to remind Dobie that
even though he is dumber and less charming than Dobie, he will win every
time because he has—in abundance—what society values.

This constant repetition of phrases and speeches defining the
characters is normal procedure in television comedy, but, like Jack Benny,
Dobie Gillis uses the idea of repetition to subversive ends. Whereas the
repetitions are usually used to reassure the audience about the show's
familiarity, *Dobie Gillis* suggests that this reassurance is a comfort only for
those who are satisfied with the status quo. For the hopelessly have-not
Dobie it represents a stubbornly stagnant social structure indifferently ignoring and holding him in his place.

Dobie's only compatriot in societal isolation is his lifelong "good buddy"
Maynard G. Krebs (Bob Denver) who, unlike Dobie, is an outcast by
choice rather than chance. Maynard is a 1950s "beatnik," but his values
are actually closer to what a decade later would come to be known as a
"flower child." One theory on the decline and fall of the flower child empire is their naïve belief that they could build a culture based on sex disconnected from money and power. Shulman and Amateau, children of the
Great Depression, had no such illusions and could conceive of a character
of Maynard's idealistically ethical values only as having no interest in sex
whatsoever.

Although devoted to the intricate and sophisticated sounds of Dizzy
Gillespie and Thelonius Monk, all of Maynard's other passions are pointedly pre-pubescent: his stupefying string and tin-foil collections, his
menagerie of toads and snails, and his enthusiasm for watching the old En-
dicott Building getting torn down (which he constantly demonstrates by
ramming his head into Dobie's stomach) and such cinematic classics as
The Monster That Devoured Cleveland (once, upon emerging from a triple
feature, the billboard behind Maynard proclaimed "Cleveland devoured
three times!").

Maynard acts as a bizarre morally progressive and socially regressive
conscience for Dobie, his line on girls being, "They take the best seats in
the movies, they won't sit on the floor and listen to jazz all night, and they
giggle about you in the girls' powder room. Girls—who needs them!"

The stylization of *Dobie Gillis* was so complete that one of its best episodes, "Competition Is the Life of Trade," was mostly written by the team of Dick Conway and Roland MacLane, who had previously functioned as the main writing forces for the vastly different sitcom *The Life of Riley*. In this episode, Dobie pants after the attentions of Delphine Quimby (Sally Todd) the new girl in town who has moved in from Cleveland. When Chatsworth flashes his foreign sports car at her Dobie is prepared to throw in the towel but in this case Herbert T. Gillis chooses to fire his son up with the tradition of American equality. He poetically explains that: "It's like getting on a bus, see. *Everybody* gets on together: men, women, children. And then they see a vacant seat and they all *race* for it on equal terms. That's the democratic way." So Dobie sallies forth to race for Delphine's seat.

The elder Gillis is flushed with the American spirit until he hears the news that a new merchant named Quimby is about to open a rival grocery store and begins whimpering, "Poorhouse here we come." The news disturbs Dobie equally when, while plying Delphine with his baroque love twaddle ("my great tawny animal"), he helps set up her father's store and suddenly realizes that he is now willingly doing the exact same work he has spent a lifetime trying to avoid in his own father's store.

Dobie's hurried escape is short circuited by the arrival of his father who welcomes Quimby (frequent *Dobie Gillis* character player Jack Albertson). Herbert Gillis introduces himself as Fred C. Dobbs, "a neighborly neighbor from the neighborhood" and advises Quimby to charge outrageously high praces on the assurance that he would still be underselling Gillis. But both father and son are foiled when Quimby sees through Herbert's masquerade and is then offered a deal by Chatsworth—the complete Osborne grocery order for a date with Delphine.

> *Delphine*: Father, I am not a chattel.
> *Quimby*: Go upstairs and put on your new dress, chattel. You know, the one I said I'd throw you out of the house if I ever caught you wearing.

Yet the American spirit of determination and fair play cannot be denied. Dobie takes his case to Chatsworth's mother (Doris Packer) who responds with her typically impervious cynicism: "Has Chatsworth been upsetting the working classes again? That nasty boy." Dobie proclaims that what Chatsworth is doing is underhanded and un–American, to which Mrs. Osborne replies, "Underhanded yes, un–American no." But Dobie valiantly persists, invoking the heritage of the Osborne line through American history, which unfortunately turns out to consist mostly of profiteering traitors. Dobie's arguments ultimately move Mrs. Osborne to split her grocery order between Gillis and Quimby since: "Where else but in America would our ancestors have had the freedom to behave as abominably as they did?"

Competition and democracy win out in the end. Both Herbert and Quimby are happy and Dobie is afforded a wage to work in his father's store. But filling Mrs. Osborne's orders keeps Dobie so busy working that Delphine goes to the dance with the idle Chatsworth and Dobie is left muttering the line his father uses about him, "I've got to kill that boy, I've just got to."

Dobie Gillis served as a rococo counter-argument to the 1950s family-comes-to-the-suburbs sitcoms. By the early 1960s, however, the post–World War II adjustment was old news and the New Frontier in sitcoms was being forged in various forms by such disparate shows as *Bewitched*, *The Dick Van Dyke Show*, and *The Beverly Hillbillies*. In fact, the debut and immediate rise to the top of the ratings of former George Burns writer Paul Henning's unheralded urban vs. rural sitcom, *The Beverly Hillbillies*, constituted the most dramatic demonstration of era changing until the similar phenomenon of *The Cosby Show* in the mid–1980s.

As would be expected with a show that was so formulaically generic and became so popular, *The Beverly Hillbillies* became a mini-industry for Henning, spawning two spinoffs: *Petticoat Junction* and *Green Acres*. The issue of spinoffs has never properly been examined in television comedy. Why it is that a ground-breaker like *The Mary Tyler Moore Show* will spin off a raft of increasingly blurred copies of itself while a safe and bland show like *Happy Days* will spin off the Lucy-like physical comedy of *Laverne and Shirley* is a matter that needs much more serious thought and discussion. But in all of the tangled history of spinoffs the fact that *Green Acres* would turn out to have more to do with *Dobie Gillis* than its parent show would probably be the biggest shocker. That is, unless you took a careful look at the credits of both *Dobie Gillis* and *Green Acres* and saw that Guy Scarpitta was the associate producer on both shows.

On *Green Acres* the Benny/Burns fulcrum is Eddie Albert who plays Oliver Wendell Douglas, a New York corporate lawyer. Oliver is an upright pillar of the establishment with his own flinty version of counter-culture convictions: "It's a rat race out there, and the rats are winning." Oliver's dream is to drop off the ladder of success and go back to the land, living the simple life, tilling the soil and producing food from the earth. "Dream" is the operative word in this show as Oliver has conjured up an image of a farm community as a bastion of noble romanticism filled with pure and forthright people heroically pitching together to form "the backbone of the nation." And Oliver refuses to even reconsider his locked-in-concrete vision when faced with the realities of life upon schlepping his socialite wife Lisa (Eva Gabor) to live in Hooterville, U.S.A.

Snookered into buying an unusable piece of land by the relentlessly mercenary Mr. Haney (Pat Buttram), the Douglases set up housekeeping in their ramshackle plywood farmhouse, under endless and pathetically inept renovation by the brother and sister carpentry family Alf and Ralph Monroe (Sid Melton and Mary Grace Canfield). Lisa and Oliver proceed to live out their psychodramas as if actually conforming to their visions. Oliver drives the tractor and plows the land on his surreal, consciously studio-bound lunar farmscape while wearing business suits and sports coats and seethes with frustration when the crops and the townspeople refuse to conform to his images. Lisa putters around the farmhouse in designer dresses, rustling up inedible hot cakes, and pouting about having to live in "HOO-ters-ville" when actually fitting in with the tenor of the community quite well.

The characters of Lisa and Oliver take on an even more ironic twist from the casting of Albert whose Scandinavian midwestern looks and sound make him seem more at home in this setting than in New York, and Gabor whose Hungarian accent and grossly dopey demeanor make her seem alien to anything either American or human.

That anyone as spaced-out as Lisa Douglas could fit into this community indicates just how far we are from the Hooterville of gently eccentric rustics depicted on *Petticoat Junction*. Hooterville is a community where every inhabitant is locked into his own singular, narrow modus operandi, be it a method of working (Alf and Ralph Monroe, the chicken coop building construction team), a derailed train of thought (Alvy Moore as the almost poetically distracted county agent Hank Kimble), or a purpose of life (the money-grubbing Mr. Haney). No matter what kind of emotional or intellectual situation Oliver brings to them, they invariably respond by offering him the one and only thing they do, and then resent his ingratitude in not wanting their offering. The only way that the Hooterville community functions at all is that everybody accepts everybody else's presentation of self as normal. Thus, interpersonal relationships simply become escalations of what the citizens are individually. That is, everybody has accepted this except Oliver—the city-slicker newcomer who never quite realizes that what he is getting is only a nightmare inversion of how he himself behaves.

Green Acres takes the notion that a community survives by agreeing on a series of functions and then carrying them through unquestioningly—what *Fiddler on the Roof* romanticizes as "tradition"—and plays it out to its ridiculous conclusion. Everything Oliver encounters is a ritualization of function divorced from meaning, patterns so formulaic and repetitious that they quickly begin to resemble vaudeville and burlesque routines turned into situation comedy.

To accomplish this the show simply codifies all of the vaudeville patter relationships that Burns and Benny had as individual components on their shows and strings them together to form the community of Hooterville: Oliver with Gracie Allen (Lisa), with Dennis Day (Hank Kimble and/or Tom Lester as the Douglas's farmhand and self-proclaimed adopted son Eb), with Frank Nelson (Mr. Haney), with Mel Blanc (Hank Patterson as snide old geezer Mr. Ziffel). The consolidation of community among these dunces comes once again from a subversive use of the television viewer's desire for repetition.

Although every one of the *Green Acres* characters is locked in his or her vacuum-sealed visions, they all somehow manage to join together against Oliver. For instance, when Oliver's conversation with Mr. Haney about his current problem inevitably leads to the solution coming from any of the number of items being offered in Mr. Haney's June white sale ("That's right, I'm selling everything that belonged to June White"), Oliver becomes more and more annoyed by the introduction of each new snake-oil item. But when he is confronted by what Mr. Haney explains is a Louis XIV leg of lamb, which looks like a plaster cast of a leg of lamb with a thin coat of bronze paint, Oliver explodes with indignation at the insult to his intelligence. However, when Lisa wanders in to join them, she immediately recognizes this as a Louis XIV leg of lamb and when the exasperated Oliver orders her to silence she merely points out in a quiet, rational defense that she hadn't seen one of them in quite a long time.

Every little movement conspires to confirm the normality of this community through the definition of community—everybody does it. If one character whistles an aimless fragment of a tune while talking to Oliver at the beginning of an episode, you can be certain that every other character he meets will be whistling the same thing and none of them will be aware of where they've heard it before. And, by episode's end, Oliver will be watching while a symphony orchestra plays the same tune on television.

In fact, the idea of watching television is very important to *Green Acres*. While Jack Benny and especially George Burns playfully worked on the self-awareness that their shows were on television, *Green Acres* uses the notion to complete its metaphor of community as a collection of mechanically mindless ritualizations. As the makers of *Green Acres* see it, their view of the process of community is very similar to the process of making and viewing television itself. For instance, characters would pause during their morning hellos to Oliver in order to watch the opening credits go by (Eb always taking particular pains to wait for "Directed by Richard L. Bare"). Or a "two weeks later" graphic would appear over Oliver while he reclines reading on the sofa and Lisa would thoughtfully ponder, "Imagine, it's already two weeks later" while Oliver grunts in foul-tempered incomprehension. Or Oliver's frequent and endless odes to the yeoman farmer would be undercut by Revolutionary War–style soundtrack music after which Lisa would beam delightedly about how much she enjoys the "fife music" during Oliver's speeches.

On *Burns and Allen* George was aware he was on television and used this knowledge to torment the bland sanity of the surrounding society through his manipulations of Gracie's other-worldly imagination. On *Green Acres* the entire community is as illogical as Gracie isolating George/ Oliver into powerlessness. Further, Oliver refuses to accept the conditions of the community he lives in, so while the rest of the cast is vaguely aware that they are living in a television show (without considering this fact to be any more unusual than Arnold the pig thinking he is human), Oliver is the only person in Hooterville who never catches on.

Numerous shows, from *Rowan and Martin's Laugh-In* to *Late Night with David Letterman,* have since played successfully on a television self-awareness, but their television smarts have always functioned as part of the show's self-congratulatory hipness. It is *Green Acres'* startling singularity to equate the television experience with the semi-conscious stupidity of its characters, and the genre-busting modernist techniques, slamming up against the verbally broad barnyard burlesque, that makes it the most intriguing example of cultural clash in the medium's history, at least until the advent of *GLOW.*

Benny and Burns defined a style of television comedy coming out of the world of the stand-up vaudeville and nightclub comedian. Their ideas were adapted and transformed by television writers and directors to invigorate the sitcom worlds of *Dobie Gillis* and *Green Acres* and made explicit the social assumptions inherent in the Benny/Burns approach.

But by the late 1950s a whole new generation of stand-up comedians, many of whom were coming out of the satiric style of Chicago's "Second City Theater" and the San Francisco "Beat" poetry and folk music scenes, had emerged and were beginning to have an impact on the mainstream. While Lenny Bruce is the romantic, martyred icon of this generation, others, including Jonathan Winters, Mike Nichols and Elaine May, The Smothers Brothers, Mort Sahl, and Shelley Berman, were also making themselves known to national audiences through such 1950s innovations as long-play comedy records and the post prime-time talk/variety television shows of Steve Allen and Jack Paar, who were particular boosters of the "new breed" of comedians.

The coming of age of the "new breed" of comedians roughly coincides with the second generation of television that brought us *Dobie Gillis.* But the same forces that made shows like *Peter Gunn* and *Dobie Gillis* possible also conspired to keep these new comedians from blending into the continuum of weekly television programming.

Like movies, radio, and records—indeed, like the country itself—television had established its base of operations and the majority of its audience in the east and then eventually drifted west, settling in California. When New York and the East were the hub, television drama was dominated by the dynamics of the Broadway theater (an era that the stagestruck television reviewers still refer to as "The Golden Age") and comedy by the nightclub and stage revue performers. With the majority of television sets in the hands of the urban ethnic east coast audience, such stylistically aggressive live performance stand-up stars as Milton Berle, Jackie Gleason, and Phil Silvers were finally able to break through into the national consciousness after repeated failures in movies and radio. However, the combination of the medium's moving west and the spread of television set ownership throughout the country not only made television trendier, hipper, and more technically stylish, but also made it almost impossible for the new aggressive live performers like Sahl and Berman to be accepted by the newly expanded, more homogenized television audience.

None of the above mentioned new breed of comedians, with the exception of The Smothers Brothers, would either concentrate any major portion of their careers on television or have any major impact on the medium. But Chicago's subversively quiet Bob Newhart, one of the greats of the new breed, not only shifted his focus onto series television but in so doing reinvented the connection between the Benny/Burns starting points and the ensemble sitcom variations they inspired.

In his prime as a stand-up, Newhart did a routine where he played a smugly content 17th-century British adman taking a phone call from Sir Walter Raleigh in the colonies. As he halfheartedly tried to repress his mirthful condesention and ridicule while repeating Raleigh's descriptions of the wonders of tobacco ("I see, you roll it up in a piece of paper, yeah, and you stick it in your mouth, unhuh, and you set it on fire. Sounds great Walt. I'm sure it's gonna go over real big."), the audience was caught in the crosswind not knowing which was more embarrassing to their self-image: the middle-class lack of imagination in the Newhart character's rejection of cigarettes or the realization that something as objectively ridiculous as smoking was actually accepted as part of our culture. This two-way pull is the basis of Newhart's comedy and the foundation of how he would reinvent the relationship between himself as star comedian and the rest of the *Dobie Gills/Green Acres*–styled ensemble societies in his sitcoms *The Bob Newhart Show* and *Newhart*.

Newhart's characters are not interested in joining the communities that either will not let Dobie Gillis rise within it to taste its advertised rewards or conform to Oliver Wendell Douglas' idealized notions of what its advertising once claimed it to be. Newhart sees his world pretty much as it is—a collection of individual Sir Walter Raleighs grabbing him by the lapels with their own obsessive, self-absorbed versions of tobacco smoking, and is secretly hoping that they will all go quietly away and leave him alone.

Both Newhart shows started slowly, jelling somewhere in the course of their second or third seasons as Newhart searched like an orchestra leader for the right combination of sounds. On *The Bob Newhart Show* it was mostly a question of discovering the right production personnel, with the writer/producer duo of former stand-up team Tom Patchett and Jay Tarses eventually becoming the key players. On *Newhart* it was more a question of blending a compatible cast, as practically every integral player including Julia Duffy, Peter Scolari, William Sanderson, and Todd Susman were added during the show's run. And in the middle of the entire enterprise is Newhart himself, the comedy Count Basie, organizing and orchestrating his ensemble of idiosyncratic character players, controlling the comic rhythm with a steady, almost invisible hand, and adding his own devastatingly understated solos as counterstatement to the surrounding mayhem.

Both Newhart shows come out of the highly respected and hugely influential MTM company, and, in fact, one can all but trace the company's history through Newhart's work for it. *The Bob Newhart Show* was the first MTM series to reach the air after the initial success of *The Mary Tyler Moore Show* and came while the production team was still flushed with the power of their structural innovations and daring themselves to explore new outlets along the trail they were blazing. *Bob Newhart* took the *Mary Tyler Moore* format of building a complex series of interpersonal relationships around the title character both at home and at the workplace and used it to reinvent the Jack Benny format of the three distinct spaces for the life of the central character which are held together by some inexplicable form of centrifugal force.

Like Benny, Newhart has a home life, a rather modest Chicago apartment he shares with his warmly sensual and good-humored wife Emily, played by the warmly sensual and good-humored Suzanne Pleshette. Besides serving as just about the most attractive example of a mutually respectful and affectionate marriage between mature adults in sitcom history, the relationship also serves to highlight Bob Hartley's (Newhart's) character quirks and flaws. Mostly they center around his emotional conservatism: on the one hand his devotion to stasis and dependency on routine (clinging to ridiculously outdated clothing and mementoes or his dread of moving to a new house or even taking a brief European vacation) and on the other his lunging, stammering inability to verbally express the depths of his feelings (usually depicted in his long-winded, roundabout anecdote analogies which his listeners never understand). In this regard Emily functions for Bob the way Rochester functions for Benny.

The Hartleys are childless (as are the Loudens on *Newhart*), but integrated into their home life is next-door neighbor Howard Borden (Bill Daily), a man so helplessly childish that, when asked if he will help supervise a group of orphans on an outing, responds that it is all right with him as long as they have their parents' permission. The only way that Howard can function at all is as the Hartley's surrogate son, and, as such, he becomes the Dennis Day in Newhart's Jack Benny model.

The backstage space for Bob Hartley is shared with his office colleagues at the medical building where he operates his psychiatric practice. This world parallels his home life in that it is dominated by relationships with a woman of infinite jest (Marcia Wallace as wise-cracking receptionist Carol Kester) and a male bachelor friend who, despite his surface sophistication, is Howard Borden's equal in immaturity (Pete Bonnerz as orthodontist Dr. Jerry Robinson).

The "supposed contrast" comes in the onstage world of Bob Hartley with his psychiatric patients, a sad sack collection of dangling ids and pathetic superegos, including such memorable folk as the terminally timid Mr. Peterson (John Fiedler), the morose, father-dominated Michelle Nardo (Renee Lippin), the pixilated flake Mrs. Bakerman (played by Dobie Gillis' mom Florida Friebus and pointedly identified as working in a grocery store), and that textbook compendium of psychological disorder, the shockingly direct Elliott Carlin (Jack Riley).

The term "supposed contrast" is used here because the sane people and the sick people all have parallel or mirror-reflection character disorders, the only difference being that the sick people admit that they cannot cope. The topper is that while all of the characters are so similar, they never really manage to connect with each other.

The Mary Tyler Moore Show established the MTM format of interconnecting the home-life and workplace characters, and *The Bob Newhart Show* was only too happy to use the innovations that the company and its flagship show were establishing as now being sitcom-acceptable. All of the characters on the *Newhart Show* are allowed to wander in and out of all three spaces. But while they are imitating the MTM approach of having everybody become more complex the more they see of each other they actually add more attachments to their individual pathologies.

Like Jack Benny, Bob Newhart is the central figure but, unlike Benny, he is both kind and generous. As a friend and doctor his apt and commonsensical if somewhat embarrassed and haltingly offered advice is always cheerfully accepted by the other characters who then adapt it to fit in comfortably with their already existing problem. For instance, when Dr. Hartley gives Michelle Nardo a hand puppet to rehearse future confrontations with her father, she gleefully works it up into a ventriloquist act:

> *Michelle*: How was that, Dr. Hartley?
> *Bob*: That wasn't exactly what I had in mind, Michelle.
> *Michelle*: That's 'cause you could see my lips moving. I'll be a lot better at it by our next session.

A good example of how *Bob Newhart Show* characters relate to each other can be seen in an episode written by Patchett and Tarses called "The Battle of the Groups" which opens with the close of a group therapy session where Michelle is complaining that she didn't get to talk. Bob apologizes and explains that he thought it was important to assure Mr. Peterson that skin blemishes can strike people who are over fifty (he couldn't find his library card and broke out in a rash) and then further apologizes for having to cancel next week's session because of a speaking engagement he has at the school where Emily teaches. The group begins to turn against him:

> *Michelle*: I think we're getting the short end of the stick.
> *Bob*: Well, if you must think of therapy as a stick, then I try to give everybody the same end.

Bob suggests that they go on a marathon, an intense all-weekend session to be held at a cabin in the woods.

This suggestion engenders so much enthusiasm that when Bob's second, newer group arrives for its session, the first group invites it to join them on the marathon. As Bob explains all of the reasons why this is not a good idea, the patients listen thoughtfully, concur that these are indeed good reasons, and then return to their progressing plans. Bob's trepidation is then doubled when Emily decides that a weekend in the country would do her good even if she would get little chance to see Bob.

Bob's forebodings seem warranted when the patients gather outside his office to begin the trip and struggle to conceal their unease and suspicion when informed that Bob will not be joining them in Mr. Gianelli's (Daniel J. Travanti) camper, but riding in his own car with Emily. But the situation does not become unmanageable until Bob goes into his office get his coat and Michelle arrives carrying her cat in a travel case.

> *Member of 2nd Group*: How come she gets to bring a cat? Nobody in our group brought any animals.
> *Bob*: No, I don't know. See I just went in to get my coat.
> *2nd Group*: I'm just wondering how long you have to be in a group to get preferential treatment.
> *Member of 1st Group*: Look who's talking about preferential treatment. We didn't get to go on a marathon until our second year.
> [The elevators open and each group goes en masse to separate ones.]
> *2nd Group*: Well, I'm not riding down with that cat.
> *2nd Group*: I'm not riding down with that group.
> *1st Group*: Come on Dr. Hartley, ride down with us.
> *2nd Group*: No, ride down with us.
> *Bob*: We're going to walk down. We'll meet you downstairs.
> *2nd Group*: Right, Bob.
> *1st Group*: How come they get to call him Bob?

At the cabin the groups split into hostile camps but in a stunning series of events they band together against Bob when they find out that he and Emily have a separate, much more luxurious cabin ("We're not all in the same boat, he's on the *Queen Mary* and we're on the *Poseidon*"). Then they turn around and become the psychiatrist for Bob and Emily when the couple quarrel about her coming on the marathon. The groups finally fall into sullen resentment when they realize that solving the Hartleys' problem is going to take the entire length of the marathon.

> *Emily*: Now I understand the pressure you were under from your sergeant, and your basketball coach, and your Boy Scout leader.
> *Mr. Gianelli*: I understood it twelve hours ago when he first brought it up.

After half an hour of continual emotional and psychological movement, the episode ends with everybody right back where they started. As the bleary-eyed marathoners gather their belongings to return home, Michelle suddenly realizes that she still never got to talk and begins telling her story to a comatose Mr. Herd (Oliver Clark) as everybody else leaves.

By the time *Newhart* came along in the early 1980s, the MTM style was suffering from hardening of the arteries. The show suffers from almost all of the ills of 1980s sitcoms, taking place almost exclusively on a single, flatly lit, underpopulated set with everybody making mechanically timed entrances and exits like variety show guest stars. What saves this show, beyond the consistent excellence of the writing and the acting, is Newhart's insistence on maintaining the three spaces he established on the first series through the depiction of the continuing characters. Further, while retaining Bob Newhart's upper middle class/brow perspective on the world, *Newhart* manages to be one of the very few shows to respond to the realities of the 1980s by having a major component of the separations between the characters being their extremely opaque differences in class status and aspiration.

The characters who belong to Dick and Joanna Louden's (Newhart and Mary Frann) Stratford Inn, those who belong to the television station that broadcasts Dick's *Vermont Today* show, and the characters that belong to the Vermont town that houses both institutions are less spatially placed than their *Bob Newhart Show* counterparts, but no less uncomprehending of each other. Indeed, while everybody seems to congregate at the Stratford Inn, all attempts at intermingling are fated for humiliating disaster: for example, super-yuppie television producer Michael Harris (Peter Scolari) using his proto–Spanish lingo and contorted strings of alliteration to play Cyrano de Bergerac for mega-hick Larry (William Sanderson), and former Madison Avenue whiz Dick trying out his community "Adopt-a-Book" campaign on the blank-faced townsfolk.

The only characters from different spaces who think they co-exist are Michael and the Stratford Inn's astonishingly self-enraptured society deb maid Stephanie Vanderkellen (Julia Duffy). And the only thing that holds them together is the reflections they see of their self-images in each other. More and more over the years Duffy and Scolari came to dominate the show with characterizations that are both perfect incarnations of society's current, shallow self-absorption (not at all hurt by Scolari's uncanny physical and vocal resemblance to David Stockman) and thought-provoking interpretations of what Thalia Menninger and Dobie Gillis would be like if they had fulfilled their aspirations. Almost single-handedly they manage to close the circle from the late 1950s to the late 1980s.

Perhaps the crowning achievement of Jack Benny's and George Burns' art is that they managed to suggest an astonishing array of poetically imaginative interpretations of human behavior while remaining the most popular and beloved mass audience comedians for over four decades. The sitcoms that followed in their path did likewise with *Green Acres* being cancelled after seven years only because of CBS's infamous purge of rural shows, and *The Bob Newhart Show* leaving the air after six years while still similarly popular only because the star pulled the plug himself.

One of the major reasons for these shows' popularity and longevity is that they never announce, underline, or congratulate themselves on their own importance, thus freeing themselves to smuggle in their commentary and analysis under the fool's banner of "light entertainment." For unlike the Smithsonian Institution sitcoms, forever hitting the drum roll for their "important statements" and then delivering solemn, self-righteous stands in favor of ecumenical brotherhood and tolerance, these shows are more interested in examining attitudes than in striking them.

4
The Sennett Tradition

I'm Dickens ... He's Fenster, Camp Runamuck, Valentine's Day, Occasional Wife, *and* The Monkees

Mack Sennett has, by and large, ceased being known as the individual who created a large body of popular and influential comedy two-reelers during the silent era, and is now almost exclusively invoked as the brand name for a long-ago discredited style of humor. "Custard pie" and "Keystone Kop" are fused to Sennett's name like corn flakes are to Kellogg's, and are now used as pejoratives to dismiss comedy that is crude, simplistic, and—corny. A descriptive analysis of Sennett's work usually conjures up hazy recollections of grotesquely buffoonish characters who endlessly chase each other, pause to smash one another with blunt or pointy objects thereby provoking all manner of exaggerated pratfalls, then regroup to chase each other some more. As a description of a typical Sennett film all of the above is true—but incomplete.

The dismantling of Sennett's reputation is still an ongoing process which, over the years, has taken many forms. My earlier assessment of how the Hal Roach model for two-reeler comedy flourished in the sound era and later became the underlying structure for television comedy while the Sennett model floundered and led to his company's demise in the early 1930s has probably contributed to Sennett's dismantling. The analysis made earlier is based on the divergent paths followed by Roach and Sennett during the 1920s. However, any accurate portrait of Sennett's unassailable contributions to the core spirit of American comedy demands a more comprehensive understanding of his stylistic approach and philosophic concerns. In particular, most analyses tend to gloss over Sennett's unyielding devotion to a working-class sensibility.

Sennett broke away from the poetic aspirations of D. W. Griffith at Biograph in 1912 in order to produce raw, physical comedies for what was then a predominantly working-class film audience. Biographical sketches of Sennett continually harp on his crude behavioral manners and lack of formal education—all of which contributed to how well Sennett's assumptions about what was funny matched up with the experiences and expectations of his audience. Although Sennett's Keystone Films was the dominating force in film comedy throughout the teens, the seeds of Sennett's destruction were sown when, after having signed up then unknown Charlie Chaplin in 1913, he let him leave the studio after only a little more than a year. Allegedly, the conclusive proof of Sennett's shortsightedness both as an artist and as a businessperson was his unwillingness to pay the immediately popular Chaplin what he was worth and his refusal to allow Chaplin to control the gag construction and pacing of the films he appeared in. While these two items are true, they do not represent the whole story.

It was logical for Sennett to have signed Chaplin because a working-class ethos was central to both of their sensibilities but it was inevitable that they would also part company because of the very different ways in which they played but that ethos. Leaving aside for the moment the enormous gap in comic inspiration between Chaplin and Sennett (or between Chaplin and practically anybody else for that matter) the working-class viewpoint meant that they shared the same attraction to aggressive, physical comedy which punctured the pomposity of power and privilege. But while The Little Tramp never relinquished his working-class perspective throughout Chaplin's phenomenally successful career, it was, from the outset, the perspective of an unhappy outsider who aspired to belong in the middle class. In other words, the kicks to the butt in Chaplin films were in the service of more noble ends.

Chaplin pursued "the girl" because in his world she embodied the values of the higher moral order to which The Tramp aspired and he humiliated snobs and bullies because they unjustly prevented the majority of decent working people from getting their fair share of physical and emotional wealth. But in Sennett films the hero pursues the heroine in order to satisfy his appetite for emotional and sexual gratification and to deny her favors to his friends and rivals. And, he conspires to bamboozle the authority figures in order to flatter his ego and escape punishment for having grabbed more than his prescribed portion of physical and emotional wealth. If the characters in Sennett films seem to be more representative of behavioral "types" than three-dimensional people, it is because, in Sennett's view, human nature is little more than a grab-bag collection of instincts and desires which, if it could be said to have any premeditated philosophy of life at all, would be something on the order of "whatever gets you through the day."

All silent comedy was primarily visual and ultimately all of the major figures in American silent comedy (Sennett, Chaplin, Roach, Keaton, et al.) can stylistically be classified under the general heading of physical slapstick. But what Chaplin was pioneering in film was a form of physical comedy that emanated out of an individual character's particular personality. So while his gags may have been similar to Sennett's, they needed to unfold with a different rhythm in order to detail the progression of the thoughts and emotions that went into them. Chaplin's gags needed a different compositional sense to draw the audience's identification towards the inner psychology of the central character. Chaplin's camera concentrated on showing The Tramp in full figure for the same reasons that Griffith would cut to close-ups, to transport the audience inside the workings of an individual's consciousness. So as it was inevitable that Sennett would rebel against Griffith, it was equally inevitable that Chaplin would rebel against Sennett.

While industrialization continued its transformation of the United States into a powerful and wealthy nation, the habitat of the motion picture continued its transformation from nickelodeon to movie palace and carried along in its wake a new generation of film patrons who came predominantly from the middle class. As the image of the motion picture's function shifted from lurid diversions for immigrants and day laborers to respectable entertainment for the average family, our cultural assumption about how the popular visual arts are supposed to relate to their audience became redefined. It is this revised definition that has not only shaped our image of what a "good" movie is ever since, but has also altered our perception of the cinema that preceeded this revision.

The practical effect of this development in the short term was, and is, that with their focus on character complexity and individual psychology, both Griffith in drama and Chaplin in comedy became the defining artistic models for popular American moviemaking. Indeed, Chaplin's phenomenal popular success led to the rise of a whole generation of character comedians such as Buster Keaton and Hal Roach's first star Harold Lloyd who established their own audience-endearing idiosyncratic personalities and who, like Chaplin, became so popular that by the 1920s they had graduated from two-reelers to creating and starring in their own feature films.

For the most part this left the major battle in two-reelers to be fought between Sennett, who throughout the 1920s increasingly turned to doing burlesque parodies of popular mainstream films, and Roach, who with his later stars, Charlie Chase, Our Gang, and Laurel and Hardy, devised his own brand of character-centered comedy. Roach's films had pretty much the same quotient of mayhem as did Sennett's, but his pacing was even slower than Chaplin's because the destruction was motivated by the quirky relationships between all of the characters and the comedy came as much out of their sustained and detailed reactions to the destruction as from what they were expressing through the aggression itself.

The practical effect in the long term is that conventional film history has recorded Roach's eventual ascension and Sennett's demise as part of an evolutionary maturity of the medium, a triumph of complexity and sophistication over crudity and vulgarity—and, this is true. Throughout his twenty-year run, Sennett made very little effort to adjust himself to technological innovations or sociological trends and his films tend to be both more interesting in theory than in practice and play better in compilation highlights than as full-length entities. But it is also true that as the mass audience became more and more gentrified, it showed an increasingly greater reluctance to look at its reflection in Sennett's dark mirror. Indeed, his harsh, distanced, almost Hobbesian view of character and society seemed to embody everything that our "every day in every way we are getting better" country wished to repress.

While the progression of film history mirrored our social history of movement from a working-class to a middle-class country, television developed in exactly the opposite direction. Since the television set was originally an expensive piece of furniture tied to an experimental medium, the television audience at the outset of its history was overwhelmingly upper and middle class. It was not until television clearly demonstrated that it would supplant radio as the basic mode of home entertainment that the price of a set dropped considerably and the audience broadened to include more and more people on the lower economic rungs. Therefore, conventional television history begins with a Golden Age and gradually degenerates until by the end of the 1950s it has become "a vast wasteland."

This route was paved by the golden rise and wasteful fall of the two comedy staples that dominated the 1950s: the New York–based live variety show which gradually disappeared as production facilities became more and more Hollywood dominated, and the "family-in-the-suburbs" sitcom which had temporarily worn out its welcome through overexposure. As the television powers that be began searching for new comedic bandwagons they hoped would become the profitable trends for the 1960s, many of television comedy's best and most experienced writers began experimenting with series that incorporated contemporary applications of the Sennett approach, his distanced characters, his basic instinct behavioral psychology, and his dark, anarchic assumptions about social organization. The transitional springboard for these leaps from the silent Sennetts to the 1960s sitcoms was 1950s television comedy's lone poet of the working-class attitude, Jackie Gleason.

Leonard Stern's television career in mainstream variety shows and sitcoms could be said to have started before the medium's creative beginning and continued until after its end. From his work writing for various 1950s variety shows leading up to his position as head writer on *The Steve Allen Show*, through his executive position at Talent Associates in the 1960s where he oversaw such seminal shows as *Get Smart* and *He & She*, on through *McMillan and Wife* in the 1970s and up till nearly the present as creative consultant for *Sledge Hammer*, Stern has become almost a pocket history of television comedy. One of the variety shows Stern wrote for was *The Jackie Gleason Show* and while he was not primarily connected with "The Honeymooners" sketches he clearly saw in them the basis for the working-class sitcom. Yet ultimately it was the very particular deviations from the "Honeymooners" format that Stern infused into his sitcom *I'm Dickens ... He's Fenster* that established it in the Sennett tradition, deviations which were made all the more apparent by ABC's decision to program the show immediately following its already established literalized knockoff of "The Honeymooners," *The Flintstones*, on its Friday night schedule.

Dickens was John Astin as Harry Dickens, a reasonably successful cog at the carpentry shop where he works. Although ostensibly the show's straight man, Harry Dickens is not only, as is often the case, its indispensable fulcrum, but also its most complex and fully realized character. At the beginning of what has turned out to be an incredibly varied and highly undervalued career in television, Astin invents some extraordinary head and shoulders gestures and employs an extremely delicate use of open-faced sincerity to convey both the innate decency and severe limitations of a well-meaning dullard. Harry is the Ralph Kramden figure but since he is basically a good-natured lump, the kind of furious half-baked schemes for social advancement that stood at the core of "The Honeymooners" would not be the source of this show's tensions.

Rather, the locus is found in Harry's relationship with the Ed Norton character, 1950s hipster comic Marty Ingles as Harry's best friend and fellow carpenter Arch Fenster. Ingles, who is distinguished by his squeaky, gravelly voice and a closed-mouth grin with pop eyes expression that he lifted from Red Skelton and would in turn be used by Jay Leno for his signature look, retains Art Carney's loose-limbed physical eccentricity and even affects a Nortonesque hat. However, Ingles updates all of this so that it will represent a bebop funkiness and thus takes the character's behavior out of its accepted role of ethnic village idiot and turns him into a mild deviant living on the outside fringe of polite society.

The tension for Harry is therefore supposed to come between the respectable, responsible home life he shares with his wife Kate (played by Emmaline Henry as the perky 1960s version of Audrey Meadows' sardonic deadpan) and the temptations that Arch's "swinging bachelor" lifestyle represents. But in reality Arch is just the most tangible icon of what is

I'm Dickens (**John Astin, left**) ... *He's Fenster* (**Marty Ingles, right**).

actually a much more comprehensive threat to Harry's adult domestic world, the whole "boys' club" ethos of the carpentry shop workplace society. The operative word here is "boys" as these male-bonding wood warriors are depicted as a rag-tag batallion of klutzy foul-ups bracketed by Dave Ketchum as the super-sensitive Mel Warshaw on the one hand, Henry Beckman as the sarcastic sorehead Mulligan on the other, and fronted by Frank De Vol doing his Charles Butterworth impersonation as the shop's impotent boss Myron Bannister.

The dynamic contrast in behavioral expectations between Harry's life with his domestic wife and with his bumbling work buddies was best demonstrated when Stern resurrected that constant staple of 1950s domestic comedy, the plot about the husband and wife arguing over whether or not a joke is funny. Indeed, in the 1950s, Stern had used this exact same argument about this exact same joke in a sketch on *The Steve Allen Show* and it is the contrast in the presentations that illustrates the point.

The joke goes like this: a guy walks into a psychiatrist's office and tells the doctor that he'll give him a hundred dollars if he will answer just one question. The doctor agrees and the guy asks whether it is possible for a man to be in love with an elephant. The doctor tells him that such a love is not possible and the guy says, "Well, then what am I going to do with an engagement ring [spreads hands wide apart] *this big*?"

In the variety show sketch, Allen brings the joke home to his wife, Pat Carroll, and his irritation at her not laughing at the joke is compounded by what she had found funny. That is, after having rearranged the living room furniture and left for the kitchen to prepare dinner, Carroll had laughed furiously when she reentered the room to see that on arrival Allen had instinctively thrown his hat where there had always been an end table and was now retrieving it from the bottom of the goldfish bowl. The argument between husband and wife continues back and forth until it is decided that the issue will be settled by a third party. The third party is telephoned, but as Allen gets to the punchline and spreads his hands apart he realizes that you cannot tell this joke to somebody who is not in the room with you. Already one down, Allen then bets Carroll that the first person who walks through the front door will laugh at this joke, but that person turns out to be their ten-year-old paper boy and after a half-hearted effort to tell the child the joke, Allen simply gives up and pays off the bet.

In the *I'm Dickens . . . He's Fenster* episode, Harry has been chosen to speak for the shop at the Safety Awards Dinner and hoping to open with a good joke he excitedly brings this one home to try on Kate. The argument between the two of them is not dissimilar to the *Allen Show* sketch, but here the third party is the clear and present Arch and while his physical proximity allows him to understand the visual element of the joke, it also allows him to absorb the abuse of being buffeted between the couple.

Had the episode ended there it would have been more remarkable as a recapitulation of the *Allen Show* sketch than as a transcendence of it. But, stung by Kate's rejection of the joke, Harry seeks vindication by telling it at work the next morning. What follows is the most stunning escalation into hostilities since Laurel and Hardy's *Big Business*.

At first the heated argument over whether or not the joke is funny ruins what little concentration pre-existed at the shop and creates accidents. Then, as spite over wounds mounts, mishaps begin occurring, in Popeye's phrase, "ax-citentally on poipose" which soon leads to full-blown fist fights. At the episode's climax the shop has divided into two warring camps stalking each other from opposite ends of the frame, brandishing carpentry tools as weapons for the imminent Armageddon, taunting each other with their contrary battle cries "It's funny!" and "It's not funny!" until Harry manages to diffuse the situation by pointing out that the joke is now superfluous since the shop has completely ruined its safety record and no speech for the Safety Awards Dinner will be necessary.

Fear of women was always a major component in the male-centered world of comedy shorts whether it took the form of Chaplin's otherworldly reverence, Laurel and Hardy's nightmare of being dominated, or any of the many points in-between. Sennett's films tended to be more male-dominated than the star comedians' or Roach's. But by its very nature the Sennett world implicates domestic and nurturing women as a threat to the male characters remaining in the uninhibited, competitive state of primal trial by mayhem which is assumed to be their normal habitat. A show like *I'm Dickens . . . He's Fenster* examines this attitude by depicting the carpenters' frustrations at not being able to cope with any adult situation at work and through Harry's struggle to maintain a happy relationship with Kate. For the most comprehensive analysis of male infantilism, however, one must turn to David Swift's series *Camp Runamuck*.

To some, *Camp Runamuck* may have seemed like the nadir of a downward spiral in Swift's career since he is still best remembered for one of the legendary series of the Golden Age, *Mr. Peepers*. Broadcast live from New York in the early 1950s, *Mr. Peepers* is remembered by television history for the quiet warmth of its humor and the subtle maturity of the characters it presented. Fortunately, the few kinescopes that are now commonly available for viewing reveal a much more interesting show than this dignified official reputation would indicate. Swift used the ways and means of early 1950s television to recreate a kind of "puny patsy" underdog comedy of the 1920s in the middle-class setting of a high school teaching community. The alleged quietness of the show actually applies only to the "eye of the hurricane" titular character played by Wally Cox, and much of the comedy comes from Cox reacting with the slowest, most hesitant takes this side of Harry Langdon to English teacher Tony Randall's belligerent preening and athletic coach Jack Warden's macho bluster.

Swift was able to use his *Mr. Peepers* prestige to help in launching his directorial career in features, first for Disney, whose predilection for sanitized versions of silent movie slapstick meshed nicely with Swift's style,

and then for Columbia which eventually led him to that studio's burgeoning television division, Screen Gems. While the studio system of mass produced movies was rapidly disintegrating under television's onslaught,
some of the studios were able to recreate their roots by retaining contract
writers, producers, directors, and actors to produce large blocks of studio-
styled television programming. In the late 1950s, Warner Bros. with its
humorously tinged action westerns (*Maverick, Sugarfoot, Bronco*, etc.) and
private-eye mysteries (*77 Sunset Strip, Hawaiian Eye, Surfside 6*, et al.)
dominated the field. But by the 1960s, the ascending studios were Universal for melodrama and Columbia-Screen Gems for situation comedy. Indeed it was Screen Gems' record of success with executive producer Harry
Ackerman's romantic and domestic comedies that allowed them to experiment with a more offbeat premise like *Camp Runamuck*.

The title location is a boys' summer camp situated just across the lake
from a girls' camp called Camp Divine. However, in many episodes the
boys did not even appear since in terms of immature, overreactive, and self-
destructive behavior they were really no match for the adults who were
supposed to be supervising them. The camp's owner and commander is
Wallace Wivenhoe, played, in the show's masterstroke of casting, by bullet-
headed, barrel-chested Arch Johnson. With his hulking presence and raspy
voice, Johnson spent the bulk of his long television career playing sardonic,
bullying heavies in melodramas. But, as Wivenhoe, who desperately wants
the respect of everybody from "the little persons" at his camp to the town
elders who control the country club he hopes to join, Johnson becomes the
ultimate waltzing elephant trying out all kinds of overelaborate gestures of
goodwill only to bellow in fits of impotent rage when they are not accepted
in the proper spirit.

The task of actually administering the day-to-day operation of the
camp falls to chief counselor George Spiffy (Dave Ketchem again). Spiffy
is the Harry Dickens figure here, the semi-steadying influence charged
with humoring Wivenhoe's moods and coaxing production from his
hapless cohorts: a young fellow counselor, the bumbling naif Stanley
Pruett (Dave Madden), the camp's erratic Doc (Leonard Stone), and its
thin-skinned cook Malden (Mike Wagner). It is Spiffy who has periodic
bouts of depression about the hopelessness of his situation. In fact, in a
two-episode story, after being egged on by his mother's digs about how
well his cousin is doing in the adult world of business, Spiffy actually quits
the camp. But after taking a job in the big city he finds that it is nothing
but a trap, a nightmare of musty Dickensian drudgery that makes the fresh
air pranks and pratfalls of Runamuck seem stimulating in comparison.

It is also Spiffy who will give in to periodic bursts of Zen-like tolerance
and call for truces in the never-ending, hair-pulling, clothes-snatching war
between Runamuck's staff and the goody two-shoes at Camp Divine.

Those exasperatingly efficient females are led by stout, Martha Raye–like Alice Nunn as Mahala May Gruenecker who constantly embarrasses Wivenhoe with her affection, and Marilyn Monroe sound-alike Nina Wayne as second-in-command and erstwhile Rhodes scholar Caprice Yeudelman, the very thought of whom sends Pruett into spastic convulsions of sexual longing.

In the show's most introspective episode, aptly titled "Slaughter," Swift, who both wrote and directed it, briefly reveals some of the motivating forces behind the characters' behavior. The story opens with the Runamuckians waving goodbye to their most recent batch of campers and preparing for the outdoor activities they've planned for their day off— Wivenhoe for his beloved golf game, Pruett for a tennis match with Caprice (if he can only stop his shaking), Spiffy and Doc into town for shopping and a movie, and Malden for sunbathing—when, from out of nowhere, the skies cloud up and unleash a torrent of monsoon-like rain.

Forced back inside they begin moping around the rec room with nothing to do (Wivenhoe practicing his putting on the carpet, Doc incessantly pounding out "Chopsticks" on the piano) until Mahala May and Caprice show up to visit. Excited by this salvation from boredom, the men gather around the women hoping to entice them to stay, but, as usual, only manage to demonstrate how clueless they are in choosing ways of relating to them. After a few awkward introductory remarks on both sides, Spiffy makes what he thinks is a harmlessly jovial observation that in their yellow slickers the women look like the label of the cod liver oil bottle. This, of course, leads to the usual escalation of insults and hurt feelings on both sides and ultimately results in an even grumpier group of guys moping around the room. Finally, Pruett, who has taken to riding a bicycle around in circles, falls on and ruins Wivenhoe's golf clubs setting off the final flurry of yelling and screaming that sends everybody storming off to their separate quarters.

While in their rooms each begins reading pulp fiction adventure books, and as they get more and more engrossed in the stories they begin projecting themselves into the narratives: Pruett as a jungle explorer hunting for an Amazon tribe, Doc as a World War I flying ace crash landing in a French village, Spiffy as a *High Noon* sheriff facing the Younger Brothers singlehandedly, and Wivenhoe as a military general sent to confront an invading Martian spaceship. As the individual reveries unfold, with the other characters playing the supporting roles in each man's fantasy, the inner workings of their self-images surface: Pruett as the sexual adventurer, Doc as the dashing outsider, Spiffy as the lone defender upholding the community, and Wivenhoe as the bastion of order surrounded by aliens. But as Swift begins rapidly intercutting the stories, they all begin boiling down to the same fear of failure and betrayal. Pruett is sold out to the cannibals by his guide Doc, French townspeople Mahala May and Caprice sell Doc souvenirs until his money runs out whereupon he is handed over to the Germans, Spiffy must not only fight the Younger Brothers singlehandedly but also winds up being shot at by his mother Mahala May and his wife Caprice, and Wivenhoe finds that his bullets have no effect on the Martians who decide to take him back home as an Earth specimen. As these fantasies career wildly towards collectively disastrous climaxes, the men all wake up screaming from their daydreams, run out onto the camp grounds, and after crashing into each other, hold together for collective comfort. Embarrassed by their display of emotionalism they then suddenly realize that the sun has come out and, repressing their experiences, march off together again as friends so that they can endlessly act out their fears and frustrations in the weeks to come.

Adult audiences have always been uncomfortable with examinations of infantilism even in distanced, if sympathetic, treatments like *I'm Dickens . . . He's Fenster* and *Camp Runamuck*. But setting these shows among blue-collar carpenters and marginal camp counselors allows the majority of middle-class viewers to disassociate themselves from the antics and deny any resemblance to their own personalities. However, Hal Kanter's *Valentine's Day* sets up a highly attractive social setting, one with which the majority of the middle-class audience was certain to identify their ambitions—and then populated it with smooth and sophisticated versions of the same overgrown children that the two previous shows had allowed us to dismiss as poor relations. In fact, the show even employed strategically placed modernist filmic devices to ensure a maintained distance between the surface seductions of the milieu and any inducement for audience identification.

Valentine's Day is the story of the highly successful young publishing executive Valentine Farrell (Anthony Franciosa), non-fiction editor at the old-line firm of Brackett and Dunstall. Handsome, young Val seems to be the personification of the New Frontier, enjoying his "swinging single" lifestyle while fending off the oversized workload dumped on him by the harried Mr. Dunstall (Jerry Hausner). In this very male version of the American Dream, Val's pursuit of romantic conquest necessitates the introduction of a new female companion in each week's adventure with the sense of permanence in his life being provided by his male-bonding relationship with his long-time friend and man-servant Rocky Sin (Jack Soo). The emotional attachment between Val and Rocky goes back to their initial meeting as Korean War soldiers where Rocky saved Val's life and thus carved out a permanent place for himself in Val's heart and household. But, after Val recounts this story to his female companion in the show's first episode, she points out, much to Val's surprise, that it had actually been Val who had saved Rocky's life. And this is our first indication that "the good life" may not actually look like its picture in the catalog when you get it home. Each day in Val's little boy's version of the pursuit of happiness is just like the Korean War incident. For each day consists of one long group game of upmanship, a whirling rotation of matches to find out who will be the last one to be caught with his pants down (in all senses of the term) and who will be in the room with him when it happens.

A typical episode has Mr. Dunstall rushing upstairs to Val's bedroom where he pleads with Val to abandon his breakfast in bed and come in to work. Val smugly rebuffs him vowing that this year he won't be talked out of his two-week vacation until a long-faced Rocky enters to tell him that he, Rocky, has been called up for two weeks of Army reserve duty. This then will be Valentine's day as he faces not only two weeks of rest and relaxation but also the comforting vision of Rocky sweating his way through boot camp redux. That is until Rocky reads the next paragraph of Uncle Sam's greetings and discovers that Val has been recalled for duty as well.

Once at the Army base Val is besieged by a plain Jane WAC (Shari Marshall) brandishing her manuscript (Mr. Dunstall's doing) and Val assigns Rocky to keep her away from him. This, of course, is Rocky's cue to lead her directly to him. Val retaliates by having Rocky assigned to trash removal detail but Rocky sneaks into the Officers' Club where, forced to pose as the bartender, he acquits himself so well that he gets himself promoted above Val. Nevertheless, Val manages to get Rocky assigned to one of the twenty-mile hikes but Rocky counters by eating strawberries thus triggering his allergic reaction and landing him in the hospital where he is fed breakfast in bed by a beautiful Oriental nurse. Game and set to Rocky—but the match isn't over. When they return to the city they are visited by the plain Jane WAC who turns out to be a beauty who had toned herself down for her own two weeks of Reserve duty. Val then smirkingly saunters off with her for an editorial conference, but not before force-feeding Rocky some strawberries.

This is the basic Sennett view of reality as played out in a stratum of society that Sennett usually left alone. Stylistically *I'm Dickens . . . He's Fenster* very carefully recreated the kind of "primitive" look of a Sennett film in its threadbare black-and-white carpentry shop setting while *Camp Runamuck* with its colorful, outdoor, studio-supported milieu added elements from some of the more elaborately staged physical gags of Keaton and classic cartoons. But in the sophisticated world where one would expect to see a more dignified brand of farce, *Valentine's Day* needed to find some strikingly expressionistic devices which would alert the audience that the forthcoming journey would be via roller coaster rather than limousine. Primarily, they were provided by two men, the first of whom was Anthony Franciosa himself.

Franciosa was one of the many intense, darkly handsome New York method stage actors who hit Hollywood around 1957 (some of the other actors were Ben Gazzara, Robert Loggia, and John Saxon) and although he had shown more of a flair for comedy than most of the others, he was still primarily noted for his fiery dramatics. Exactly why nobody had previously thought of using his flailing gesture, bulging eye histrionics and goofy Cinemascope smile in the service of broad comedy is hard to say, but luckily for *Valentine's Day* Franciosa was gleefully willing and extremely able to turn the title character into a suave but dopey cartoon of the romantic leading man he usually played. Indeed it is astonishing to see the rapid progression of expressions when, after another of Val's frantic dashes down the staircase as he tries to make up lost time on his way to work, he is stopped by Rocky offering him a coffee cup at the foot of the stairs. "What's this?" Franciosa inquires suspiciously to which Soo explains that since time is short he has combined the tomato juice with the coffee. After a few hesitant glances searching for support from Soo he chances a gulp whereupon his face lights up with joy of this new taste sensation only to have it collapse almost immediately as nausea overtakes him and he emphatically commands "Don't *ever* do that again!" as he turns his attention to the front door. Ultimately, Franciosa's frantic emotionalism playing off of Soo's sardonic minimalism created both a stylistic clash and a philosophic blend as they wound up covering every possible approach to their single-minded purpose.

The other key player was the director, former Ernie Kovacs colleague Barry Shear. Shear's strategy was to simulate the pacing of a Sennett highlight reel but periodically freeze the frame on one of Franciosa's huge comic reactions (so much to choose from) or Soo's barely perceptible smirks and then use New Wavish transitional spins, wipes, or cuts to leap from one emotional climax to the next. The result was not only to increase the distance the show kept from portraying the characters as identity figures but also to create a strange kind of empathy for them as they grew more and more to resemble panic-stricken mice caught in a rigged maze.

Like Leonard Stern and David Swift, Hal Kanter had a long television history as a writer who had worked for such disparate talents as Arthur Godfrey, George Gobel, and Danny Kaye. That he would become such an enthusiastic participant in the Sennett cycle is not something one would assume from those earlier credits and, in retrospect, seems downright surprising considering that he is now best remembered for his later work as creator/producer of *Julia*. Yet Kanter seems like a natural when one compares his work to the long histories in traditional sitcoms of executive producer Harry Ackerman, producer Bob Claver, creators Lawrence J. Cohen and Fred Freeman, and story editors Stan Cutler and Martin Donovan all of *Occasional Wife*, a show that not only retained *Valentine's Day*'s freeze-frame strategy but raised the stakes by adding an off-screen narrator/commentator in the person of Los Angeles Dodgers baseball announcer Vin Scully.

The employment of a narrator could not of course stem from silent films like Sennett's, but it does call to mind the Pete Smith Specialties and Behind the Eight Ball shorts of the 1940s. However, those narrators served to reduce the characters to behavioral ciphers, figures out of an instructional manual demonstrating all of the many forms of failure. In *Occasional Wife* Scully makes only occasional intrusions and functions in a way very similar to his role as a sports announcer.

As a baseball broadcaster, it is Scully's function to act as a multifaceted conduit between the players on the field and the fans at home. He must give a factual account of the prosaic and repetitious movements on the field while at the same time remaining faithful to the romantic traditions that the sum of those movements represent. He must objectively recount the results of a game that is based on regularized failure (the best of hitters succeed only thirty percent of the time, the best of teams win only sixty percent of the time) while becoming the ambassador of personification for the unspoken players to their emotionally committed fans. More than any other current practitioner of his trade, Scully is able to combine warmth with irony, and poetry with common sense to portray a game that is equal parts futility and grandeur. Scully brought all of this to his work on *Occasional Wife*, making the show's furious activities both a ridiculously childish game and a serious metaphor for all of the hostility that lies under our most mundane activities. Only Scully could introduce this week's plot by saying that it was a typical day in the characters' lives, "a day destined — to get worse" and infuse that teaser with equal doses of attraction and repulsion.

In fact, it is Scully whom we hear first at the beginning of each episode informing us that "This is a modern fable of the big city. It's about a swinging bachelor with a problem...." This bachelor is Peter Christopher (played by Michael Callen as the latest thing in Tony Curtis hustlers) who does not mind having to give up his bus seat to parents and children or losing out on the family discounts offered by travel agents, but definitely considers it a problem when his bachelorhood blocks his career path. Peter is a rising young executive at Brahms Baby Food ("every meal's a lullaby") but Mr. Brahms (played by Jack Collins as Edward Andrews with an Irish lilt) considers it disloyal to the company for his employees not to be producing future customers. So Peter is faced with the edict, "no marriage, no promotion."

Drowning his sorrows at a local watering hole, Peter falls into conversation with Greta Patterson (played by Patricia Harty as Doris Day's iron-willed kid sister) who works there as a hat check girl in order to support

Michael Callen and Patricia Harty negotiate their relationship in *Occasional Wife***.**

her ambitions of becoming a fashion designer. When Greta casually remarks that it is a shame that Peter can't just wear a phony marriage ring as she does to discourage drunken come-ons, a little light goes on above Peter's head and a high concept is born. Or, as Scully puts it, "she went on salary as his occasional wife."

The operative words here are "on salary." Peter agrees to foot Greta's art school bills and household expenses in return for her being on perpetual call to pose when needed as his wife. But budget battles break out immediately. When Greta insists on a new, more realistic phony wedding ring, Peter takes her to a jewelry store and, in a sly parody of the title sequence from *Breakfast at Tiffany's*, tries to talk her into the closest thing he can find to a Cracker Jack ring while the salesperson (Lindsay Workman doing a fine John McGiver impression) offers droll heckling from behind the counter. Finally, Peter rents her an apartment two floors above his and they settle in to negotiate over the furnishings: Peter bartering up from Salvation Army in order to get concrete concessions on working conditions, Greta bartering down from designer stores in order to get drapes thrown into the deal. Clearly, the revisionist view of marriage as a primarily economic arrangement is strongly at work here, but this show goes even further than that. The underlying assumption on *Occasional Wife* was that *all* interpersonal relationships were basically business accommodations with each new narrative development analyzed by every participant to see if it bettered or worsened their future bargaining position. While "nothing personal, just business" has lately become one of the more tiresome verbal cliches in corporate Hollywood movies, *Occasional Wife* existed almost thirty years ago to offer weekly demonstrations of what a shark's picnic life would actually be if our society lived exclusively by that credo.

Peter, our protagonist, is a charming, young, red-blooded American male. He is the sort of man who forms the backbone of our business world, the sort of man who when backed into a corner sees nothing wrong with having Greta's utilities turned off in order to compel her cooperation. For instance, in one episode Peter signed on with the manager of a rival baby food company who had finally persuaded its owners that the firm needed an infusion of new blood. Since he no longer needed to pretend to be married at this job, Peter fired Greta and sent Mr. Brahms a letter of resignation. However, when the opening round of new blood infusion turned out to be the owners replacing the manager with one of their young nephews, a twisting-in-the-wind Peter resorted to hiring a waterfront thief to help him steal the letter from Mr. Brahms' office. Exhausted but relieved, Peter returned home with the letter only to have Greta get hold of it for use as a bargaining chip in her rehiring negotiations.

Greta, the title figure, is equally committed to the traditional values of individual will and personal triumph in the marketplace of success and is not above withholding Peter's phone messages as leverage for a higher household allowance. Impatient with her progress at art school, Greta once planned with some colleagues to start their own dress manufacturing company and persuaded (read coerced) Peter into becoming a financial backer. Peter also wound up housing the manufacturing facilities since Greta was hosting a visiting aunt, and as production trampled over Peter's privacy, visions of joining The Great Society danced in Greta's head.

However, Greta found that she could not produce dresses cheaply enough to meet the going market price and Peter wound up being called home from the office to settle a wildcat workers' strike in his living room.

But Peter and Greta's personal ambitions are more often than not put on indefinite hold since the occasional couple must spend most of their time furiously running in place trying to plug all of the holes in the leaky dikes Mr. Brahms hands them while at the same time keeping their own dirty secret from tumbling out of the closet. Once Mr. Brahms put Peter and Greta in charge of discouraging a client's "stage mother" wife from pushing her untalented daughter (Sally Field) into an acting career. After much agonizing they concluded that some kind of variation on the truth might actually be effective here so they proposed to Peter's friend, an avant-garde theater producer (Severn Darden), that he audition the daughter and tell her the truth, that she had no talent. However, when the producer saw how rich her family was he hired the daughter and induced the mother into becoming the play's financial backer (Freeze on Darden's smirky grin. Scully: "Why is it that the bad guys always seem to be having all of the fun?"). When Peter tried to cover himself by explaining to Mr. Brahms what the plan had been and how it went awry he nervously concluded that the client could not blame him for what happened. And Mr. Brahms agreed with this analysis, the client would blame Mr. Brahms—and Mr. Brahms would blame Peter. This episode ended happily for Peter as a self-described "soppy" and pointedly offscreen reconcilation between mother and daughter got him off the hook. Both Greta and Scully marveled at how he had lucked out yet again, but Peter was not always so fortunate.

Once, while Peter and Greta are tolerating (in Scully's words) "that All-American ritual, dinner out with the boss and his wife," the entire party sat glumly enduring one of the restaurant's special features, tea leaf readings from inhouse fortune teller Madame Celeste (Rose Marie). When the good Madame predicted an upcoming marriage for Greta, Mr. Brahms scoffed that she was already married. The incident led to an escalating "oh yeah" argument that culminated with Mr. Brahms wearing his dessert in his lap, Madame Celeste getting the old heave-ho, and Peter and Greta trying to blend into the wallpaper.

Madame Celeste turned up at the office the next morning to demand that Brahms help her get her job back with a line of reasoning that alternated bullying insults with abject appeals for sympathy for her plight as the sole support of her son, a first-year Columbia law student. A sweaty palmed Peter tried to forge a compromise. But when the issue came down to the Madame's reading of Peter's instant coffee (she believed in keeping up with the time) and he turned up single again, negotiations broke off with the Madame storming out charging discrimination.

This engendered one of the show's rare occasions where Peter and

Greta actually felt empathy for somebody other than themselves. Moved by the Madame's plight as a working mother, they are tottering on the brink of confessing to Mr. Brahms when the law student son Rudolph (Richard Dreyfuss) actually turns up in his three-piece suit with accessory earring to forcefully represent his mother's action for slander, libel, and defamation of Gypsy. Brought to his senses, Peter instantly snaps back into his usual mode of scrambling for self-preservation and refuses to settle the issue by producing his marriage license on the legal precedent of *Stewart vs. Allison* (the previous night's late movie had starred James Stewart and June Allyson).

His skin saved, Peter arrives at work the next morning to find that his livelihood is once again threatened. Brahms Baby Food is now under siege from a combination outdoor picket, indoor sit-in Gypsy demonstration. Peter is dispatched to reach a settlement with Madame Celeste—or else. But at her Gypsy Mobile Unit Madame Celeste is busy dashing off a letter to the Attorney General and preparing for her appearance on local television to plead her cause. With her pressure campaign going so well she is no longer willing to accept merely getting her job back, she is also demanding a large cash settlement as well.

Squirming in desperation Peter tries to affect a theatrical pose of moral outrage. He solemnly asks her if she is familiar with the term "extortion." But when she cheerfully assures him that she is quite familiar with that term, he finds that he must sink to the bottom of his bag of tricks for a solution. And since it is at the bottom that his own sensibility is most comfortable, a brainstorm is not long in coming.

Later that night Greta is humoring Mr. Brahms into watching *Three Gobs, a Gal, and a Gunboat* on the late movie and they discover that the show is now called *Gypsy Flicks*. That is, "the show that combines cheap old movies with expensive advertising" with your co-hosts, Madame Celeste, and, in a phony baloney moustache and the cheesiest Gypsy costume, Peter Christopher. Since the show also combines positive messages about Gypsy life with Madame Celeste's assertions that she can foretell a long and happy future for every baby who eats Brahms Baby Food, our occasional couple now seem about to live happily ever after.

However, when Madame Celeste and Rudolph drop by much later to visit the Christophers, they have both good news and bad news. The good news is that having been transformed into a celebrity through *Gypsy Flicks*, Madame Celeste is now off to Hollywood to become the new Kim Novak. The bad news is that Rudolph's new client is one Jerome D. Pitzloff, a Lithuanian palm reader who claims that he too can read the future in Brahms Baby Food (as long as the food is placed in the baby's palm) and who wants to know why Brahms has done so much for Gypsies and nothing for Lithuanians. Again Peter tries the moral outrage bit:

Peter: Madame Celeste, aren't you ashamed to allow Rudolph to cash in on your fame?
Madame: Oh I never take any interest in my son's career.
Peter: Since when?
Madame: Since about two minutes ago.

But this time his bag of tricks is empty. So as the camera freezes on Peter and Greta's pained expressions, it is left to Scully to provide this week's moral lesson: "It was a wise Gypsy who first said 'you can't win 'em all.'"

I'm Dickens . . . He's Fenster set up a tension between the possibility of a kinder, gentler domestic world for Harry Dickens and the "man's world" jungle represented by Arch Fenster's "swinging bachelorhood" and the pratfall camaraderie of the carpentry shop. *Camp Runamuck* merely suggested the possible domesticity with Camp Divine so it could concentrate on the inner workings of the boys' club, while *Valentine's Day* trod lightly on the male bonding between Val and Rocky in order to play out the predatory life of the sophisticated bachelor. *Occasional Wife* differs from these three shows in its toning down of the physical buffoonery, but it does so only to better demonstrate what an entire culture set up along Sennett's philosophical lines would look like. In fact, the use of the "normalized" look and feel inherent in the Ackerman–Screen Gems style to sugarcoat its poison becomes the show's crowning glory since, by doing so, they also normalize the behavior it depicts. *Occasional Wife* may well be the iciest series ever presented on network television (unless you count the "Fractured Fairy Tales" on *Bullwinkle*) because it presents itself as no different from any other romance of attractive young people in the big city. The audience sat watching all of the desperate lies and schemes, waiting for the traditional tonal turn, where Peter and Greta discover that their social ambitions are trivial because they have fallen in love, to kick in. However, the unbelievable truth was—it never did.

Occasional Wife disguised itself as just another Screen Gems romantic comedy in order to propose that our modern-day culture was actually more thoroughly Sennettized than the historical period Sennett represented. Another Screen Gems series was concurrently using a modernist reinterpretation of Sennett's original gag construction and pacing to propose that it represented a more creative alternative to our modern-day culture which could force a more sympathetic bond between a dubious public and its "dangerous" title characters, *The Monkees*.

Unlike the four previously cited shows, which were helmed by television comedy veterans whose experience of Sennett came from firsthand personal knowledge, *The Monkees'* creative team was composed almost entirely of young insurgents (including future film producers and directors Bert Schneider, Bob Rafelson, Paul Mazursky, and James Frawley). And, as contemporary 1960s artists, they participated in that era's insurgent

They get the funniest looks from everyone they meet. Hey, hey they're The Monkees: (left to right) Davy Jones, Micky Dolenz, Peter Tork, and Mike Nesmith.

viewpoint of using history as an analytical tool to create fresh perspectives on present-day reality. In singling out Sennett as the core text of their historical rereading, the *Monkees* team was sharing in a sensibility that had already been popularized by Richard Lester.

Indeed, both at the time of its production and in the annals of standard television history, *The Monkees* has been all but creatively marginalized for its obvious borrowings from Lester and his Beatles films, although Lester and The Beatles have suffered little for their borrowings from Sennett and 1950s American rock-and-roll respectively. But the admittedly naked similarities seems to have blinded people to the very different uses that *The Monkees* was making of these elements. For while the show was most certainly influenced by Lester, it was more by *The Running, Jumping, and Standing Still Film* than *A Hard Day's Night*, and more the Victor Spinetti sequences in *A Hard Day's Night* than The Beatles. And while The Beatles, whose name has more to do with their love of Buddy Holly than any identification they felt for the animal kingdom, were acknowledged in their films as the enormously popular, critically respected musicians that they were, it was crucial to their show that The Monkees, whose name reflects their social status, were an obscure, almost destitute band that was ignored by the entertainment industry and disdained by polite society.

The carpenters of *I'm Dickens . . . He's Fenster* and the counselors of *Camp Runamuck* were low-prestige workers whose slapstick antics reflected their lack of stature. But they were still included as part of the collective "we" in American society. *The Monkees* was one of the few instances where the characters of an American television series represented a cultural "otherness" for the majority of the audience. *Occasional Wife* set up a distanced artifice to reflect the harsh realities of the "Fractured Fairy Tales" philosophy that highlights the most animalistic side of human nature. On the other hand, *The Monkees* set up a poetic, uninhibited artifice to reflect the liberating spirit of *The Adventures of Rocky and Bullwinkle*, comically overwrought, in-jokey pulp-fiction serial stories where the title characters are the only animals in an otherwise all-too-human world.

As on *Rocky and Bullwinkle*, the characters exude a show business self-consciousness to the extent of continually wandering outside of the half-baked stories in order to demonstrate how confining these worn-out folkways of popular narrative are. While the "act naturally" Beatles were constantly being compared to The Marx Brothers, it was the cultural analyst Monkees who used them as the structuring principle for the group's internal cohesion with frenetic Micky Dolenz functioning as Groucho, laconic Mike Nesmith as Chico, child-like Peter Tork as Harpo, and heartthrob Davy Jones as Zeppo.

But more than that, the show became television's extension of the counterculture's love for dressing up as iconic figures in American folklore and acting out revisionist versions of our cultural history. As practiced, it was a way whereby one could both embrace the spirit of an everlasting childhood where the game of cowboys and Indians never ended, but also an adult philosophical statement redefining what it meant to be a cowboy and/or an Indian in both historical and contemporary political terms. *The Monkees* took its second-generation view of Sennett-styled comedy, using it in the speeded-up, jump-cut, surreal compilation form in which it had been handed down. The show then added a contemporary sensibility to the prankish, cartoony effects in order to transform Sennett's brutish viewpoint into an instrument of spiritual liberation from a mundane, middle-of-the-road mindset. Further, by linking the most extreme sequences of this visual games-playing to the soundtrack performances of the band's teenage rock-and-roll, it created a very tangible definition of the kind of spirit that music was trying to weave into our culture.

In many ways *The Monkees'* redefinition of Sennett was the rock-and-roll variation on the in-joke goofiness that Soupy Sales had infused into his various kids shows. Borrowing elements from Rocky and Bullwinkle, Soupy Sales, and specific devices from classic animation, *The Monkees* was extremely conscious of how, as representatives of teenage culture, they were tied in to the history of children's television programming. Numerous episodes touched on the theme of children and the entertainment industry, one of which had the Monkees guesting on *The Captain Crocodile Show*.

The group turns up at the studio figuring to play a few songs for the kids and then moves on. But the good Captain (Joey Forman) turns out to be a show-biz paranoid, a basket case of insecurities and evil traumas who is convinced that the Monkees have been sent to take over his show. Captain Crocodile represents traditional Sennettism as, in the name of "fun, fun, fun," he employs pies in the face and exploding musical instruments to humiliate the Monkees in the eyes of his audience and prevent them from competing with him for the children's affection.

Then the Monkees counterattack with their own version of Sennett humor. First they crash the network board meeting that has been called to determine whether they should remain on the Captain's show. Micky pushes his way in posing as a ratings service exec who crunches everybody under a barrage of indigestible numbers. He is followed by Mike who allegedly wanders in as the kindly old janitor who only tunes in the Captain's show to see The Monkees. Finally, Davy and Peter cap the charade hardselling the network brass as "widdle" kids who will hereafter refuse to eat their vegetables unless The Monkees are returned to the air. Buckling under this onslaught, the Captain is quickly unraveling into a jangly nerved mass of jelly reduced to playing with his ball bearings and displaying his wide variety of twitches. He decides to go the limit and unleash his intensely loyal Crocodile Corps kids on The Monkees with instructions to kill. And so we cut to the ever-popular, always decisive chase.

As the soundtrack swells with the stirring strains of "Your Auntie Grizelda," the ferocity of a typical Sennett chase is here converted into an inventive game version. The film speed is by turns quickened and slowed, the characters continually change costumes from shot to shot (with the ever-hounded Monkees changing to represent other American "others" such as Russians and Mexicans), and the continual running around turned into a running round of follow-the-leader up and down a detached five-step staircase that has been plopped down in the middle of the proverbial nowhere. Usually it is through merely getting the comic villains to participate in these parody versions of violent confrontations that they are philosophically disarmed and thus defeated. However, in this case, since the children are not really the villains, the chase leads back to the television studio where the Monkees improvise a story for the kids and the Captain reveals his true colors when he yells at them for not following orders.

Through its use of Sennett techniques to make its characters more heroic and likable, *The Monkees* became the only one of these five shows to garner enough popularity to be picked up for a second season, a popularity it quickly dissipated through its experiments with various forms of alternative narrative structure during that second and final year. Ever since film, and ultimately television, became defined as middle-class media, the trick for Sennett and all of his successors has been to smuggle in all of the distanced characters and harsh viewpoints while maintaining friendly relations with the mass audience. Therefore, it is not surprising that during this early to mid–1960s cycle many Sennett influenced shows were called but few were chosen to remain as long-standing friends of the families.

In many ways the ritualized world of *Green Acres* can be counted as part of this Sennett cycle and its success in tying all of its buffoonery, acid social views, and modernist distancing devices to a collection of endearingly cartoony characters and an anachronistic rural setting constitutes the cycle's greatest popular achievement. However, the only other show from the cycle that found long-running popular favor was one of its least resonant and least representative. While former Bob Hope writer Sherwood Schwartz's *Gilligan's Island* painted its surface with a simplified layer of Sennett slapstick, the heart of its popularity lay with its all but literalized sentimental impersonations of Laurel and Hardy enacted by series leads Bob Denver and Alan Hale, Jr.

Still, for both better and worse, the Sennett style has had a greater impact on the past 20 years of television comedy than the relative obscurity of these five shows would indicate. On the down side, usable devices and strategies from these shows were co-opted by middle-of-the-road television and alchemized to the point where they have become philosophically inverted. But then one can almost see the historical inevitability of *The Monkees'* outcast horseplay transforming into the smug, moralizing wheezes of doctors and military officers on *M*A*S*H*, and one need only look at the current incarnations of *I'm Dickens . . . He's Fenster* and *Valentine's Day*, namely *Home Improvement* and *Dream On*, to see how the 1960s romanticized universalization of child-like innocence curdled into the 1980s narcissistic personalization of wallowing in arrested adolescence.

On the other hand, we are now also seeing the most creative new voices in television comedy rebelling against such moist moralism and self-absorption and using the Sennett style as the foundation for their antidotal insurrections. To date the analytical, politicized roughhouse comedy of England's Comic Strip has far outdistanced their American counterparts, but fresh ideas cast from the Sennett mold seem to be surfacing with satisfying regularity. This style, which had until recently seemed to have become a dead language, is now yielding most of the vital new ideas on the scene, with the final irony for a form so caught up in the ethos of male aggression being that the ultimate Sennett show may turn out to be *The Gorgeous Ladies of Wrestling*.

5
I Found It at the Movies
Sid Caesar, Carol Burnett, and Don Adams

In a recent interview Billy Crystal pinpointed the moment when he first decided to become a comedian. He vividly recounted a childhood memory of watching television with his parents and seeing Sid Caesar come strutting onto the screen barefoot, in a pathetically tatty costume, and with a pointedly phony bald wig as accoutrements for his impersonation of Yul Brynner in *The King and I*. Crystal described how he collapsed in hysterics as Caesar's expression of regal arrogance turned into an explosive exaggeration of comic pain and surprise as he bellowed out, "All right, who left the cigarette butt on the palace carpet?"

It is emblematic of our present generation that Crystal's initial exposure to, and early appreciation of the arts and crafts of comedy came from watching television. But it is equally emblematic that what he recalls watching is one of the seminal figures of the previous generation doing a movie parody.

It is possible to understand the stylistic and philosophic differences between the two generations from the ways in which they related to the pop culture visual mediums of their youths. Growing up during the prosperous, suburbanized 1950s and 1960s, television served as a matter-of-fact everyday presence in the home of a Billy Crystal. Television presented a scaled-down, everyday world that blended into the home life surrounding it and invited a feeling of security in the viewer—a feeling that you could indeed become what you beheld because the people and events you were watching belong to the same kind of world that you inhabit.

The experiences and expectations of a young Sid Caesar however were quite different. Growing up in the urban melting pot during the

Great Depression, practically everything surrounding Caesar was some kind of reminder of his individual insignificance and his closer collective identity with his immigrant ethnic heritage than with the mainstream American tradition that was marginalizing his life. And his relationship with the movies was just another one of those reminders. Movies were not everyday home companions but rather special events that involved active excursions to dark and exotic venues where you had to pay cash money for the privilege of seeing the show. Further, the overwhelmingly larger-than-life shows that you saw were not representative of the life you were leading but rather of an idealized world, a world you could only strive to inhabit in your wishes and dreams. The Depression-era children would come home from the movies and play act their own versions of the stories that they saw, and it was by reconstructing the movies on their own terms that they were making their own realities understandable to themselves—and the gap between those realities and the grandeur of the movie world to which they aspired.

As these children reached adulthood the deterministic forces of the Depression were easing, only to be replaced by the equally overpowering forces of World War II and the post-war prosperity that followed in its wake. And so before they had gotten a chance to catch their collective breath and make a mature reexamination of their childhood self-images this generation found that they had somehow become adult, middle-class suburbanites with immediate family responsibilities, future-defining jobs, and television sets. But through all of these years of rafting through the historical tides, going to the movies remained a constant in their lives as the familiarity of the studio system's genre plots and contract stars provided a steady stream of idealized images for these grown-up children to compare against their own experience.

The exploration of this gap between our daily lives and the movie images we love became a central issue for many of the comedians of the Depression/World War II generation. Of course, there were many different ways that this gap could be approached and many different ways that those images could be interpreted, a point best illustrated by comparing the work of the aforementioned Caesar with that of the television comedian whose professional style and personal background most closely resembled Caesar's, namely Jackie Gleason.

Both Caesar and Gleason were New York ethnics who grew up watching the movies of the late silent and early talkie eras. Both developed a wide range of comic characters some of whom, like the silent comedians, were presented in pantomime. However, unlike the prototypical silent comedians, neither man conveyed either an underdog quality or an "everyman" universality in their appearances. Both were big men with dark, almost menacing features and harsh urban accents to their gruff voices. In fact, both men carried with them the aura of a great reservoir of internal anger just below the surface that was under imminent threat of explosion. And one of the salient features of both mens' performance styles was the surface explosion of that anger. But it is the very different ways in which they expressed their anger that highlights their contrasting self-images and their contrasting approaches to character which, as it happens, made understandable the very different ways that they utilized their devotion to movies.

One rarely, if ever, thinks about Jackie Gleason directly in relation to the movies. The overriding memories of Gleason's work center on the large cast of comic characters he created, and the only one of them who was even tangentially connected in any specific way to the movies was late-night television host Stanley Sugg who hawked the full line of Mother Fletcher's snake oil products between snippets of films that invariably starred "the ever-popular Mae Busch." And, ironically, Sugg has now become the most obscure of Gleason's stock company of characters—probably because he was lifted lock, stock, and vocal inflections by Johnny Carson for the "Art Fern's Tea Time Movie" sketches on *The Tonight Show*. Yet if you look carefully at all of the other fondly remembered Gleason characters, you can see what a close student of movie comedy he had been.

The most pronounced influence can be seen on those characters who relied either extensively or exclusively on pantomime. Gleason's "pathetic victim" characters such as Fenwick Babbitt and The Poor Soul take gestures and reinvent plotted sequences from all of the silent "underdog" comedians ranging from Chaplin and Harry Langdon to a variety of now forgotten lesser figures. Even more pointedly, Gleason's self-assured, tipsy playboy character Reginald van Gleason III is an almost total recreation of Raymond Griffith's persona both physically and behaviorally. The influences of silent film comedy appear much more nakedly in these characters because Gleason saw them primarily as abstractions, the first two as the kind of stepped-upon little guys that the Irish kid from Brooklyn could never stop being in his own mind, and the latter as the kind of wish fulfillment idealization that the Brooklyn kid could only dream of becoming. In a way these characters *were* the movies to Gleason, the movies as seen by the more verbal, very concrete, and painstakingly particularized Gleason-created characters that belonged to his home-base Irish-Brooklyn neighborhood.

The more verbal a Gleason character was, the more specifically placed within and descriptively informational about the neighborhood he became. The windy story teller, Joe the Bartender, narrating the continuing adventures of such perennial patrons as Fatso Fogarty and Crazy Guggenheim, set up a whole James T. Farrell universe which ultimately served as the sociological/psychological underpinnings for the other neighborhood characters that Gleason personally portrayed, Rudy the Repairman, Charlie Bratten, and Ralph Kramden. In many ways the world inhabited by these neighborhood characters is as harsh and tragically determined as anything we see in Farrell's writings, but Gleason is able to turn it into comedy largely though applying the techniques he picked up from those comedians he watched in his youth.

The Kramdens and the Nortons of "The Honeymooners," Gleason's most original and most completely individuated set of characters, were strongly influenced by Laurel and Hardy. The most striking device from Laurel and Hardy's arsenal that Gleason employed almost endlessly was one character's blank stare of negation standing against the other character's flailing emotional appeal for approval. One could point to the continual replayings of the totemic scene where Alice Kramden (Audrey Meadows) stands in stone-faced incredulity listening to Ralph's furious whinings as he begs her to accept his latest hare-brained scheme to achieve social status and monetary reward. But one could point to an equal number of scenes where it is Ralph standing immobile in bug-eyed disdain while Ed Norton (Art Carney) winds down another sputtering episode in his collection of circular-thinking brainstorms which always end with even Norton realizing that he has been talking nonsense and Kramden adding his inevitable coup de grace, "You are a mental case." Indeed, the Gleason pantomime principle applies even here. When "The Honeymooners" stop talking and switch over to more physical comedy, the silent movie comedy basis becomes even more apparent. In an episode in which the Kramdens and the Nortons take charge of a fleabag hotel, Ralph and Ed engage in a long, silent sequence in which they attempt to clean up the lobby where they are so patently impersonating Laurel and Hardy that you can almost hear the Leroy Shield music in the background.

Gleason's strategy, then, is to integrate the ideas and techniques of the comedy he grew up watching into the adventures of his neighborhood-rooted characters in order to make the frustrations and despair of their ordinary lives theatrically entertaining for the audience. The saving grace of that comedy seems to be the only thing that keeps Gleason from violently acting on the rage that drives both him and all of his characters. Gleason is so completely rooted to his origins in the working-class neighborhood that he carries with him at all times the inbred resentment of being confined by that social definition. And since he and his characters cannot conceive of their lives in any other terms, all of that resentment is directed outward, towards the people and things they see as holding back their progress towards success. When Rudy the Repairman takes phantom swipes at the rich and middle-class people whose homes he is wrecking and savagely mutters, "You dirty—!" or when Ralph Kramden shakes his fist in frustration and threatens to send Alice to the moon after she has demolished yet another of his plans for upward mobility, Gleason is giving voice to what those characters do not want to believe but privately know to be true: that their immutable self-identities are traps which will keep them permanently locked into place among society's nonentities. This whole attitude can be summed up by Ralph's other recurring threat towards Alice, "Don't steam me, 'cause I'm already steamed!"

All of this is in sharp contrast to the way that Sid Caesar operated. "The Honeymooners" eventually came to overwhelm everything else Gleason did in part because he invested so much specificity in documenting their lives. We came to know so much about the Kramdens and the Nortons (their histories, their jobs, the other people in their building) that it was almost inevitable that they would outgrow their segments on Gleason's variety show and be spun off as a full-fledged sitcom. That is the form in which we now remember "The Honeymooners." As originally conceived, it was simply *The Jackie Gleason Show*'s version of what was a staple of 1950s variety shows, a weekly serial of sketches that featured the show's regular cast members chronicling the adventures of a specific married couple. On *Your Show of Shows* this was the saga of Doris and Charlie Hickenlooper as portrayed by Imogene Coca and Sid Caesar. If we compare the way that the Hickenloopers and Kramdens were presented, the contrasting approaches of Gleason and Caesar are placed in stark relief.

The Hickenloopers were almost as relentlessly universalized as the Kramdens were specified. From the incidental details in the sketches, we can surmise that the Hickenloopers live in New York but we are never told where. Charlie is occasionally pictured working at a desk in an office but we never find out what he does or for whom. And, we sometimes see them interacting with other characters who are supposed to be their personal friends but they are not carried over from sketch to sketch and no specific social milieu is ever established. In fact, the one thing that we do know about them, their urban identity, is also mitigated by naming them Hickenlooper after the then well-known Republican senator from Iowa. The focus then is not on how the characters relate to the social order but how they interact with each other in the classic, almost fetishized situations that create conflict between any husband and wife (i.e., husband goes out to play poker with "the boys" without informing wife or wife totals car in traffic accident and must prepare husband for the shock of bad news). This is not to say that the Hickenloopers are not as fully characterized as the Kramdens. It merely points up how the conscious decision to keep the Hickenloopers sociologically vague is as revelatory of Caesar's approach as the Kramdens' overspecificity is of Gleason's.

Caesar's New York Jewishness is as transparently a part of every character he played as is Gleason's New York Irishness. But while Gleason's

Sid Caesar plays the German professor and Imogene Coca plays romantic rapture in *Your Show of Shows.*

comedy was the external conflict between the neighborhood boy and the rest of the outside world, Caesar's was the internal conflict between the neighborhood boy and every other kind of person he was able to imitate. Caesar was always playing characters who were divided against themselves. All of the self-evident aspects of Charlie Hickenlooper's personality speaks to an overdetermined past in the parochial ethnic ghetto but all of

the details of his daily life point towards an undefined present in the up-
wardly mobile melting pot. As such, while a Gleason character such as
Ralph Kramden will direct all of his frustrations outward, a Caesar
character like Charlie Hickenlooper will often turn his rage inwardly onto
himself. One can see how strikingly this operated when the Hickenloopers
did their version of that 1950s perennial, "husband and wife argue about
whether the joke he told her is funny."

In this instance the joke is about the little boy who keeps circling the
same block over and over again and when asked by a policeman what he
is doing, explains that he is running away from home but his mother won't
let him cross the street by himself. After Doris interprets the story literally,
expressing sympathy for the boy and worry for the mother who is waiting
at home, Charlie makes a painstaking effort to retell the story so that Doris
will see that it is a joke. He stops each time she interrupts the story to
mollify her objections with ever-increasing frustration ("I agree with you!
Up to this point it's a very serious story!") but he finally gives up in disgust
hurling the expected "You have no sense of humor" accusations at her as
he retreats. But then, alone in his own single bed, he unexpectedly turns
on himself. Maybe he told the joke wrong. Maybe he left something out,
he muses to himself, and that is why Doris did not get it. His new resolve
to try the joke again only leads to the phoning of a third party to whom
Doris tells the joke with the events described in the wrong sequential order
which ruins the punchline. Charlie is so enraged by her butchering of his
joke that he grabs the phone from her and begins to tell it himself. But he
is now so completely out of control that the version he is telling is even
more misshapen than Doris's version. As he reaches for what he suddenly
realizes is a non-existent punchline, he pauses in thought and again turns
on himself. Slamming down the phone he begins yelling, "That's not a
funny joke! I don't think that's funny at all! And I'm gonna tell Harry
tomorrow, 'That's not a funny joke!'"

Caesar has always been cited for how well he does foreign dialects, for
how well he can, using non-words and nonsense syllables, impersonate
through speech patterns and body gestures the characteristics of what is
supposed to be the typical Frenchman, or Italian, or German. Indeed his
talent in this area is extraordinary, but the component of these impersonations which is rarely mentioned, the component which in fact makes these
characters funny, is that while he is taking on all of the characteristics of
these European types he is, at the same time, steadfastly remaining what
he actually is, the typical New York Jew. The constant battle between what
he is and always will remain and all of the many things he can both envision
himself being and convincingly impersonate is what makes his dialect
characters work, and explains why he is so strongly attracted to and so
brilliant at doing movie spoofs.

In a surviving segment from *Your Show of Shows'* precursor *Admiral Broadway Revue,* Caesar does a monologue which he describes as his impression of a boxing movie. What he actually does is an analytical take on one of the most primal of the "assimilate to American monetary success vs. keep the moral ethnic faith" conflicts, Clifford Odets' *Golden Boy,* with a smattering of its updated version, *Body and Soul,* thrown in for contemporaneousness. Caesar whizzes through the character's internal struggle to choose between cash and culture with such a wide array of leap-of-logic lunges between those polarities that the argument all but disintegrates into its essential absurdity. Even more to the point, by portraying the character as a dim-witted pug closer in spirit to Maxie Rosenbloom than John Garfield, he exposes the melodramatic phoniness of the whole setup. In a theatricalized setting one can almost accept a tough/tender John Garfield agonizing over whether to become a boxer or a concert violinist, but Caesar's stark monologue brings him back to his documentary roots and as he stumbles through his soliloquy ("Nah, nah, I dought wanna be a fighta, I wanna be a chemistry teacha"), the unbridgeable gap between the slick movie aspirations and the hard neighborhood realities come hilariously into focus. In fact, for an even more concise distillation of Caesar's approach one need only return to Billy Crystal's example, Caesar striking an exotic, heroic pose as the King of Siam only to be brought back to earth by some neighborhood stumblebum who left a cigarette butt on the carpet.

Both in his personal life and in signature roles like those in *Body and Soul* and *Humoresque,* John Garfield embodied the agonies in the contradictory drives to both assimilate in pursuit of the American Dream and retain roots in his ethnic value system. And it was Garfield's portrayals of these roles that are now considered to be the vital link between the Group Theater ethos of the Depression and the "method acting" revolution of the post–World War II world. So it was not coincidental that just as Caesar had parodied the Garfield image in that 1949 boxing routine, many of his best 1950s film parodies were comic exaggerations of classic method performances. From playing Montgomery Clift's Pvt. Pruitt in *Your Show of Shows'* legendary spoof of *From Here to Eternity* to taking on Marlon Brando's showiest performances in *A Streetcar Named Desire* and *On the Waterfront,* Caesar delighted in sending up the method's internal contradictions, such as characterization being drawn from the actor's personal psyche while his ego remains subservient to the author's character, or a torturously public display of theatrical craft leading to a higher level of naturalism.

These battles to reconcile self-expression with artistic interpretation and play-acting with ordinary experience fit perfectly into Caesar's approach and he feasted on every opportunity to parody method performances. "On the Docks" is a typical example where Caesar contorts Brando's gestures designed to express Terry Malloy's almost "feminine" sensitivity

within his brutish inexpressiveness to the point where Caesar begins looking like a bashful five-year-old while threatening to bash his brother's head
in. The innate condition of being two people at the same time that play-
acting an already existing movie afforded fit perfectly into Caesar's mode
of operation and he never tired of exploring new facets of this condition.

Beyond the movie parodies, the Hickenloopers sketches, and the
mime and dialect routines, the other recurring feature on Caesar's shows
was a never-ending parody of an early rock-and-roll singing group, The
Haircuts. Viewed today these segments which feature Caesar, Carl Reiner,
and Howard Morris as a trio of pompadoured jumping jacks, are almost
painful to watch. They have very little feel and even less sympathy for what
they are spoofing, leaving the three men to run an endless treadmill recycl-
ing their single schtick of mocking untutored performers who are substituting exuberance for talent. The only thing that saves some of these bits
is Caesar's tentative discovery of the links between method actors and
rock-and-roll singers (it is not coincidental that a constant criticism of
both groups was that you could not comprehend their diction) such as in
a long, convoluted recitation segment to one of The Haircuts' moronic
songs where Caesar narrates the story of his night out with his girl, giving
us the litany of their trek through the whole New York subway system and
each course of their seafood dinner while groping to discover what exactly
is the point of his story.

The rationale for so many segments with The Haircuts may seem baf-
fling now, but in the mid to late 1950s all of the major variety shows were
doing the rock-and-roll waltz. It behooved Milton Berle to bring out Elvis
Presley and Steve Allen to present Jerry Lee Lewis in order to stay abreast
of the musical trends, but the intensity and frequency with which they proclaimed their personal distaste for the music seemed almost to be a prophetic understanding of what it would wind up doing to the traditional
variety show.

Radio and 1950s television variety shows had an unspoken dependence on America's acceptance of swing as its national musical idiom, a
combination of jazz and pop that united musical tastes and defined a
rhythm for consensus entertainment. In point of fact, swing had already
fragmented into progressive instrumental bebop and commercial pop
vocals by the time television came along but enough of its common glue
spirit remained to propel the variety shows—until the rock-and-roll revolution. Rock-and-roll fragmented the audience along generational lines,
leaving the comedians who fronted the variety shows alienated from the
music that would normally be part of their show.

Further, at the same time that rock-and-roll was changing the rhythm
of music, the gradual shift in television production techniques from live
New York telecasts to videotaped presentations from California was also

altering the established rhythm in variety presentation. And, as if that were not enough, a new rhythm in comedy was also being developed by the beat- and bebop-influenced new breed of stand-ups who wrote their own material and were not particularly interested in adapting to variety ensemble. Taken all together these trends destroyed the unspoken consensus for the traditional variety show format. By 1961 all of the now legendary 1950s shows hosted by comedians were off the air and only a few shows hosted by mainstream pop singers remained.

Through the mid–1960s television slowly adjusted itself to these cultural changes and a new era of variety shows began to evolve. Shows such as *Shindig, The Lively Ones*, and *Where the Action Is* indicated ways in which rock-and-roll music and the videotape format could be combined which would be acceptable to a consensus audience, and certain new-breed comedians such as The Smothers Brothers became interested in adjusting their performance style to accommodate series television. By the late 1960s a variety renaissance was underway, with shows such as *Rowan and Martin's Laugh-In* exploring the comedic possibilities in the videotape format and both The Smothers Brothers and Sonny and Cher using the California folk/rock scene as a springboard for comedy. Yet while those are the shows that we now remember in relation to this second wave of variety, the series that outlived all of them was one that took advantage of this genre revival to reinvent the traditional format, *The Carol Burnett Show*.

Both Burnett and her producer/husband Joe Hamilton were veterans of Garry Moore's late 1950s variety show. When the revival gave them the opportunity to do their own show, they seized it in the name of the 1950s shows, in general, and *Your Show of Shows*, in particular. In order to accomplish this, they had to reestablish the sense of stage space that the live shows had had for an audience that was now accustomed to the pre-recorded filmic techniques that the other new shows were exploring. Thus, the introduction of the now famous opening sequences in which Burnett comes out onto the bare stage, the house lights come up, and she engages in question-and-answer sessions with the studio audience. Thus the re-emergence of the *Your Hit Parade*–style endings with the entire company congregating back on stage to wave goodbye to the folks at home. During the first few seasons the show even used vaudeville-styled title cards to name and introduce each new segment of the show.

None of this was done in the interest of nostalgia. It was necessary for Burnett to reintroduce the stylistics of the 1950s variety show because her comedic interests were in doing the very things that those shows established: the married couple sketches (first in the Caesar tradition with the universalized suburban couple Roger and Carol, then in the Gleason tradition with the highly specified Southern Gothic family that was eventually spun off as a sitcom for Vicki Lawrence), the mime routines with her charwoman character, and, and, most emphatically, the movie parodies. However, Burnett had been focusing her attention on a very different group of movies because her comedic concerns and stylistic approach took her in the direction of a very different aspect of film culture.

Like most female comics of her era, Burnett's style was to a large degree formed under the overwhelming influence of Martha Raye who, along with her contemporaries Joan Davis and Judy Canova, brought female physical comedy aggressively into the swing era. Building on the stage work of Fanny Brice and Charlotte Greenwood, Raye gracefully speeded the tempo of all of the physical, facial, and vocal gestures in her version of the self-deprecating, man-chasing character to the point where her constant turnabouts from wild and eccentric pursuit to sudden bouts of introspection and back again began to resemble a seamless stream of emotional consciousness. In the 1940s, this influence led to the battalion of manic jitterbug comedienne/singers (Betty Hutton, Betty Kean, Peggy Ryan, Cass Daley, and others) and by the 1950s to stage and television musical comedy performers (like Dorothy Louden, Charlotte Rae, and Burnett). But as huge a presence as Raye was, equally important to Burnett's development was Caesar's *Your Show of Shows* co-star, Imogene Coca.

There is a strong facial resemblance between Coca and Burnett and Burnett clearly studied Coca's work carefully. Burnett's comic "come hither" sensual expression is identical to Coca's for instance, and she also picked up on Coca's way of suddenly running her voice up three or four octaves to comically overemphasize a change in emotional moods. But Burnett was not watching Coca in order to find devices she could successfully copy, she was following the work of a comic talent who was using much the same emotional and psychological approach that she intended to explore.

In *Your Show of Shows*' spoof of aviation test pilot films, *Sneaking Through the Sound Barrier*, Caesar plays test pilot Jim Johnson as a spoof version of the ultimate stiffbacked Wasp. However, the defining Caesar moment that identifies his technique comes when he is told of the dangers he is about to face and suddenly he turns into one of the Bowery Boys ("Whydya tell me that!? I was just going up for a flight. I wasn't nervous. *Now* I'm nervous!").

This is followed almost immediately by Coca's defining moment where she breaks down into operatic hysterics, pleading with Caesar not to take the plane up and ending by burying her head tearfully in his chest. Caesar simply whispers, "I must," and Coca's head immediately bounces back up to reveal a beatific smile with spaced-out eyes as she contentedly coos a calm and dutiful, "Alll riiight." If the center of Caesar's comedy was that he was both inside and outside of the character at the same time, the center of Coca's comedy was how ferociously she could envelop the emotions of the character and with what speed and dexterity she could shift from one emotional state to another.

In some ways *The Carol Burnett Show* can be understood as what *Your Show of Shows* would have been had Coca been its central presence. Yet left to her own devices, Burnett was not simply content to engulf the emotional states of the characters in the movies she parodied but instead aimed to skyrocket them into the stratosphere. And while Caesar's attitude was best expressed through the ambivalent stances of 1950s Method actors, Burnett's allegiance was to the emotional extremist grande dames of the 1940s. Indeed, Burnett's ability to home in on the high-tension emotional buttons that those movie stars were pushing and enlarge the effects to the point where the actorly manipulation became absurdedly naked was truly uncanny. For example, Burnett was equally adept at lampooning the campiness in Joan Crawford's "queen bee" monsters or in putting on a short skirt, squeaking up her voice and highlighting the underlying monstrosity in the innocent Shirley Temple goody-good girl. In fact, it was that ambidextrous ability to demolish either end of the madonna/whore trap that gave such comic resonance to her classic dismantling of Bette Davis' "tour-de-force" twin portrayals in "A Swiped Life." That, and the cockamamie foghorn which incessantly lumbered in to underline every unsubtle shift in the story. Yet for all of the wide range of actresses and performances that Burnett lampooned over the years, the one that she never tired of playing, that she returned to in sketch after sketch, was Gloria Swanson's creation of Hollywood's undisputed queen of psychotic megalomania, Norma Desmond in Billy Wilder's *Sunset Boulevard*. Indeed, the *Burnett Show*'s concept of a Dean Martin celebrity roast for Norma Desmond is as audacious as anything done by SCTV.

The 1940s films, which contained the juiciest meat for Burnett to devour, were the films she had grown up watching and play-acting in her youth. They remained the films she chose to recreate in her adult career because these 1940s films possessed many distinct elements peculiar to their era that could not be recreated in spoofs of the then current cinema. The institution of the Production Code in 1934 left American films with a truckload of dilemmas about how to portray some common realities of sex, violence, and the ambiguities of morality without incuring the wrath of the censorship boards. *The Thin Man* and *It Happened One Night* came along right after the code went into effect and very clearly directed Hollywood down the road of substituting banter for sexual tension and creating metaphoric gestures and objects to represent states of mind.

By the time that the 1940s rolled in, this system of signs and metaphors had become so commonplace and so entrenched into such a deep level of abstraction that the uninitiated practically needed a code book to figure out what was going on. For example, much has been made of the many ways that cigarette smoking was used to indicate the sexual relationship between the characters, but the devices used to define a sexual relationship in the 1940s could be as explicit as a phallic cigarette or as deep a reach as a character deciding whether he will or will not be having onions on his hamburger—and therefore whether he wanted his breath fresh enough for later intimate contact. In fact, "hold the onions" became a popular comic catchphrase on radio and in cartoons for just this reason.

Relying so heavily on this elaborate system of metaphors, 1940s films began to take on the aura of extended dreams. They developed a slow, almost hypnotic pace (the length of the average "A" film increased by about half an hour during the 1940s) leading up to almost operatically intense emotional climaxes. If you were not in on the meanings of the metaphoric events in these narratives, the characters' responses to them would seem laughably overwrought particularly within the genres that Burnett found most fertile—the domestic melodramas which were condescendingly referred to as "women's pictures," and the thickly romantic crime films that came to be known as "film noir."

Your Show of Shows constructed its Depression-era or contemporary film parodies by picking out individual scenes from the film and recreating them in more or less real time so that Caesar could first establish the character and then wander in and out of its expected movie responses. In contrast, Burnett compressed the 1940s films' dreamlike narrative until the metaphors separated into a ridiculously naked collection of wheezy theatrical tricks and then elongated the emotional climaxes until they became self-contained orgies of hysteria in every sense of the word.

Burnett was extremely conscious of how these movie metaphors functioned even when she was not specifically doing a movie parody. A sketch in which she and her husband (Harvey Korman) both hire the same hit man (frequent guest star Steve Lawrence) to do each other in boils down to that time-honored routine of the struggle over the gun whose discharging instigates the long, tension-packed pause before we find out who has been hit. Only here the struggle is played out among three people, and after the gun goes off they all seem to be groping themselves for wounds for what seems like an eternity before Burnett finally finds a telltale spot, gets the other two's attention, indicates herself with a jaunty "Yo," and spins to the floor. She reused the idea in one of her Norma Desmond sketches. In this instance, she concentrates on the idea of how a long, elaborate death scene becomes an actor's ultimate moment of commanding audience attention as she goes through a grandiose flurry of grimaces and staggers only to be interrupted by an irritated Steve Lawrence who tells her to knock it off because the bullet hit him.

In fact, it seemed that Burnett was committed to exploring every one of the many meanings of movie death scenes. Dying, representing the ultimate orgasm, got star billing in her send-up of Wilder's *Double Indemnity*. Here, with Burnett as the femme fatale and Steve Lawrence (again) as insurance investigator Walter Leff, they make a feast of the film's sex and death climax as they grunt out different versions of "I love you, Baby" and stagger and flop all over the set like kids romping through a playground while taking four or five turns at blasting away at each other.

But perhaps the ultimate *Burnett Show* death scene comes when she makes mincemeat of William Wyler's alleged "subtle" deep-focus sequence where Bette Davis sits calmly in the foreground while Herbert Marshall is having his heart attack on the background staircase in *The Little Foxes*. Here Burnett is prepared to patiently sit out Roddy McDowall's agony on the stairs. But when he begins to have too much fun resurrecting himself over and over again, sliding up and down the bannister and convulsing on the floor like the fourth Stooge, her patience, just like that of the orchestra who must continually rev up to accompany McDowall's antics, begins wearing thin. Burnett is finally forced to troop back to the staircase to witness these shenanigans and "evil eye" McDowall into submission. When the bitten dust finally settles, Harvey Korman leads the rest of the cast back into the room inquiring, "What happened? We heard all this 'dying music' in here."

While it may not have been absolutely necessary for Burnett to couch her show in anachronistic 1950s stylistics in order to do her movie spoofs, the time warp aura did make it easier for the audience to accept her preoccupation with the melodramas and musicals of the 1940s. Burnett paid a small price for that decision since while her talent was always hugely respected, she was then considered to be somewhat quaint in comparison to such super-contemporary shows as *Laugh-In*. In retrospect, Burnett's penchant for pushing melodrama so hard that it turned into slapstick horror seems almost prophetic. Imagine what a *Carol Burnett Show* of the 1980s would have made of Stephen King and slasher movies.

While the decision to recreate the stylistics of a 1950s show was a philosophic choice on Burnett's part, her insistence (and Caesar's) on doing movie parodies left no other choice in terms of program format than the theater-staged variety show. It could be argued that the aesthetics of the variety show sketch combines the worst elements of theater and television in that the close-up naturalism of the television camera emphasizes the inauthenticity of the theatrical sets, while the live physicality or the theatrical performances are undercut by the sketch format's usual ten- to twelve-minute time limitation. Yet, ironically, these were the very qualities that made for successful movie parodies. The ridiculous gap between the means of the original production and the spoof version helps the comedian expose how a movie's lavish budget and technical expertise are used to gloss over its dubious notions of logic and philosophy and reconnects both comedian and audience to its primal purpose in movie parody by returning us all to the children we were, play-acting our own version in the back-yard.

If you return to Billy Crystal's childhood remembrance, the salient points that stuck in his mind were the tackiness of Sid Caesar's costume and the phoniness of his bald wig in his pathetic attempt to impersonate the King of Siam. But while all of these factors played to the strengths of performers such as Caesar and Carol Burnett, they were almost impene-trable obstacles for Don Adams.

Adams first came to national attention as a stand-up comic in the late 1950s. His early appearances on *The Steve Allen Show* reveal a talent that has already focused on an extremely specific attitude but is searching for its most perfect form of expression. In two early appearances he begins with fairly typical material about issues such as apartment hunting in Manhattan. His style of presenting this material is somewhat hushed and tentative, his timing on the punchlines a tad awkward. But then he hits us with a non-existent segue "Which of course brings us to the movies" and follows it with a quizzical "What did I just say?" double take and all of a sudden we seem to be dealing with a totally different comedian.

The heart of these *Allen Show* routines then become parodies of ex-positions we have heard in genre movies since time immemorial. In both cases he is playing authority figures, a Bengal Lancers–type Army officer and an ace police investigator, trying to impress a room full of people of the length and breadth of his expertise—which unfortunately seems to consist entirely of tortured interpretations of how their roles are usually played in standard-issue movies. For instance, the detective's explanation of how he identified the killer sounds like and unedited compilation of every denouement in a "locked-door" mystery ever filmed:

> Inspector, when you gave me this case I knew it was going to be a tough nut to crack. But after working twenty-three hours—every day—for the past twenty-eight years I've narrowed the suspects down to the people in this room. And I'm delighted to see we have such a splendid turnout. The room is packed. . . . Very clever how he covered his tracks. Yes, but he forgot one thing. He forgot about the magnus begolia. Yes, the magnus begolia, a very rare flower that is only found on the southern tip of Tibet. But what he didn't know was that the magnus begolia only blooms at night! After that, the case was fairly simple.
>
> He was the only one who had the key to Madeline's closet. He was the only one who knew the secret of the Chinese vase. He was the only one who could have gotten on board the *Star of Passion* and gotten back in time to forge the passport of Henri Duvall and still make the sixth race at Jamaica. The only one who had a fanatical devotion to cats and an un-canny knack for brain surgery. . . . This, and the fact that he never shaved, led me to believe that he was wearing a mask!

At the end of this mind-boggling explanation it turns out that he has not only identified the wrong killer but he is explaining this all to the wrong police inspector.

Unlike Caesar, whose character is constantly clashing a movie existence with a neighborhood existence, or Burnett, whose character is constantly trumping a movie existence with the consequences of its logical emotional conclusions, there is no internal conflict in the Adams persona. His character is completely committed to seamlessly inhabiting the romantic, authoritative role of the movie action/adventure hero. The conflict comes from the surrounding world's stubborn refusal to conform to its role in the time-honored script he is playing out. As such, like Bob Newhart, his monologues imply a narrative context with other characters playing off of what he is saying, but the specifics of his approach all but preclude the narrative taking the form of variety show sketches.

Since Adams' comedy depends on his character's total commitment to his movie-inspired self-image, he must maintain an actorly devotion to staying in character at all times. Thus, it would be almost impossible for him to slip into and out of the diverse duties of a variety show host. Indeed, even in these *Steve Allen Show* monologues Adams only seems comfortable after he has donned his now familiar voice of the movie hero. (While these monologues give tangible evidence of how Adams derived the voice from William Powell in his Philo Vance/Nick Charles mode, they are also reminiscent of James Cagney's staccato singing of the title song in *Yankee Doodle Dandy*). Further, since the comic conflict comes from a realistic environment refusing to respond to the movie cliché expectations that Adams has for it, the self-consciously "let's pretend" milieu of the variety show sketch would be self-defeating.

Adams needed a narrative setting that looked realistic enough to pass for an action show yet was out-of-synch enough to cue the audience for comedy. Luckily the James Bond spy movies came along. Most television police, private eye, and military shows are prudently scaled-down versions of their big-screen counterparts. But the mid–1960s spy movies with their revealings in "jet-set" values and lifestyles and their emphasis on space age weaponry were simply beyond television's budgetary reach of facsimilation. The dramatic television spy shows devised a number of strategies to finesse this gap ranging from *The Man from U.N.C.L.E.* and *The Avengers*, continuously escalating the fantasy quotients in their storylines, to the reliance on documentary-style location shooting in *I Spy* and *Secret Agent*. But for Adams this was not a problem to be solved, it was an opportunity to be seized. He found his perfect vehicle in portraying Secret Agent 86— Maxwell Smart on *Get Smart*.

The fact that *Get Smart* could not duplicate the expensive toys used in the Bond films was constantly emphasized. For instance, the Bond films' elaborate network of communications devices is replaced by Smart's plebeian shoe phone on which he has continual operator interferences and message-unit shortfalls and the never-to-be-forgotten Cone of Silence, a double-headed bubble of cheap plastic that was supposed to shield its inhabitants from prying ears but only found new and creative ways to garble their conversation every time it was used. The gap between *Get Smart* and the parent Bond films became emphasized enough to also duplicate the gap between variety show sketches and more traditional movies, therefore freeing Adams and company to move in the direction of those sketches' looser pacing and broader acting. And, having stripped the spy film of its gaudy front, *Get Smart* was able to play the genre's New Frontier patina off against the traditional comic book and Saturday afternoon serial adventures that were underneath it.

Smart worked for the United States' spy network known as CONTROL while all of the villains worked for its evil counterforce KAOS. Most spy movies and television shows set up this melodramatic euphemism for the Cold War antagonism and some of the name dichotomies were even more antic than *Get Smart*'s. Yet with this choice of names Adams was again demonstrating an understanding of what constitutes the primal seduction of the action movie for its predominantly male audience. The wish-fulfillment fantasy of being able to take dynamic control over the people and events in one's life has always been the basis of the American action film's overwhelming appeal to the worldwide mass audience. And this is true both of the run-of-the-mill films that simply feed the fantasy and of the artistic innovators in the field who offer an exploration of control (Howard Hawks), a critique of control (Alfred Hitchcock), or a rebellion against control (Raoul Walsh).

From those early monologues onward, Adams was continually exploring how action movie authority figures use elaborate strategies of language manipulation to demonstrate their claims to control. While the malfunctioning shoe phone and Cone of Silence are narrative extensions of the breakdown in communications that occur in the monologues, *Get Smart* took advantage of another device that was much more central to series television to make language manipulation the centerpiece of its strategy. Television has always favored the installation of catchphrases to emotionally bond shows to their audience, and during its five-year run, *Get Smart* became the king of catchphrases. But the show was not developing its steady stream of ritualized dialogue merely as a form of audience endearment, but rather as its most forceful piece of evidence to demonstrate how language is used to claim control.

Just as diminutive nicknames are created for everyday products (e.g., "fries" for French fried potatoes, "air" for air conditioning) in order to convince ourselves of our familiarity and mastery of the consumer culture, so Maxwell Smart could trot out a tried-and-true reaction to whatever surprising development he encountered. No matter how exotic or ridiculous the obstacle KAOS put in his path, it was just "the old communications equipment in the French bread trick" and therefore nothing that the wise and experienced Maxwell Smart could not control. Further, if any, lessons were to be learned from any of his adventures, Smart was always ready to sum each of them up with the same all-purpose epitaph for the villain: "If only he had used his genius for niceness instead of evil." Each successive "and loving it" after Smart is cautioned about the mortal dangers he will be facing or "would you believe. . .?" routine while he is trying to bluff the villains served the subversively contradictory purposes of flattering the audience for their insider anticipation of the catch-phrases while also demonstrating how pathetically inadequate such movie-programmed responses are when encountering new experiences.

Yet with all of the built-in advantages of the spy genre and the almost limitless ways in which Adams exploited them, *Get Smart* would not have worked if Adams did not have that realistic foundation off which the movie fantasies could play. Just as Bob Newhart's reflective passivity needed the supporting cast of extroverted eccentrics who could nevertheless develop a rapport with him, so Adams' aggressive acting out of the movie hero needed the grounding of intelligent and sympathetic co-stars whom the movie hero was trying to impress. In this regard, character actor Ed Platt, veteran of countless Eisenhoweresque authority figure parts in 1950s movies, did yeoman's work playing the Chief of CONTROL. Platt was always able to maintain an innate dignity and sense of purpose while doing every possible variation of slow-burn exasperation at Smart's physical and verbal bumbling.

But in the final analysis the show was actually held together by Barbara Feldon who played Smart's constant companion in adventure, Agent 99. As the one person above all that Smart was trying to impress, Agent 99 had to respond to all of the variety show sketch and stand-up monologue elements that Adams worked into Smart's character and adventures. Feldon had to react as Smart's colleague, his love interest, his sidekick, his damsel-in-distress, his parental figure, and other roles while carrying the load of making the narrative aspects of the show credible. It was Feldon's unheralded triumph to maintain a seamless veneer while constantly shifting gears in response to Adams' various comic ploys and establish the personality of an intelligent and attractive professional for 99 as well.

In fact, Adams was never able to reassemble the delicate chemistry that made *Get Smart* the perfect vehicle for his particular style of movie spoof comedy. His follow-up sitcom *The Partners* put him in the unromantic role of a uniformed policeman which completely changed the dynamics of how he played out his movie persona and quickly failed. Adams then followed with one of the most bizarre shows in television history, *Don Adams' Screen Test*. On this game show, which Adams hosted and produced, contestants teamed with actors to recreate selected scenes from film history. Ultimately, Adams' greatest post–*Get Smart* television success came in recreating the bumbling, hardware-smitten, secret agent character by providing the voice for the title character in the children's cartoon series *Inspector Gadget*.

While Don Adams' post–*Get Smart* television career has not exactly been stellar, neither Sid Caesar nor Carol Burnett have been major comedy players on the tube for the past twenty years as well. Although all three have continued their careers doing fine work in various other forms and functions, it may well be that the dynamics of both movies and television have changed so dramatically over the past quarter century that the concept of televised movie spoofs is no longer viable. Many of today's corporate Hollywood megaproductions are so overblown and so overcalculated that they contain spoofs of themselves within their own contours. Indeed, a whole new genre of film has emerged, including such efforts as *Airplane* and *Hot Shots*, which are little more than elongated variety show sketches and exist solely to spoof the conventions of those blockbuster films.

At the same time television's own history has lengthened and its cultural influence has become so pervasive that the niche once filled by variety shows doing movie spoofs has now been taken over by SCTV-styled comedy sketch programs that parody television itself. The next generation's Billy Crystal may be out in today's viewing audience deciding to take up comedy as a profession based on a side-splitting take on *Beverly Hills 90210*.

6
ALF in the Family

The People's Choice, Topper, Bewitched, ALF

In one of his maddeningly smug but insightful comments on art and film aesthetics, Jean-Luc Godard once said of Lumière and Méliès, twin fathers of French cinema, that it was the former chronicler of unstaged street scenes who was actually the fantasist and the latter trick photography magician who was truly the documentarian. He meant that by presenting a concrete, literal picture of a particular point in time, Lumière was depicting a world which, to someone viewing it 50 years after its passing, would seem unreal. Méliès, on the other hand, in imagining a world of developments which were impossible during his own lifetime (e.g., space exploration), was creating a vision which would become our contemporary reality.

Godard is ever-ready to make seemingly perverse pronouncements in order to startle the self-satisfied status quo, but, as usual, there is also a larger and very serious intention behind the statement. To Godard our insistence on placing fantasy and realism in separate, disconnected boxes not only betrays an appalling lack of artistic vision but is also, on the most prosaic level, a simple misreading of life as it is actually experienced. The fact is aspects of fantasy and realism are constantly interweaving in most artistic recreations of life be they "art films" like Godard's or "mindless fluff" like television sitcoms.

The generic structures of sitcoms as they established themselves in the 1950s broke down into three basic categories: (1) the family in the suburbs (e.g., *Father Knows Best, Leave It to Beaver*); (2) the show biz celebrity family—both urban (*Make Room for Daddy, I Love Lucy*) and suburban (*Ozzie and Harriet, Burns and Allen*); and (3) the adventures at the workplace (*Private Secretary, Our Miss Brooks*).

All three of these sitcom genres presented themselves as straightforward and realistic although, naturally, each show created its own individual tone. But look at the power structure within the character groupings on these shows reveals that on family shows, all moral power flows up to the father who was acknowledged by everybody as the presiding authority. On workplace shows, the central character was usually a professional woman who, though not always acknowledged, was clearly depended on by both superiors and subordinates to guide the operation.

Yet while the proposition of whether father does or does not know best is debatable, unlike his depiction on these shows, the sociological facts were that he was rarely present at home during domestic crises. And, in terms of workplace shows, women were still reeling from having been thrown out of the workforce in droves after World War II. In many respects the popular success of all three of these sitcom genres came from the ways in which they embodied wish fulfillment fantasies for both sexes. And, in many respects, the popular successes of the counterargument fantasy sitcoms, most notably *Topper* and *The People's Choice*, came from their explorations of realities which the straightforward shows dared not contemplate.

The People's Choice, like the family shows, also presented itself as a realistic, if highly stylized, commentary on the burgeoning post-war move to the suburbs. Using names of which John Bunyan would have been proud, *The People's Choice* was set in developing New City, California, and concerned the adventures of one Socrates "Sock" Miller (Jackie Cooper), a gentle, shy, honest-by-default birdwatcher who somehow manages to land himself on the city council. Councilman Miller becomes the thorn in the side of Mayor Peoples (played by heavy, jowly Paul Maxey like a fugitive from the tank-town road company of *The Front Page*), whose grandiose plans to expand both his community and pocketbook are constantly foiled by Sock's bumbling interference. What Mayor Peoples does not know is that much of Sock's bumbling stems from his engagement, then marriage, to the mayor's demure daughter Mandy (Patricia Breslin) which they are keeping secret until Sock is financially able to move from his house trailer on the outskirts of town and into a respectable home within the community.

The People's Choice would have been one of the better 1950s sitcoms if it had stopped there. But the show was taken into a completely different category with its constant cutaways to snide running commentary on the proceedings from Sock's pet basset hound Cleo. Supplied with the voice of radio/television character actress Mary Jane Croft (who was showing her versatility by also playing the Nelsons' next-door neighbor Clara Randolph on *Ozzie and Harriet* during this time), Cleo served as the igneous intrusion into the ongoing shenanigans as the camera cut to her weary, poker-faced puss for "what fools these mortals be" wisecracks about Mayor Peoples' greasy perfidy or Sock's flustered confusion. Not even the quasi-regal Mandy was spared. For instance, in one episode while Mandy was accusing the retreating Sock of not liking her cooking, the audience suddenly got the picture of the dog-faced hanging judge Cleo as Croft voice-overed: "I once ate one of her potato pancakes and it gave me hairballs."

In some respects Cleo mirrored the way that George Burns functioned on *Burns and Allen*. (Incidentally, while *The People's Choice* was the joint creative effort of Cooper and producer Irving Brecher, it came through Burns' McCadden Productions.) In other ways Cleo was more like the comic relief "best friend" characters that Eve Arden and Oscar Levant used to play in 1940s movies. In both cases Cleo shared in the sense of powerlessness that the characters had within their worlds. She realized, as they did, that she had as much in common with those who are helplessly watching in the audience as with the main motivating characters she is on screen to support. Just like those detached, ironic human characters, Cleo's remarks are as much a way for her to maintain an internally sane perspective on her social "otherness" as it is external commentary on the ongoing activity she is only allowed to observe.

Further, by identifying Cleo as a dog whose thoughts are heard but not spoken, *The People's Choice* also linked her to the cartoon tradition of animals serving as surrogate children. All of the major icons of animated cartoons, Bugs Bunny, Daffy Duck, the early Mickey Mouse, Pluto for the later Mickey Mouse, have held high the banner of childhood imagination and gameplaying in defiance of the overwhelmingly powerful forces of adult conformity. In comic strips this idea is domesticated and all but made literal by characters such as Garfield and Snoopy who, for all practical purposes, are their human owners' children. Cleo, thus, becomes the live-action version of this concept. She is television's version of the animal as underground children who spend their time alternately creating their own child world fantasies and shrugging fatalistically at their human owners' follies in thought-bubble commentaries.

Just as Sock's marriage to Mandy is a secret to the rest of the world, so their child Cleo is a secret even to them. And Cleo uses the fact that all of the grownups ignore and patronize her to create an alternative vision to what the people choose which she shares with the audience and nobody else.

Like most of the 1950s sitcoms that were not about a family unit in the suburbs, *The People's Choice* had strong connections with 1930s/1940s "screwball comedy." Some attempts were even made to adapt individual screwball comedies into continuous series, the most notable success being *Topper*.

Topper did not start out as a screwball comedy but as a whimsical

Thorne Smith fantasy novel which the Hal Roach film transformed into the not uncommon screwball comedy structure of two flighty socialites who enlighten a stuffy, middle-class professional man to a more liberated view of life. The only difference was that in this case the two socialites happened to be ghosts. But in adapting the Roach adaption for 1950s television, the Bernard L. Shubert and John W. Loveton series had to modify the characters again, and by so doing turned the property into a very uncommon television sitcom structure.

As Cosmo and Henrietta Topper, the recessive, most proper bank vice-president and his fluttery wife, Leo G. Carroll and Lee Patrick do almost Rich Little–like impersonations of Roland Young and Billie Burke from the original film (and its two sequels). But the presentation of George and Marion Kerby, former owners of the Toppers' home who return as ghosts and stay on to enlighten Cosmo (who is the only mortal who can see and hear them), had to be refashioned to fit the format of weekly half-hour television.

The kind of sophisticated, sensual hedonism that Cary Grant and Constance Bennett brought to the first *Topper* movie would not have worn well week after week. And, even if it had, it would not have been acceptable to the more prosaic and practical minded television audience of the 1950s. As played by the husband and wife acting tandem of Robert Sterling and Anne Jeffreys, the Kerbys were transformed from irresponsible upper-class swingers, who become Topper's inadvertent role models, into his wildly imaginative and incorrigibly adventurous surrogate children.

Jeffreys turned Marion into a rambunctious and flirty tomboy forever trying to coax her "Toppy" to join in the fun. Sterling turned George into a pouty, sensitive would-be leader of men counseling "Topper, old man" with his sage advice about which wrong conclusion to jump to. Together they could be counted on to materialize at any inopportune moment, always in dress-up costume for the ongoing discussion (if Henrietta was chiding Cosmo for being out of shape they would appear in sweatsuits and carrying gym equipment; if bank president Mr. Schuyler [Thurston Hall] was telling Cosmo about visiting European dignitaries, they would appear as old world royalty complete with beard and monocle), pestering Cosmo for his attention while he was trying to deal with the grownups. When Cosmo became annoyed with their Cleo-like heckling and they escalated to moving objects around the room, Cosmo would shrug in embarrassment and with a weak grin mutter some lame puns about light housekeeping while his most proper peers began wondering about his stability.

The Kerbys were always on the lookout for the kind of melodramatic adventure that the Toppers' sexless, measured existence sought to deny. They would jump at the slightest sign of plot thickening to construct the most elaborate conspiracies which demanded the immediate heroic attention

Not your average 1950s family. Leo G. Carroll and Lee Patrick as Cosmo and Henrietta Topper sit in front of their shadow children, Anne Jeffreys as Marion Kerby ("the ghostess with the mostest"), Robert Sterling as George Kerby ("that most sportive spirit"), and Buck as Neil, their alcoholic dog in *Topper*.

of Cosmo and themselves. Cosmo would try to humor them with the same kind of dry irony he used on the adults:

> *George*: Can't you just see the newspaper headlines: "Topper Captures Spy Ring."
>
> *Cosmo*: We must be reading different papers; mine says: "Topper's Body Found Floating in River."

But despite all of his sophisticated adult polish, Cosmo is always drawn into their schemes and they usually wind up benefitting him spiritually if not physically.

Cleo was perpetually ignored by the adult humans in her world and the Kerbys' literal invisibility rendered them completely inconsequential to everybody except Cosmo Topper. However, since the Kerbys do appear in adult human form to their father figure Cosmo, the advantage that they have over Cleo is the refuge they can take in this one person who, despite all of the contrary social pressures, consistently acknowledges the legitimacy of their feelings and their stake in affecting events. Besides, like all good 1950s children, the Kerbys came equipped with their own dog, the alcoholic St. Bernard Neil (Buck). It is in this two-way relationship between the Kerbys and Cosmo that *Topper* breaks out of the patronizing, condescending "kids say the darnedest things" approach and creates a structure where, for all of their limitations, the children have as much to teach as to learn.

The 1950s have always been the favorite whipping boy of sociologically based critics committed to exposing the smug conformity of American middle-class culture. There is certainly enough of this conformity to go around for a hundred such critics. But while the examples of conformity in 1950s television may strike as a tad more naked in their chauvinism, the fact remains that most chroniclers of this era tend to oversimplify its diversity, leading many to believe that it was all *Giant* and Mitch Miller with no *The Girl Can't Help It* and Fats Domino.

Television criticism has always been the bastion of arrogantly sloppy generalists and to this day the conventional wisdom is that there were no challengers to the dominating *Father Knows Best/Leave It to Beaver* mode. The prevailing mood of the era made shows like *The People's Choice* and *Topper* create much more elaborate metaphors for their fantasy families but the alternatives they offered to the traditional family power structure were real enough.

While the 1950s have been oversimplified in cultural history, the sixties is a term which has been haphazardly thrown around to cover all sorts of developments. In point of fact, the 1960s actually encompasses two separate eras neither of which began in 1960 or ended in 1969.

The early 1960s represented a break more in style than philosophy from the 1950s: very much the way James Bond differed from Joe Friday or John Kennedy differed from Dwight Eisenhower. In television, this period was represented by the least understood and examined turning point in the medium's history: the transition from black and white to color. As with the rest of the culture, this period of television saw the same people who had been prominent during the 1950s redesigning the presentation of their vision, and, in so doing, creating the concrete context for the attitudinal shifts that occurred late in the decade.

One of the shows most aesthetically and philosophically central to this transition to color was *Bewitched*. The show, in fact, derived a whole new look and feel by combining the talents of two people who had come out of very different 1950s sitcom traditions: executive producer Harry Ackerman, the assistant producer of *Leave it to Beaver*; and producer/creative consultant William Asher, the director of *I Love Lucy*.

Like many of the shows from this period, *Bewitched* began life in black and white and changed over to color early in its run. However, *Bewitched* always seemed to have been in color for it inaugurated a look and feel that became identifiable with Ackerman's long string of sitcoms (including such shows as *Gidget* and *Love on a Rooftop*) that all but defined the genre's visual feel for the next ten years.

The look of *Bewitched*'s world might be termed "good taste Holiday Inn." The shiny, white, modern-age appliances and bold, cheerfully colored decor combined with the high-key Columbia studios lighting to create an aura of confident and optimistic acceptance of a brave, new era where a constant progression of new technology and expanded consciousness would be the norm.

Most of the significant early 1960s sitcoms (*Bewitched, The Dick Van Dyke Show, The Beverly Hillbillies, My Favorite Martian*) were in one form or another about transition from a more traditional style of living to this new viewpoint. In fact, *Bewitched* and *The Dick Van Dyke Show* can be seen as two alternative versions of adjustment to the college-educated, upper middle-class, affluent society.

The *Van Dyke Show* is structured as the new era version of its production company's flagship series *Make Room for Daddy*. Rob Petrie (Van Dyke), like Danny Williams (Danny Thomas), divides his time between his life at home with his family and his career with colleagues in show business. But while Danny's home is an apartment in New York City, Rob's is a house in suburban New Rochelle. And while Danny's problem is that he is a performer/celebrity both at work and at home, Rob's is that he is a family-oriented office worker (a writer for a television show) burdened by the heightened emotionalism of show business. Indeed, this tension between the new-age suburban society and the old world, big city show-biz community is highlighted in the character groupings. Rob's domestic relationships are dominated by perky 1960s types like Mary Tyler Moore (the show's Jackie Kennedy figure) and Jerry Paris, while his office mates are vaudeville veterans Morey Amsterdam and Rose Marie.

Bewitched organizes these tensions in a much different manner, and the key figure here is Asher. It might be said that as *The Dick Van Dyke Show* is to *Make Room for Daddy* so *Bewitched* is to *I Love Lucy*. *Lucy* was the show-biz family sitcom that reversed all of the genre's conventions. The show's center was not the headlining performer at the Copa but his non-professional spouse and the unspoken secret of the show's audience appeal was that while Ricky Ricardo (Desi Arnaz) was the performer, Lucy

It's a witch's world. Elizabeth Montgomery, Agnes Moorehead, and Dick York in *Bewitched.*

Ricardo (Lucille Ball) was actually the creative genius of the family. The show's vast audience was willing to swallow Lucy's scatter-brained social blunders in order to see what kind of inspired improvisations she would employ to overcome them as well as Ricky's Vegasoid production numbers in order to see what kind of creative chaos Lucy would make out of them.

In transforming this premise to the now more tangible world of the new frontier suburban couple, a completely new rationale had to be invented so as not to intimidate the audience about the wife's superiority; she's not normal, she's a witch.

As *Bewitched*'s superior Samantha, Elizabeth Montgomery was every bit the Jackie Kennedy figure that Mary Tyler Moore was, and much more than Moore she projected the graceful *oblige* of a friendly and democratic aristocrat. In becoming the domestic wife to rising young advertising executive Darrin Stephens (Dick York, and later played by Dick Sargent), she would clearly have had to abandon the manor to which she was naturally born, but the supernatural extent of her inherent abilities comes as even a greater shock to Darrin than it does the audience. What's more, the problems and complications caused by this "mixed marriage" become dangerous primarily because everybody surrounding Samantha refuses to accept the terms on which she chooses to define herself.

Samantha is trapped between the conflicting needs of the two people who love her most. In one corner is her snobby jet-setting mother Endora (Agnes Moorehead). To Endora, the exotic Samantha is disgracing the superiority of her heritage by co-habiting with a mortal. In the other corner is the fair-minded but conformist go-getter Darrin. To Darrin, Samantha is the emasculating "Sam"; she is constantly posing all kinds of threats to his head-of-the-household status with her unusual powers.

Indeed, Darrin is also caught in a double bind. Privately he admires his wife's abilities enough for him to endure Endora's insults and the unpredictable consequences of his witch-wife's simplest, most innocent acts. But publicly he is terrified that exposure of his peculiar marital situation will ruin his credibility with his opportunistic boss Larry Tate (David White) or lead to social segregations through the machinations of snoopy next-door neighbor Gladys Kravitz and her morose, cynical husband Abner (played by veteran Brooklynesque character actors Alice Pearce and George Tobias). Incidentally, the Kravitzes served the same function that Rose Marie and Morey Amsterdam did for *The Dick Van Dyke Show*.

It is of paramount importance to this show that all aspects of Darrin's emotional tightrope act converge at the point of his job in the advertising industry. For *Bewitched* tells us that maintaining a non-threatening and friendly rapport with the public and persuading other people to accept your own point-of-veiew without seeming to have pushed them into it—in short, advertising—is what the new era is all about. And Darrin soon comes to realize that the practical result of Samantha's powers is that she is actually better at advertising than he is.

Whereas Cosmo Topper could only offer ironic wordplay to explain away the Kerbys' antics to a culture whose highest priority was propriety, both Samantha and Darrin could invent the most preposterous explanations for the other-worldly events surrounding them. And, as long as the explanations tied into an advertising concept (the not yet manufactured car in the driveway is a showcase test model; the spaceship in the backyard is a new toy soon to be on the market), everybody was willing to accept that this was just another ingenious ploy to acquaint us with yet another addition to modern technology.

In the justly famous two-parter where ditzy Aunt Clara (Marion Lorne) summons up Benjamin Franklin (Fredd Wayne) to fix an electric lamp, Franklin goes strolling all over town inquiring of passersby the meaning of modern life. The only really unsettling aspect of this for the citizenry is that they cannot quite figure out what that vaguely familiar fellow in the eighteenth-century get-up is advertising. Larry Tate immediately assumes that Franklin is Darrin's brainstorm for the Franklin

Products account. And, in relation both to his career status and community ties, Darrin sees no possible way to correct him.

Franklin gets in trouble only when, after viewing the state-of-the-art hardware at the modern edition of his own innovation, the community fire station, he endeavors to test out the fire engine, plows into a hydrant, and causes a mid-town traffic tie-up. The politically ambitious city D.A. (Mike Road) is not anxious to endanger his media image by prosecuting the old duffer unless he can strike a self-righteous pose by conclusively proving what he already cynically assumes: the Ben Franklin impersonator and his contrived joyride are both part of a ploy to grab public attention. What's more, Larry Tate is more than happy to reenforce that assumption by making the even more cynical offer to merge the D.A.'s run for higher office into the whole Franklin Products campaign.

It is up to Samantha to retrieve everybody from the tar pit, and she does so through her own higher form of advertising, through her witchcraft. She all but literalizes the intentions of advertising by placing subliminal, unconscious thoughts into people's heads (thoughts which truly mystify their holders as soon as they come out through their holders' mouths). Through these transformations, Samantha is able to turn community protests, school lectures, and media broadcasts into platforms for Franklin to explain his communal civic intentions. Once heard, Franklin's social values generate a groundswell of public approval and Samantha completes the process by putting thoughts in the D.A.'s mind that allow Franklin to express this same political idealism to judge and jury, who then award him the verdict.

Samantha's witchcraft advertising is like Franklin's political message in that it seeks to return the process to its original intentions. She uses subliminal suggestion not to implant self-serving invitations to convivial conformity, but to allow people to break their routine long enough to hear someone whom they would ordinarily ignore.

This political use of advertising is relatively rare for the series. More typically Samantha tries to de-pollute advertising's psychological application. The majority of advertising seeks to feed people's fears and anxieties in order to link its product or service to the healing process for the supposed breakdown in self-esteem it is, in fact, manufacturing. Numerous *Bewitched* episodes would begin with somebody, often Darrin, already beaten into self-doubt by conflicting social pressures and Samantha inventing some kind of imaginary service or product which she gives away to them as the "magic" provider of the inner strength they refuse to acknowledge.

Bewitched would also approach advertising from the other end of the telescope as in the episode "Man of the Year." Here Endora, the eternal heckler, surrounds Darrin with a spell whereby everybody who comes in close enough contact with him will be thoroughly impressed by everything he says. The now literalized herd instinct proves so strong that even after Darrin realizes that these half-formed thoughts from the top of his head are not works of improvisational genius and the spell has been removed, the advertisers remain attached to the ideas they bought while under the influence (although they cannot quite figure out why they like them). Samantha is forced to recast the spell so that Darrin can resell everybody on the good ideas he has since worked out.

Like *I Love Lucy*, *Bewitched* got most of its mileage out of setting up the most conventional and overfamiliar married couple sitcom plots and letting the structural reversals its format has worked into the genre spin these plots into unchartered territory. In "Sam Goes to the Moon," the age-old "husband thinks wife has it soft doing housework" plot goes into overdrive. Darrin knows that Samantha need but wiggle her nose to make the housework do itself (thus going conventional aristocracy one better since wiggling noses, unlike servants or staff assistants, need not be paid). It was always a point of honor to Samantha that she did the housework in conventional mortal manner. But in this episode when Endora shows up insisting that Sam join her on a shopping trip to Tokyo and couches this as a question of filial loyalty, Samantha finds it necessary to finesse the household duties in order to keep everybody happy.

Only there is no way to keep everybody happy. Having to constantly defend himself against witchcraft leaves Darrin in a state of continuous short-fuse paranoia. Feeling his mortal malehood threatened by Sam's obvious fudging of the housework, he backs her so far into a furious corner with his prosecutorial inquiry into how she spent her day that she finally stomps off yelling that she went to the moon.

On a conventional married couple sitcom this figure of speech would simply be a throwaway line in the working out of the husband's conflicting desires to be both the family power figure and the co-equal in love and respect with his wife. But here Darrin realizes that Samantha may indeed have gone to the moon and spotting a package of tea she bought in Tokyo, he becomes convinced that she has brought back samples of moon dust. The playing out of Darrin's conflict becomes a psychologically profound mixture of the literal and the metaphoric as he comes to realize that his immediate desire to make a killing marketing and advertising the exclusive rights to moon dust would also result in the killing of his wife by drawing societal attention to her condition and her talents. By episode's end Darrin is preparing for sleep having awakened from his nightmare of interplanetary moguldom and Samantha is brushing her hair while gazing up at "the lady in the moon." When Darrin asks her how she knows that it is not the commonly understood man in the moon, she tells him that she said she had not been to the moon *that day* but she didn't say that she had never been there.

Bewitched ran for eight years and spanned both the early 1960s and the period of societal implosion that is now generalized as "the 1960s." In fact, as it wended its way through the decade, *Bewitched* usually provided much more telling commentary on Aquarian idealism than most of its trumpeted "relevant" competition. For instance, in the episode where Steve Franken and Hamilton Camp played two canine-based aliens who scrooched mean-spirited busybody Gladys Kravitz (now played by Sandra Gould after Alice Pearce's death) with their niceness guns, they turned her into a literal flower child.

But the cumulative effect of the multilayered debate about national and personal purpose raised during the 1960s was to fracture that shared sense of identity, ideals, and aspirations that the growing mass communications industry had done so much to define for American society during its rise to superpowerdom. The unraveling of what came to be called "the national consensus" has since been the motivating force behind most of American culture for the past 20 years and the volumes still needed to be written about its ongoing effects are beyond the scope of this book. However, its effect on network television, the pop-culture medium most dependent on a consensus audience, was an unstated crisis that resulted in structural changes in most genres designed to create a new "television consensus" out of the viewing public.

The initial response in the 1970s was to treat the new internal, domestic threat to consensus much like the external, foreign threat of World War II was treated in the 1940s. The nuclear family sitcom all but disappeared but the family members were reconstructed into "we're all in this together" World War II "melting pot" platoons that became the palsy-walsy workplace gangs at *WKRP in Cincinnati* or the *Taxi* garage. Indeed the almost interchangeability of the military family and the workplace family became nakedly apparent when the Army unit of *M*A*S*H*, which had provided much of the structural bedrock for this format, transformed itself into a corporate office for a series of IBM commercials without having to change anything except the costumes.

The family at the workplace shows became a perfect gathering spot for a culture that was now devoted to both "family values" and "singles lifestyles," and is a structure that is still going strong as we near the year 2000. But, by the dawn of the 1980s, it was also becoming apparent that television comedy itself was fracturing into two very distinct camps of style and attitude.

While comedy is far too complex a subject to be summed up by any one principle or set of axioms, there are principles which, while not definitive, can be said to be true as far as they go.

If one accepts the premise that comedy is created out of the tension between what is and what ought to be, then 1980s comedy can be divided almost equally between the throwback to consensus items like *Family Ties* and *The Cosby Show* (which see very little difference between what is and what ought to be and get most of their comedy out of ridiculing that which deviates too far from the middle of the road) and the "all I know is what I saw on television" media captives like *Late Night with David Letterman* and *Moonlighting* (which have no vision of what ought to be and can merely regurgitate parody versions of what is).

This is not to say that these two approaches speak different languages. Even the most traditional family show does pop culture "in" jokes and no mass market network show completely turns its back on maudlin moralizing. As divergent as their tactics are, their strategies are actually quite similar in that both styles are grounded in a highly self-conscious preoccupation with television history. Yet there is hardly a show alive that has managed to combine the consensus square with the media hip. Hardly a show, that is, except for *ALF*. This is primarily because *ALF*'s link to television history is connected by Tom Patchett, a man whose work has been primarily concerned with forging just such a combination.

In the 1960s, Patchett and his partner Jay Tarses' stand-up act showed a fascination with both the creative and tawdry aspects of American pop culture long before it became a dominant theme in comedy. Their best-known routine involved a hapless customer at a roadside chain restaurant, referred to as Howard Jackson's, which was famous for its ice cream. The customer finds that every item he could possibly want has been shorn of its generic name and magically transformed into HoJack's—as in "up the price." Repeatedly frustrated in his efforts to get reasonably priced chocolate or vanilla ice cream (HoJack brown and HoJack white), he throws in the towel and merely asks to use the washroom only to be told that he will have to pay for the privilege of using the HoJack john.

As writers/producers for *The Bob Newhart Show*, Patchett and Tarses learned the genre structures of sitcom and were encouraged to integrate their pop-culture orientation into the scripts. This gave *The Bob Newhart Show* a much more contemporary feel than the more prestigious social issue sitcoms of that era. Patchett and Tarses even managed to rework their ice cream customer sketch into an episode when Bob and others in the cast visited one of the then popular fast-food–styled super parlors. All of the ice cream concoctions are given silly names and the patrons are given even sillier service—a spotlight hits each person as his order is being served while a chorus of hammy waiters chant an advertising jingle connected with the item's name (for The Great White Whale, "You can't eat it! You can't eat it! You can't eat a whale!"). The ever-private Bob thought he could avoid this spectacle by ordering a single scoop of vanilla ice cream only to have the spotlight hit him and the waiters taunt, "Single scooper, single scooper, this man is a party pooper!"

When Newhart voluntarily retired from his series, Patchett and Tarses went on to do the hugely undervalued *Tony Randall Show*, where Randall, like Newhart, provided a strongly defined central anchor of comic moral sanity to build the pop-culture riffs around. But after the *Randall Show*'s untimely demise, Patchett and Tarses groped unsteadily through such shows as Mary Tyler Moore's abortive variety series and the workplace family sitcom *Open All Night*, searching for a more contemporary formulation of their viewpoint.

It was in *Buffalo Bill*, a rather bold attempt to build the pop-culture comedy around an abrasive central character who bordered on the repugnant, that they began to see how their viewpoint could relate to 1980s culture. However, they also saw that they wanted to take this new concept in vastly different directions and parted company on less than amicable terms.

Tarses, taken with the possibilities of greater literary and psychological depth in a flawed central character, seems determined to become the Stan Kenton of sitcom with *Buffalo Bill*'s successors *The Slap Maxwell Story* and *The Days and the Nights of Molly Dodd*, shows that all but define the term "overwritten." Patchett, continuing along the Jimmie Lunceford route, has sought to balance the more abrasive central character against the Bob Newhart anchor and, repartnering with Paul Fusco, came up with *ALF*.

ALF manages to combine the two styles of 1980s comedy in a way that bounces back at both of them. Structurally it is almost a funhouse mirror reflection of *Family Ties*, giving us the middle-aged parents who have not surrendered their 1960s humanist values and are trying to cope with their three ultra 1980s offsprings. On *Family Ties* the oldest child and show's central consciousness exists to render David Stockman and his philosophy adorably cute for a wannabe audience. On *ALF*, however, the central consciousness child is both the oldest and the youngest, the most individually creative and media consumer gullible, the most family tied and the most painfully physically and emotionally "alienated." In fact, he both is and is not part of the family, being the adopted visitor from the planet Melmac, Gordon Shumway, a.k.a. AlienLifeForm.

The parents, Willie and Kate Tanner, are the upholders of the traditional, but the very particular tradition of Patchett. And, as wonderfully played by Max Wright and Anne Schedeen, they are a completely realized version of Bob and Emily Hartley in the 1980s. Like Bob Hartley, Willie Tanner exudes the quiet decency of a man committed to a life of compassionate and deeply private personal relations in a culture increasingly engulfed by people who are packaging their personalities as advertised products they want to snooker you into buying. Like Emily Hartley, Kate Tanner tempers her sensual warmth with a no-nonsense devotion to the genuine and the practical. Neither the characters nor the performances are flashy attention-grabbers, but they form the backbone of the show, providing a context of attractive normalcy through which the title character's responses to American culture can be measured.

Physically, vocally, and philosophically, ALF owes a great debt to Jonas Prohaska's Cookie Bear character from *The Andy Williams Show* which was probably the best, and least remembered, of the Chris Bearde/ Allan Blye hippie-dippie variety shows of "the 1960s" (*Smothers Brothers, Sonny and Cher,* etc.). In effect, those shows were taking the 1950s Steve Allen approach—gleefully seize on the most infantile burlesque silliness and then reinterpret it with an almost surreal beat-like analysis—and update it to the counterculture 1960s. This tradition was carried into the present primarily by Jim Henson and his various Muppet shows which lead almost directly to the "high concept" premise of *ALF*, which is basically E.T. becomes a Muppet and stays on to become part of the suburban family.

Forced to remain within the Tanners' house exclusively, lest, like E.T., he be turned in for government research, ALF is left to interpret life on Earth almost entirely from what he sees on television. As such, he is learning how to become the perfect contemporary American, since the lifestyle imposed on him is that which the culture is increasingly turning to by choice.

The factual mistakes he makes are all perfectly logical: identifying the Miss World Beauty Contest as United Nations coverage is far-fetched only if you never look at how the news is presented; and citing Colonel Klink of *Hogan's Heroes* as the cause of World War II is ridiculous only if you ignore the kind of melodrama made out of history. But what ALF picks up most quickly is the concept of attitude, an approach of life that is best summed up by his oft repeated catch phrase, "No problem!"

Craving attention and affection in his isolated corner of the world, ALF gleefully embraces all of the totemic mythology we hoodwink ourselves with about success in American society. ALF's unquestioning conviction that celebrity equals achievement continually leads the very private Willie into ridiculous and humiliating exposure in front of audiences of strangers. And ALF's devotion to the conventions of melodrama, such as his frantic theory that the Tanners' missing baby might have been eaten by a dingo as in *A Cry in the Dark*, is a constant frustration to the clear-eyed Kate.

Overall, ALF dresses his persona for success by taking on all of the pushy aggressiveness of a supersalesperson, the self-centered mindset of an industrial mogul, and the snappy lingo of an in-crowd trendsetter. In short, ALF embraces the personality of that revered 1980s icon, the stand-up comic.

Stand-up comics are hardly new to the world of family sitcoms. Indeed, one of the genre's founding fathers, *Make Room for Daddy,* and the show that initiated the genre's revival in the 1980s, *The Cosby Show* (the Sheldon Leonard and Jay Sandrich connections between these two shows are not coincidental), are built around stand-up comics. But while Danny Thomas and Bill Cosby came to sitcom from the world of stand-up night club comedy, they worked in a format that allowed for a transformation of their style and viewpoint into an ensemble mode.

Most stand-up comedy begins with the emotional/philosophic assumptions that parallel the physical/visual reality of the form, the comedian standing alone against the rest of society. The strategy of most stand-up monologues is to string together a disconnected series of jokes in an order and with a rhythm that will create a mosaic viewpoint of the outside world which the audience will be seduced into sharing. Cosby and Thomas, however, work in a style that is often referred to as storytelling rather than joketelling. They attempt to paint a detailed, recognizable social picture with the humor depending not so much on detachable, individual punchlines as a continual interaction between themselves and the world they have described.

Showing the worlds that Thomas and Cosby are telling about is merely the next logical step, so their adaption to the sitcom mode is relatively easy. But, unlike Bob Newhart, whose stand-ups actually structured the unseen others in his world as the dominating power with himself as the reactive agent, Cosby and Thomas overwhelm the world they describe with the force of their own personalities. On their shows they are stars in their own households interacting with everyone around them but almost trampling their families and friends under the weight of their enormous presences. Perhaps one of the inadvertent meanings of the title *Make Room for Daddy* is an acknowledgment of one of the show's ever-present themes—how much physical and emotional space Thomas devours.

ALF and its title character masterfully show how the "world according to me" mindset of the stand-up comic is a logical reaction to the experience of childhood and how the television generation culture of the 1980s has all but made their merger inevitable. ALF's physical appearance reflects the child's emotional self-image of hapless clumsiness and self-conscious, inexperienced differentness that keeps him in the margins of life going on around him. He tries to overcome this by overwhelming, and thus joining, the audience he feels alienated from by displaying his superhumanly artistic understanding of their culture through his hilarious collection of jokes.

ALF works best when it teeters on the edge balancing the inherent pathos of ALF's plight with the bulldozing tactics he uses to overcome it. One of the best examples of this is when ALF rearranges Willie's party for his boss into a masquerade so that he can attend it, meet some new people, impress them with his snappy insults of their costumes, and bluntly bully the boss into giving Willie the well-deserved promotion that Willie has been too timid to ask for. Cornering ALF in the kitchen, Willie once again allows his pride in ALF's artistic ingenuity to overwhelm his chagrin at being the only person at his own party not to know it was a masquerade. He winds up asking ALF how he managed to get the zipper for his costume, and ALF matter-of-factly replies: "Remember that old jacket you were thinking of throwing out? Well, hang on to it, I ripped this out of your new raincoat."

Like ALF, the entire fantasy family genre walks a fine line between imagination and ridicule. If the premise and characters are accepted as "real" by the viewing public, then these shows are free to smuggle all kinds of subversive notions about family in from out of the closet. If they are not accepted by the viewing public, then their fate is to be held up to everlasting shame as the stupidest ideas to ever insult our intelligence.

Like most mass culture art, the heart of these shows is essentially reassuring. The fantasy families never cross the line between proposing reorganizations of power within the family to questioning the purpose of family itself. But for a culture that is increasingly burying itself in the narrowing notion that believing a fantasy long enough will turn it into reality, paying closer attention to fantasies which suggest broader possibilities for reality may be time well spent.

7
The Granfaloon Family

The Mary Tyler Moore Show,
The Odd Couple,
and Their Idiot Children

The year 1970 was extremely pivotal, falling around the midpoint in the history of network television to date. As such, this becomes a very convenient time to reflect back on the influences leading to the creation of the two seminal sitcoms that debuted that year, *The Mary Tyler Moore Show* and *The Odd Couple*, and explore the ways that these two shows (and the two other seminal early 1970s sitcoms *All in the Family* and *M*A*S*H*) influenced everything that has come in their wake.

Perhaps it is a function of how we explain our country's history, the breaking away from established European society to create a completely new form of government, but innovations in practically every walk of American life are usually presented as having been generated out of pure inspiration with no connections to the history and traditions on which they were built. Innovations in the arts are no exceptions to this rule.

Take, for instance, *The Mary Tyler Moore Show*. While most assuredly a groundbreaking series on numerous levels, the show can also be described as the next logical evolutionary step in many established sitcom traditions. In tracing the development of the "life in show biz/life at home" show with *Make Room for Daddy* on the one hand and *The Jack Benny Program* on the other in the 1950s, on through *The Dick Van Dyke Show* and *The Joey Bishop Show* in the 1960s, all of the elements that would come together in *The Mary Tyler Moore Show*'s particular mix are apparent. Similarly, in looking at the "single working girl" shows from *Private Secretary* and *Our Miss Brooks* in the 1950s through *That Girl* and *The Doris Day Show* in the

1960s, not only can the style and content of Mary's show itself be identified, but also, in the last two named series, the style and content of Mary's
much-heralded opening credits sequence. However, for comparison purposes, this section does not start with any of these long-running series, but
with an unsold pilot from 1966 called *My Lucky Penny*.

My Lucky Penny concerned a poor, young dental student named Ted
Penny (Richard Benjamin), his manic, get-rich-quick-scheming neighbor
Freddy Rockefeller (Joel Grey), and the title character, Ted's formerly
rich bride Jenny (Brenda Vaccaro) whose Lucy-like determination is to
boost her beloved Ted to success if for no other reason than to justify
allowing her name to become Jenny Penny. The show was based on the
constant collisions between ambition and security, imagination and sanity, Rockefeller and Penny, being played out by having Vaccaro's and
Grey's contrasting forms of steamroller energy continually crisscrossing
around Benjamin's extreme deadpan stasis.

While *My Lucky Penny* never made it to CBS's fall of 1966 schedule,
ABC's schedule that fall included a quieter, friendlier version of the same
concept in Harry Ackerman and Bernard Slade's *Love on a Rooftop* with
Peter Deuel, Judy Carne, and Rich Little in the Benjamin, Vaccaro, and
Grey roles respectively. However, in television old pilots never die; they are
simply redesigned and pitched again. And so it was that *My Lucky Penny*'s
writer Arne Sultan was back with Richard Benjamin the following year for
a show that did make the CBS schedule, *He & She*.

Benjamin's immovable centerpoint was only slightly toned down
from the previous show but, as the title indicates, the irresistible opposing
force was singled to the creative, Lucyesque wife who was now played
more for grace than intensity by Benjamin's real-life wife Paula Prentiss.
If CBS's objection to *My Lucky Penny* had been that it social focus on only
three people had been too narrow, *He & She* certainly had the answer.
Dick and Paula Hollister (Benjamin and Prentiss) were placed in a much
wider behavioral net both at work and at home.

At home, the third character from *My Lucky Penny* was now conceived
as a bridge between the title figures, a mutual friend who has traits of both
a he and a she. Harry the fireman (Kenneth Mars) worked in the firehouse
next door but he participated all too conspicuously in Dick and Paula's
domestic problems, as did their serenely incompetent building super Andrew Hummel (Hamilton Camp). Away from home Paula worked at the
airport for Traveler's Aid. Dick was a successful cartoonist, the creator of
the popular "Jetman" comic strip and consultant to the television series
based on the script. Complications here usually stemmed from Paula's
headlong dives into Good Samaritanhood and Dick's trials with his nud-
nik business associates—the strip's sharklike syndicator Norman Nugent
(Harold Gould); television's Jetman, the white-haired, ego-engulfed,

penny-pinching, womanizing actor Oscar North (Jack Cassidy); and Dick's perpetually frazzled, bald-headed, tenor-voiced accountant Murray Mouse (Alan Oppenheimer). Those last two characters are somewhat familiar to *Mary Tyler Moore Show* fans. Oscar North was so much the progenitor of Ted Baxter that Cassidy eventually wound up guesting on the *Moore Show* playing Ted Knight's brother. And, during the 1950s and 1960s, about the only way that Alan Oppenheimer could be distinguished from Gavin MacLeod was by the latter's larger girth at that time.

Many of the key production people for the *Moore Show*—Allen Burns, David Davis, Jay Sandrich—first came together on *He & She*, and, to a great extent, the much and justly admired sophistication of the *Moore Show* can be seen in the writing and acting from this earlier series. But, ironically, one of the *Moore Show*'s most heralded innovations—the complex interaction between the ensemble cast—is exactly what is missing in *He & She*.

This is partly a function of Mary Tyler Moore's acting persona. Like most enduring television leads, Moore possesses an attractive blend of emotional definition and passive mystery which keeps audiences coming back week after week to share what happens to her. But perhaps more than anybody else in television history, Moore has an all but unlimited capacity to switch from her own leads and solos to providing obbligato or support rhythm for practically any personality that joins the band. Her uncommon gift for developing a rapport with such a wide array of styles allowed her show to build bridges between her female neighbors at home and her male co-workers in the office, and created reasonable conduits for characters who under any other circumstance would avoid, as much as possible, each other's company.

In contrast, *He & She* truly had to huff and puff in order to get its disparate personalities gathered for interaction, and as the season progressed the show continued to introduce modifications aimed at fusing the ensemble. Paula's work at the airport was phased out, allowing her to be at home or drop in at Dick's office more frequently. Oscar North wound up purchasing the building that the Hollisters lived in, necessitating his constant visits to their apartment. The show was quite definitely aware of its problem, but without a centripetal force character, the plots always wound up looking a little clumsy in comparison to the writing and the acting. Benjamin was too detached and ironic a figure to be the central glue. And while Prentiss had both the temperament and the talent to fill the role, the concept of the show directed most of her energy to playing off Benjamin.

Retrospectively, it was unfair to ask either of them to fill the void since the unstated premise of the show was that all of the people in Dick and Paula's lives were actually impositions on the title relationship. Even the lugubriously loyal Harry, with his overwrought gestures of devotion, was depicted as more of a burden than a comfort. What *He & She* was aiming at was the redefinition of the married couple sitcom that Bob Newhart and MTM Enterprises achieved—after *The Mary Tyler Moore Show* created the ensemble cast model from which they could deviate.

While many elements that went into the *Moore Show*'s breakthrough can be traced from these earlier shows, there were also a number of new elements that went into the mix. As important as Moore's acting skills were to the concept of her show, even more significant were the social changes that she and her collaborators picked up on while constructing the show's structure. What had happened between *He & She*'s debut in 1967 and *The Mary Tyler Moore Show*'s debut in 1970 was the realization of how the coming-of-age of the baby boom generation had changed societal attitudes towards both work and home and, most specifically, the impact of the introduction of the "happy news" format in local programming.

Throughout the 1960s the constant expansion of the networks more deeply into daytime and late night plus the growing popularity of off-network syndicated shows continued to erode the number of hours that affiliate stations could use for their locally produced programming. These shows not only served the function of providing area residents with programming slanted to their individual concerns and tastes, but also formed a more personal connection between the viewer and the tube since many of the audience participation game, sport, and talk/information shows made it possible for everybody and their neighbor to appear on the air. For the individual stations, these shows provided a proving ground for local talent. But, more importantly, the relative success of these shows provided the ratings and revenue difference between themselves and the area's competing stations. By decade's end, however, the stations were basically reduced to producing only the local newscasts which, as the other local programming disappeared, now began to carry all of the functions formerly assigned to a variety of shows. As the newscasts took on added importance for the stations, consultants were brought in to repackage them in more entertaining forms which culminated in 1969 with the introduction of the "happy news" format.

Happy newscasts were designed to make the show more friendly and personal for the viewer. This was done by making the newscast more closely resemble the already popular fictional television genres. Newscasters, who had heretofore been presented as aloof, almost professorial experts from the world of important people, were now shown as regular Joes who had emotions and personality quirks just like everyone else. Instead of having each reporter and report cordoned off into its own separate space, the "news team" now sat together on the same panel, bantering with each other in between stories and commenting on each other's report. Before long the producers found that the "team" functioned best for the viewer when it was presented as a kind of family: the anchors taking on the roles of the mature, stable parents; the weather and sports people as the squabbling kids; and the arts critic as the eccentric aunt/uncle. Soon after, commercials for the newscasts began appearing, picturing the news team engaging in off-hours group activities like touch football designed to show what a fun bunch they were and how well they worked together.

Eventually this led to the news stories themselves being presented as full-blown melodramas using narrative fiction film construction and editing for maximum emotional identification and with the most successful stories being expanded into "docudrama" television movies. But the overwhelming success of happy news as originally presented stemmed from its understanding that the new generation of young adults no longer lived at home with their parents but in their own singles apartments, thus making the people they saw every day at work their most frequent companions.

The Mary Tyler Moore Show took all of these elements—the single, young adults, the happy news team, the closer dependence on fellow workers—and built it around its star's talents to create the new sitcom family of neighbors and co-workers. Despite Moore's huge range of empathy in order to devise a place where everybody knows your name and is always glad you came, however, the show found it necessary to soften the edges of its character collection.

While there is a smooth continuity of character type and writing style from *He & She* to *The Mary Tyler Moore Show*, everybody is much more user-friendly in the latter. Whereas Rhoda Morgenstern (Valerie Harper) and Phyllis Lindstrom (Cloris Leachman) often imposed their neuroses on Mary's generous nature, she was never asked to cope with the kind of basket-case histrionics that Harry imposed on Dick and Paula. And while the Hollisters found it expedient to suffer Oscar North out of business and social necessity, Ted Baxter was accepted as a full-fledged member of the Mary family. It is the difference between these parallel characters that offers the key to what now seems to be the permanent changes that *The Mary Tyler Moore Show* has made in the sitcom genre.

Oscar North is vain, petty, miserly, condescending—and he is very good at it. His ploys to pad his bankroll and or screen time, to impress women, and to humiliate the other characters succeed as often as not, but win or lose, the smirky, sneering smile that was Cassidy's trademark is never knocked off Oscar's face. On the other hand, Ted Baxter is a bumbler. He aspires to all of Oscar North's vices and irritates everybody with his behavior, but he is so childishly ineffective and so easily outmaneuvered that he actually winds up being rather endearing. What's more, like every other character on *The Mary Tyler Moore Show*, Ted has

Pioneering a more feminine/feminist sensibility in sitcom social organization—Cloris Leachman, Mary Tyler Moore, and Valerie Harper (left to right) in *The Mary Tyler Moore Show.*

glimpses of introspection that offer very public revelation of how his faults function as ill-conceived attempts to win acceptance and affection. In time Ted Baxter's ineptitude made him such a lovable duffer that the show found it necessary to take another shot at the Oscar North character with Sue Ann Nivens (Betty White).

The sense of communal compassion that gave dignity to even its most caricatured characters and allowed them all to be equal partners in the gang can be seen as part of the feminine/feminist temperament with which *The Mary Tyler Moore Show* was enriching the genre. And as if to prove the point, the arrested adolescent males of *Saturday Night Live* seemed to take great pleasure in going out of their way to take cheap shots at *The Mary Tyler Moore Show*. But even while the *Saturday Night Live* audience was groaning in rejection of these gags, one could see the reason for their existence. As the family at the workplace concept gained strength throughout the 1970s, rounding off the edges of the characters had become the quick and easy shortcut for the less deeply felt shows to fit everybody into their accustomed grooves. By the time *SNL* came along with its own innovation, the romanticized celebration of excess, it was basically a rebellion against the "niceness" that the *Moore Show*'s innovations had set in motion. One can only wonder if the egalitarian creators of the *Moore* model had second thoughts when their "Ted Baxter–lovable buffoon" principle was used to make gangworthy such 1980s backlash figures as Dan Fielding of *Night Court* and Kirk of *Dear John*.

The other seminal sitcom introduced in the fall of 1970, *The Odd Couple*, did not stem from a long pedigree in sitcom history but rather from the Neil Simon stage play of the same name and the film made of the play. However, in transforming the property into a continuing series, producer/writer Garry Marshall did pay very close attention to television history in other genres.

In many respects *The Odd Couple* took what might be termed the Lone Ranger and Tonto principle of action-adventure shows and turned it into situation comedy. A popular action-adventure structure, particularly in series form, presented the action hero as an intelligent but primarily elemental and instinctive person, a representative of the average person who becomes heroic through an applied abundance of physical strength, emotional energy, and moral courage. He is counterpointed by his sidekick partner who shares in the action but who primarily provides the intellectual analysis necessary to overcome the villains and the philosophical rationale of the necessity for the adventure. The sidekick partner's intellect often takes him out of the cultural mainstream and gives him the coloration of minority otherness which the society accepts as a necessary junior partner in the common goal of defeating the villains.

The play and film versions of *The Odd Couple* came out during television action-adventure's most liberal period, a time when these intellectual sidekicks had almost reached equal status with the series leads and their otherness was celebrated as a hip alternative to the more conventional lead—to the point where these characters, be they Russian (*Man from U.N.C.L.E.*), African-American (*I Spy*), female (*The Avengers*), or alien (*Star Trek*), had become the most popular members of their casts. In turning *The Odd Couple* into a series, Marshall and company retained the equal status for these characters and put them into a domestic marriage.

As slobby sportswriter Oscar Madison and fussbudget photographer Felix Unger, the urban Jack Klugman and the urbane Tony Randall formed a new kind of sitcom relationship in that both were intelligent yet comical, sympathetic yet deeply flawed, and neither one dominated nor followed the other. Clearly Oscar was posited with the characteristics that our society identifies as masculine and Felix with those identified as feminine. But by following the action-adventure model and taking the curse off by having the characters be of the same gender, *The Odd Couple* was able to suggest ways that married couples could deal with the frustrations of co-habitation beyond the power games of social and sexual status.

The Odd Couple's alternative view of marriage combined with *The Mary Tyler Moore Show*'s expansive view of family opened up many new avenues for the sitcom format, and, for a few years, it appeared that the genre would grow immeasurably. However, another view of immeasurable growth is cancer and the long-term results turned out to be much different than anybody in 1970 could anticipate.

In the short term, *The Odd Couple* began a long association between Marshall and Paramount Television which over the next decade produced such shows as *Happy Days, Mork & Mindy*, and Marshall's best show, the working-class female version of *The Odd Couple, Laverne & Shirley*.

Debuting in mid-decade, *Laverne & Shirley* took advantage of recent genre developments to build a much more elaborate "family" around its title characters, but it was the way in which Penny Marshall and Cindy Williams redefined the couple that made it a landmark series. Marshall takes Oscar Madison's belligerent bluntness and turns it into Laverne's defensive shield against her social insecurity, while Williams explains Felix Unger's dictatorial prissiness as the external result of Shirley's internal war between her moral rectitude and her emotional extremism. But as good as they were individually, they were even better as a team. Marshall and Williams developed a style of patter, a fast-paced, under the breath synchronization of intertwining speech and gesture that they were able to carry over into the pratfall comedy which cemented the verbal and physical gags into an unbroken stream of objectified behavior.

In many respects *Laverne & Shirley* represented the high point of 1970s' television comedy. Besides its intrinsic merits, it has come to be a kind of historical touchstone for female team humor. It updated Lucy and Ethel's physical antics to a rock-and-roll tempo, provided a low comedy parody of Mary Richards (Shirley) and Rhoda Morgenstern (Laverne) in its own present-day commentary, and created a structure of internal chemistry and verbal/physical rhythm which contemporary comedians such as French and Saunders have built on. However, in other respects, *Laverne & Shirley* turned out to be the end of the line for the verities of situation comedy as they had been known to that date.

Both *Laverne & Shirley* and its parent show *Happy Days* were set in an amorphous late 1950s/early 1960s time warp for the very practical reason that in style and in content they were ignoring the enormous conceptual changes that *The Odd Couple, The Mary Tyler Moore Show*, and also *All in the Family* and *M*A*S*H* had brought to the genre.

The Odd Couple was written by Neil Simon who, at that time, was producing the most popular and arguably most entertaining of what was known as the "tired businessman's plays." Throughout its heyday the Broadway theater was sustained by a style of farce that had a much more sophisticated surface than film or television comedy since it was geared to a wealthier and more cosmopolitan audience. However, within its own world these plays served the same kind of function and held the same level of status that sitcoms have had in television history. By the early 1970s the economics of the Broadway theater had begun its astonishing upward spiral and the baby boom generation of television viewers had passed through a college education into upper middle-class income status. So it was only natural that as the changing nature of the Broadway marketplace caused the tired businessman's play to disappear from the theater it would re-emerge for the next generation of its now expanded audience as a new style of television comedy, just as screwball comedy had disappeared from films and had become the original basis for television sitcoms in the 1950s.

The process began innocently enough when Mary Tyler Moore and Klugman and Randall insisted that their shows be filmed in front of live audiences in order to energize the performances. It was the same process that Lucille Ball and Desi Arnaz had insisted on twenty years earlier, and with the help of cinematographer Karl Freund they had invented a highly cinematic way of doing it. A major stylistic change took place, however, when Norman Lear's *All in the Family* began being presented in front of a live audience, but shot on videotape.

Norman Lear and Bud Yorkin's Tandem Communications with its flagship *All in the Family* and Grant Tinker and Mary Tyler Moore's MTM Productions with its flagship *Mary Tyler Moore Show* came to dominate the next decade of television sitcoms. Both companies accelerated the spinoff syndrome by creating two new series each out of their initial hits, but from that point on their line of shows became a study in contrast. With few exceptions that MTM shows, just like *Mary Tyler Moore*, had its characters gather together as voluntary workplace families while the Tandem (later T.A.T.) shows, just like *All in the Family*, took place in the living rooms of nuclear family homes even when the family consisted of a single mom with daughters (*One Day at a Time*) or a single white dad with adopted black sons (*Diff'rent Strokes*).

Philosophically, it could be said that Tandem became the masculine counter-structure to the feminism being pioneered by MTM. The comedy in a typical MTM episode would stem from the discomfort and embarrassment of the characters as they tried to adjust themselves to each other's personality eccentricities with the capper being that for all of the effort, nothing is really settled in the end. A similar Tandem episode would have each character staking out a separate, locked-in-concrete position on a social issue that related to the family's situation. Here the comedy came from the insults and put-downs they hurled at each other, leading up to a single moral truth that they would all have to reckon with to one degree or another.

That Tandem would accelerate the movement towards theater stylization was almost inevitable given Norman Lear's New York orientation, the centrality of the living room setting for the shows, and the emphasis on topical references. Indeed, topical humor, the nudge-nudge sexual innuendos, and the extended body function jokes Tandem was introducing into the world of television sitcoms were the very elements that constituted Broadway's claim to sophistication.

Whether the Broadway style of comedy actually is or is not more "adult" than screwball comedy, MTM style, or any other form of humor is open to debate, but the long-term effect on television of this style combined with the videotaped in-front-of-a-live-audience technique is not.

When viewing the live in-studio dramas and on-stage variety shows of the 1950s, even in their now distanced form as kinescopes, one is immediately struck by their enormously edgy, almost dangerous physical presence. One can almost feel the sweat on the performers and the texture of the props even when the shows themselves were much less than stirring. The dramatic shows strove for a filmic camera technique and the variety shows, which were presented as theater stage performances, tried to have a filmic coverage of the action through choices of camera shots. But beyond whatever was accomplished artistically, the filmic camera techniques did not intrude on the theatrical immediacy, in fact they enhanced the viewer's sense of an in-person, three-dimensional experience. All of this was lost in the transition to a three-camera setup, videotaped format.

The attempt to simulate a stage setting on videotape produced only a flatly lit, one-dimensional space that was neither good theater nor good television. Further, the adaption of theatrical stage business, the pausing for applause during all of the lateral stage entrances and exits, the freezing in place by the actors waiting for the laughter to subside after each mechanically built-to punchline, completely destroyed the rhythm of film comedy without convincingly substituting its stage alternative. Unfortunately, in this half-realized form, the mechanics and preoccupations of stage comedy have come to completely dominate television. Although some of the technical kinks have since been smoothed over and many shows have returned to shooting on film, the style and tone of 1980s television comedy basically ranged from the super-traditional Broadway of *Kate & Allie* to the mildly experimental off–Broadway of *The Tracey Ullman Show*.

As the 1970s progressed, the outputs of MTM and Tandem began to resemble each other a bit more. Whereas MTM shows continued by and large to be about workplace families, some, such as *WKRP in Cincinnati*, were being presented on videotape and dealt more heavily with social issues. And while the Tandem shows continued to be the videotaped chronicles of living-room family wars, some of the shows, such as *One Day at a Time*, began taking on a more feminist slant both in production personnel and performance cast.

What was, in fact, acting as a kind of connecting rod between the two production companies was the fourth seminal early 1970s sitcom, *M*A*S*H*. This show's main structural innovation was to demonstrate how the family at the workplace format could be formulated to accommodate specific political content. As initially conceived, *M*A*S*H* attempted to duplicate the original Robert Altman film's sprawling cast of characters, but low ratings forced the show to refocus its approach. A number of characters were quickly eliminated. Hawkeye Pierce (Alan Alda) emerged as the show's central focus, and, most importantly, the show used the hierarchical structure inherent in its military format to place the remaining characters into fixed moral and utilitarian positions for audience identity and identification.

Mary Tyler Moore's acting persona made a workplace family believable and *M*A*S*H*'s military cum corporate structure made social and political tensions between the family members all but inevitable. But how were the new civilian, unMaryed families going to be able to follow in their footsteps? Well, they did—and then again, they didn't. During the early 1970s novelist Kurt Vonnegut invented the term granfaloon to describe the wildly eclectic groups of celebrities from different fields who would be herded together for conversation on that era's talk shows. About the only thing that all these people had in common was that they had all been invited to appear on the same show, yet through the very fact that they were all on the television screen together it was assumed that there was a logical, internal cohesion to the group that would yield valuable insights on whatever topic happened to be thrown up for grabs. Regardless of the amount of fictional television Kurt Vonnegut was watching, the fact is he might as well have been describing the character collections of practically every sitcom of the past fifteen years.

The blood relatives in the Tandem shows and the military draftees in the Mash unit were being forced to live under the same roof. Given an alternative most of them would have sought out more compatible companions and much of the hostility and sarcasm these characters displayed stemmed from their frustrations in not being able to escape each other. However, there is no earthly reason why the disparate collection of comic "types" who work at the *Night Court* or the *Taxi* gargage would build their lives around each other and without a Mary Tyler Moore to act as touchstone, a new gimmick would be necessary to clothe the emperor. It was found. It was the odd couple.

Comedy couples have always operated on some kind of tension of opposition that also bonded them together in a recognizable relationship. In stand-up the straight man's grounding in a conventional understanding of reality battles the funny man's unconventional understanding (be it super-literal—Lou Costello, wildly poetic—Jerry Lewis, or a combination of both—Gracie Allen) and their skill in developing a rhythm of speech and gesture mold them into a yin and a yang for the audience. In narrative form this is often translated into an unstated undercurrent implying that the basis of both the tension of opposition and the bond that holds them together is some sort of family relation. With Martin and Lewis it was a big brother/little brother relationship; for Abbott and Costello it was the stern father with his mischievous son; and both Klugman and Randall and Marshall and Williams worked just as carefully setting up their interpersonal balance. But for granfaloon social issue television it was necessary simply to throw out a premise—single mothers with children in the same house, for instance—give a list of characteristics to one character, an alternate list guaranteed to create conflict to the other and you had the perfect odd couple, 1960s free-spirit Kate and Allie the over-controlled worry-wart.

The upshot of all of this expanding family, flexible coupling, and social rumination was that the mainstream was now so amorphous that it could strangle whatever development the social order could throw in its path. There was not a class attitude, political persuasion, societal problem, or psychological quirk that could not be presented as a conflict between some kind of odd couple within the family which would then reach some kind of reconciliation because they were, above all else, an odd couple within the family. Back in the 1950s such now scoffed at mainstream shows as *Father Knows Best* and *Leave It to Beaver* were no less smug about the superiority of the values they were purveying vis-à-vis any kind of alternative than are today's shows. Those shows assumed that everybody wanted to belong to a middle-class nuclear family in the suburbs, but they were so specifically placed that alternative views like *The People's Choice* and *Dobie Gillis* were left free to exist in their own little netherworlds. Today, you all but have to go outside the genre to escape the middle.

In many respects the most representative series of the entire era is *The Facts of Life*, the final generation of Lear-Tandem sitcoms, which during the course of its nine-year run managed to encompass almost every one of the period's tendencies. It began life as a spinoff taking the housekeeper character from *Diff'rent Strokes* played by Charlotte Rae and making her a house mother at Eastland, a private girls' school in Peekskill, New York. Like *M*A*S*H* the show initially introduced a huge community of characters in its single setting, expecting Rae's central, familiar presence to hold everything together for audience identification. But also like *M*A*S*H* the show soon began stratifying and whittling away characters until it wound up stabilizing with two odd couples who between them managed to cover all of the social archetypes and idealized mythologies about race and class currently at work in the culture: idealist Jewish writer Natalie (Mindy Cohn) with perky black performer Tootie (Kim Fields), and proletarian ethnic tomboy Jo (Nancy McKeon) with rich Waspy tease Blair (Lisa Welchel).

As such the show became sort of the Norman Lear version of *Little Women* and the fact that the final adjustment to the cast which produced this format was the addition of the tomboy named Jo seems to indicate that the show's producers were highly conscious of the parallel. With this format firmly in place, the show was now able to pose practically every problem of growing up female in modern America as some sort of conflict between two of the characters and then resolve it by reaffirming that underneath all of the wisecrack insults they all belong to the Eastland family.

An emblematic episode had the ever-battling Blair and Jo traveling to New York City to visit old friends. While Blair and Jo trade their usual insults, this time centering around the ridiculous amount of luggage Blair brought for the trip, they are joined at the station by Blair's equally high-toned friend Dina (Dana Kimmel) and Jo's Bronx neighborhood pal Jesse (Alexa Kanin) which only escalates the sniping into stereo. But after the two pairs of old friends go their separate ways, trouble follows.

At Dina's home she is outraged that while friends are due for lunch her cook is nowhere to be found. However, she is even more distressed when Blair cheerfully pitches in with her school-found kitchen experience and begins to whip up what looks like a borderline inedible batch of—ugh—tuna salad. What's more, when the cook returns with still plenty of time left to prepare and serve the more elegant food that has been planned, Blair does not share Dina's anger about the cook's absence. In fact, after the cook explains that she had had to make an emergency trip to the dentist, Blair goes so far as to offer her polite sympathy. This is too much for Dina. She accuses Blair of being a traitor to her class and blames the school for having changed her.

Meanwhile, at her old Bronx neighborhood community center, Jo is remarking about how things seemed to have changed in the neighborhood and Jesse is grumbling that it is the fault of the new people, the Hispanics, who are ruining everything. When Jesse refuses to help out some Hispanic checker players, Jo tells her that this is now their community center as well as hers. And when Jo stops Jesse from spray painting graffiti on the Hispanics' wall mural, Jesse accuses Jo of abandoning her people and blames Eastland school for changing her.

At episode's end the now sadder Blair and Jo reunite at the station for the return trip home. As they gather themselves together to head for the train Jo silently helps Blair with her luggage. In future episodes they will continue their steady stream of insults about each other's lifestyle, habits, and attitudes in an odd-couple friendship that could have only been manufactured in a Hollywood story conference. But the point has been made emphatically clear: Blair and Jo's home is now Eastland school and having become part of the school family it does not matter what social or philosophic viewpoint they are supposed to represent, when the chips are down they will both stand up for the same comforting, middle-of-the-road values that the family and the school represent.

Although *The Facts of Life* all but summed up its era's sitcoms, it was a show that was constantly ridiculed by the mainstream television critics. Far from being the most graceful show of its era, it is still difficult to see why it took more abuse than any sitcom this side of *Three's Company* until you notice that much of the hostility took the revelatory form of taunting the cast members about their adolescent chubbiness. Certainly *The Facts of Life* was no worse than the much acclaimed *Cheers* whose concept of complexity is to cram as many odd couples as possible (Sam and Diane, Diane and Carla, Sam and Woody, Cliff and Norm, Frasier and Sam, Frasier and Carla, ad infinitum) onto its main set, and whose notion of sexual sophistication is endless dramatizations of Smokey Robinson's "You've Really Got a Hold on Me." But then *Cheers* could be claimed as a by-product of even more recent developments.

M*A*S*H producer Gene Reynolds' next show was *Lou Grant* which took Mary Richards' old boss into a *M*A*S*H*–like setting that featured the multiplicity of characters in a Los Angeles newspaper office. Like *M*A*S*H* the idea was to mix jokiness into serious issue themes but as this was an hour-long, essentially dramatic show with a large cast of characters at its disposal, the series soon established a structure of having two plots per episode running parallel to each other in order to create some ironic underlining and help slam home whatever Aesopian moral was to be learned that week. *Lou Grant*'s time-slot successor *Cagney & Lacey* picked up on this structural technique even more relentlessly as its way of adjusting to the brave new world of Steven Bochco television which might be described as nighttime soap opera + (*enter your show's genre here*).

Bochco took the then reigning nighttime soap opera shows such as *Dallas* and *Knots Landing* and applied their multiple plotlines, sexual entanglements, and preoccupations with money and status to whatever new genre he touched. When applied to the traditionally blue-collar, macho police action show in *Hill Street Blues*, the impression was given of having completely restructured the genre. But as the technique was applied to the traditionally upscale daytime soap opera venues of the medical profession (*St. Elsewhere*) and the legal profession (*L.A. Law*), it became clear that the main difference between these shows and *Dynasty* was that they were aiming at the tastes of different demographic groups.

Cheers might be considered the ultimate soap opera sitcom, a vogue that in and of itself did not last out Bochco's run as television's Wonder Boy. However, the ideas of parallel plotlines and stories that continue over many episodes have been permanently embedded into the sitcom form, and what is more, the concept of creating new shows by mixing and matching genres from the serendipity of television history has all but enveloped the medium. Enter the age of the television show itself as granfaloon.

Recently the game of Rock-and-Roll Mathematics was invented to demonstrate the creative exhaustion of the form. The game works by coming up with an equation to prove that each new act is simply a synthetic combination of elements from earlier, more original artists. This game could very easily be transferred to television. For instance:

The Mary Tyler Moore Show + *Buffalo Bill* = *Murphy Brown*
or
The Golden Girls − *The Facts of Life* = *Designing Women*

Of course, there have been recent sitcoms that are not robots in disguise. There have even been interesting attempts at creating the anti–*Facts of Life* (*Square Pegs*), the anti–*Cheers* (*Frank's Place*), and the anti–*Cosby Show* (*Married . . . with Children*). Indeed, numerous Fox shows like *Married . . . with Children* and *Open House* seem to exist almost exclusively to explicate the subtexts in popular network shows.

It is just possible that network television and its situation comedy format has also exhausted itself as a creative force. A look at the history of popular culture art forms in America, minstrel shows, vaudeville, burlesque, network radio, shows their life spans lasted anywhere from thirty to fifty years before they were overtaken by the ever-changing climate. In counterargument one could point to the century-long life span of the movies, but, in point of fact, silent films are a far different art form than talking pictures and all of the criticisms that could be leveled at the past decade of network television are equally valid in relation to Hollywood studio films.

It is just possible that the continued growth of cable networks, revitalized local stations, and new technologies that are just now coming into creative focus will be the future vehicles for pop-culture art. Still, it would not be wise to stop paying attention to what is happening on network television, since, as I said, it is just possible.

Part II
Modern

8
Defining Our
Television Heritage II

This Day and Age

In Joseph L. Mankiewicz's *The Barefoot Contessa*, a party guest comes up to Humphrey Bogart and reports on a shockingly outmoded viewpoint which has been expressed to him. How could such a view be held, the man asks, in this day and age? To which Bogart replies, "What makes you think we're living in *this* day and age?"

One hesitates to label anything "modern" in this or any other day and age. First, there is simply the historical inevitability that time will overtake everything regardless of what you call it, and the hubris connected to all claims of modernity always leads to those clumsy post-modern, futuristic, post futuristic, neo-quasi-kinda-sorta-future but still up-to-date labels to justify the original definition.

A much more significant warning signal is the American culture's unshakable faith in viewing history as a straight, unambiguous line towards ever-increasing, always more sophisticated progress. And so to define something as modern is to imply that it is not only more current than what is "traditional" but by the very nature of its modernity, it is more complex and in all ways better.

Even by specifically defining modern television comedy as those people and programs which simply do not fit themselves within the structure of the traditional variety or situation comedy formats, a romanticized image of rebellious outsiders who break all of the rules and thus offer a more artistically challenging vision than do the complacent traditionalists is conjured up.

While there is some truth to that last notion and it seems particularly enticing in an era when the traditional forms are wearing holes in their treadmills, it is important to understand that what is defined here as modern television comedy is a tradition in itself with a history as long as the classic forms due, in large part, to the fact that it is interdependent with those classic forms. In fact, it is possible to view the most recent shows as reactionary rejections of the current state of traditional television period. These new series demonstrate what can be accomplished within such seemingly archaic forms as (1) in-studio host presentations of local film series (*Just Say Julie*), (2) the stylistics of early 1950s television wrestling (*G.L.O.W.*), and (3) pre-television two-reeler theatrical comedy shorts (*The Comic Strip Presents* films).

One reason why an individual performer's show would wind up outside the parameters of the traditional variety or sitcom forms is that his or her performance style simply could not function within either of them. Such was the case with Groucho Marx. As early as 1934 Groucho was trying to find a permanent radio vehicle, but his comic style, which was based on his ability to overpower any artificially imposed structure with intricate verbal analysis, simply could not be adjusted to fit within any type of continuing variety or sitcom show. It was only when he was placed in the looser, more improvised structure of the quiz show and then allowed to extend what on other such shows was a brief, introductory interview with the contestants to the point where this comic bantering between Groucho and the contestants all but eliminated the quiz itself, that he found success with *You Bet Your Life*.

Many of television's early modernists had come up through radio and were steeped in the mechanics of the traditional forms. Bob Elliott first met Ray Goulding when one was an announcer and the other a sports reporter on a local radio station. Their on-air banter led to the creation of formally written comedy routines and thus the performance team of Bob and Ray. Their routines usually played off of established daytime radio and television formats including all manner of talk/interview shows and most particularly the daytime soap opera. Indeed, perhaps their best known series of continuous sketches which they brought over from radio to television, "Mary Backstyge, Noble Wife," an inversion of the popular radio soap "Mary Noble, Backstage Wife," is the direct ancestor both in form and performance style to *Mary Hartman, Mary Hartman*. And Bob and Ray continued to play off the soap opera format right up to the time of Ray Goulding's death as their final Public Radio series featured the continuing adventures of "Garish Summit," a satire of the "conspicuous consumption" nighttime soaps such as *Dallas* and *Dynasty*.

The almost monotonous, conversational tone used while expressing absurdist emotional states, which *Mary Hartman* re-introduced in the 1970s, was actually Bob and Ray's very studied play off of the hugely popular personalized style of Mary Margaret McBride and Arthur Godfrey. In

Ray Goulding and Bob Elliott a.k.a. Bob and Ray.

fact, McBride was specifically targeted in their "Mary McGoon" household hints interview segments. And just as Godfrey would use the commercial portions of his shows to draw the audience closer to him, Bob and Ray would take the concept of personalized commercial pitches for crucially important products such as Einbinder fly paper or any number of great buys from the Bob and Ray Overstocked Warehouse to couch ludicrously impractical consumerism in a folksy tone which sounded like a pair of Godfreys who had very discreetly lost their marbles. Paradoxically, while one might logically assume that the issue of sponsorship would be an oppressive strait jacket for the modern sensibility, the reality was that they were even more reliant on the vicissitudes of sponsorship than were their traditionalist counterparts.

Just as the histories of both traditional and modern jazz could begin with Louis Armstrong, so the histories of traditional and modern television comedy could begin with Jack Benny. Almost from the beginning of his radio career, Benny found ways to transform the commercial segments into integrated comedy elements of his shows. His most successful strategy was having Don Wilson bring out the Sportsman Quartet to sing ever more outlandish variations of the sponsor's jingle which became yet another element of his show over which Benny lost control and about which he had to yell "Now cut that out!" Benny's successful transformation of the commercials formed a tradition for comedians to take liberties with the sponsor's message. This extended to the point where, by the late 1940s, an acerbic comic commentator like Henry Morgan could claim in mock outrage that his sponsor was cheating the public because his product, Life Savers, had a hole in it.

Morgan was one of a number of brittle personalities who never found a regular niche on television outside of subordinate roles as a panelist on quiz show or as a semi-regular guest on conversation programs. A comic relationship to commercial sponsors, however, was the salvation of many other modern sensibilities. Although NBC tried various time slots and format for them in the early 1950s, Bob and Ray could never sustain an audience large enough to carry a continuing series. Much of their later work was done on stage and radio but, ironically, their longest-running and most fondly remembered work on television turned out to be writing scripts and providing the voices for the characters Bert and Harry Piels in a series of animated commercials for Piels Beer.

Furthermore, Ernie Kovacs, television's foremost visual formalist, would have suffered the same fate as Bob and Ray had he not developed a close working relationship with the advertising account executive for Dutch Masters cigars. Not only did his continuous, loyal sponsor allow Kovacs to resurface over and over again on network television, but it also permitted him to create the commercials that would appear within his shows, segments that were almost indistinguishable from the "entertainment" which surrounded them.

The use of commercial messages as the vehicle for comic visions no doubt pre-dates radio and there is also no doubt that a study of the still anonymous writers, directors, and designers who have done important creative work within this form is long overdue. One person whose vision is clearly recognizable in the dozens of commercial campaigns he has created and is certainly not anonymous is Stan Freberg. His distinctive voice and face, which fairly ooze irony, became familiar to the public in the 1950s from his musical parody record albums and occasional television specials. But the main body of his work was in television commercials. The master of combining a ludicrously bombastic overkill message with an undercurrent of sarcastic subtext, Freberg was able to get away with staging a Campbell's Soup commercial as a Busby Berkeley production number starring Ann Miller (complete with snappy song lyrics like "Let's face the chicken gumbo and dance,") only to end it with Freberg regular Dave Willock, playing her husband, throwing in the tag line, "Emily, why do you have to make such a big production out of everything?" Whereas Godfrey would turn a Lipton tea commercial into an orgy of audience bonding, Freberg would weave a plethora of screwball riffs around a stentorian reading of the slogan "Salada Tea—it's not half bad!"

Freberg's first significant television job was working with Bob Clampett on his puppet show *Time for Beany*. Clampett had been one of the major contributors to the Golden Age of Warner Bros. cartoons and just as some of the greatest film comedy had come out of the alleged children's ghetto of cartoons, so did live children's television programming prove to be an excellent vehicle to smuggle in underground anarchy, satire, and behavioral observation. Indeed the historical developments in children's shows almost act as a shadow history of the prime-time variety show since these actually were variety shows directed at children.

In comparing the histories of live prime-time variety and live children's variety, it can be seen that just as the adults had Milton Berle and the stage revue shows and Dave Garroway and the personality shows so were these parallel figures for the children. There was even an Ernie Kovacsesque children's show in Jack Barry's *Winky Dink and You* where the viewer, with the help of crayons and the specially purchased "magic screen," helped to compose the scenes in which the show's characters would perform.

The Milton Berle figure in children's television was Bob Smith. He structured his show along the lines of the nineteenth-century tent shows and circuses as they might have been interpreted by Olsen and Johnson. His specific model was Buffalo Bill Cody's Wild West circus, and so he became Buffalo Bob Smith—the glad-handing, always genial, but often befuddled tour guide of Doodyville on *Howdy Doody*. The show strove to provide its young audience with the aura of slapstick grandeur as Buffalo Bob, Clarabell the Clown, Chief Thunderthud, and a host of other western circus characters ran all over the studio pulling practical-joke pranks on each other, the results of which would often spill out into the bleachers of children in the studio audience known as The Peanut Gallery.

These human, adult circus-performer characters would also interact with the marionette residents of Doodyville led by the western-clothed title character, Mayor Phineus T. Bluster, Dilly Dally, and some kind of a hybrid animal called Flub-a-Dub.

The enormous popularity of *Howdy Doody* spawned many similar shows most of which emphasized one or another aspect of Smith's carnival style. Veteran burlesque comic Pinky Lee moved over to a children's program that picked up on *Howdy Doody*'s slapstick humor and *Super Circus* zeroed in on the spectacle element. However, the show which most closely captured the total picture was *The Rootie Kazootie Club*. Although this show did not have a large cast of human characters, it did replicate the child surrogate puppet community (which here featured the title character, a street-kid shoeshine boy, his girlfriend Polka Dottie, and his animal friends Gala Poochie Pup and El Squeeko Mouse) whose adventures spilled out into the in-studio audience of children and was presided over by a human interlocutor, the surprisingly sardonic Todd Russell.

The Dave Garroway figure was Burr Tillstrom whose *Kukla, Fran and Ollie*, coming out of Chicago, offered a more contemplative, verbally sophisticated alternative to the raucous East Coast shows. The Kuklapolitan Players, which featured the likes of Oliver J. Dragon and Beulah the Witch, posited a world which was mythological in nature and from that fantasy base was thus able to develop more detailed comic characters whose humor derived from their recognizable character flaws. As such, they interacted more intensely with their human interlocutor, Fran Allison, who served as a kind of mother confessor for them, a universally respected voice of reason who would sympathetically listen to their problems.

Moving even further down that road was New York puppeteer Shari Lewis. A former musical prodigy barely out of her teens, Lewis was more of a big sister to her naïve yet wickedly clever puppet friends. What's more, she entered their world on a more personally engaged level. Since Allison, like Smith and Russell, did not operate the puppets on her show, she stood apart from the world of the Kuklapolitan Players who performed on their own separate proscenium arch "Punch and Judy"-styled stage. Lewis both created and operated her puppets and so she could not only converse with them on an eye-to-eye level, but also share the same stage space with them. She was therefore able to break down and barrier between the adult human figures and the self-contained childlike puppet world and present herself and her puppets as equals who respond to the same problems and the same reality.

In later years, Lewis complained that her close identification with children's television inhibited audiences from accepting her doing more adult comedy routines with her puppets. She went on to continue her musical career and, in fact, did work adult venues with her alter ego puppet Lamb Chop, but she also eventually reconciled her relationship to children's television and in 1991 created a new series for PBS, *Lamb Chop's Play-Along.* Still, in many respects, Lewis's complaints are eminently justified.

On radio, nobody saw that Edgar Bergen was human and Charlie McCarthy was a dummy so they were ultimately judged not by the texture of their skin but the content of their characters. Their bumbling father/smart-aleck son relationship was considered the equal to any other radio comedy team and their prime-time variety show was as popular with adults as it was with children. But on television, Bergen's most faithful disciple Paul Winchell, while able to move back and forth between children and adult variety shows, was never approached with the same level of respect that Bergen had earned. Similarly, Jimmy Nelson, who had first come to prominence doing onstage sponsor commercials on *Texaco Star Theater*, was also unable to break through the invisible kiddie barrier and continued to do most of his best work in commercials, primarily his long-running series for Nestle.

In fact, all television programs that were not part of the network prime-time lineup were looked on as children of a lesser god. But while this attitude bred natural resentments, it also offered artists the same kinds of opportunities that children got when grown-ups were not paying them any attention. It is highly doubtful that Dave Garroway's brand of super low-key, jazzy commentary would have survived on television had he not been moved out of prime-time to become the first host of the *Today* show. As originally presented, *Today* was a loosely structured omnibus of conversation, music, and commentary—closer in spirit to Public Radio's *All Things Considered* than the present over-produced, smiley-faced soft news compendium.

And *The Tonight Show*, as originally presented by Steve Allen, was a completely unpredictable mixture of songs, skits, interviews, and experimental media stunts. Allen shared Ernie Kovacs' fascination with the idea of presenting burlesque and vaudeville-styled content through abstract technological means. But while Kovacs concentrated on the formal and analytical aspects of this mode, Allen was more interested in how it would spontaneously interact with a live audience. Some of David Letterman's experimental toyings with the camera and soundtrack can be directly traced to Kovacs. Other Letterman stunts such as random on-air phone calls and the journeys onto the streets outside the studio are pure Steve Allen.

Allen's eventual journey was the opposite of Garroway's. He reined in some of his wilder notions and added enough structure to the spontaneity to be able to "graduate" to a prime-time variety show. Everything on

Steve Allen raw!

daytime or late night was considered B television in the 1950s, but the national consensus audience that gave rise to such smug complacency had, by the late 1960s, disappeared. The Generation Gap was a far too simplified term to cover the kinds of attitudinal cleavages that were then dividing the American public among all ages, races, and class origins. Television tried to look on this as just another minor rupture which it could help mend together from its vantage point in the middle. But, in terms of the subject at hand, it was actually being challenged by a whole new breed of comedian who considered all of television to be arthritically out of touch with the new, developing attitudes towards social conditions. The parallel response in the world of rock-and-roll was the abandonment of AM top forty for FM album rock. And, to the hip, new voices in comedy, television was very definitely AM.

George Carlin and Robert Klein were probably the two brightest and most creative talents in stand-up comedy during this era. Both comics had centered their philosophic approach in playing off of and analyzing popular media forms. Carlin, with his "wonderful WINO" radio station routines and spoofs of game shows starring that genial guy himself, Guy Himself, and Klein, with his recreations of early talkie Our Gang comedies and halftime marching bands doing their salute to mayonnaise, were hot items on the talk and variety show circuits. Had these two comics stayed in television they would most certainly have been the major forces in modern television comedy. However, almost simultaneously, Carlin and Klein let their hair hang down, dropped out of television, and went on to become superstars in what turned out to be comedy's version of FM, the college campus performance circuit. This was the venue where you could look and dress as you pleased and be as political and profane as you chose. Further, just as the rock music performers were no longer confined by the limitations of a 45 rpm record while performing in concert, so the college circuit comedians could expand and experiment with their material without having to worry about the next act on the bill or the upcoming commercial break. The concert scene was where the creativity and excitement were happening.

It was not until the mid–1970s that television began acknowledging and provisionally catching up with the live-stage stylistics of stand-ups like Carlin and Klein and groups such as the Second City troupes and Firesign Theatre. After the Vietnam War protests and the student uprisings had begun to fade into history, the counterculture attitudes and the comedians who had become associated with those movements no longer frightened the mainstream audience. Television was prepared to forgive and forget by including unreasonable facsimiles of counterculture comedy as part of their new, improved consensus mix. The process, which still continues today, of traditional television forms absorbing over-bleached versions of these comic styles and values into its ever more amorphous "family" had already begun. However, while this all-consuming family has continued to co-opt more and more of modern comedy territory with prime-time "cover versions," the genuine articles have continued to secure stronger and stronger beachheads on every new alternative to network prime-time.

First there was *Saturday Night Live* telecast by NBC during late night which featured a regular cast of Not Ready for Prime Time Players from the Second City and National Lampoon stage shows. While their brand of broad "sex, drugs, and rock-and-roll" humor was, by this point, familiar to devotees of the college circuit, it created a bombshell on television and greatly expanded the permissible range of expression for television comedy of all types. Further, *SNL* introduced a number of new comedians to television such as Andy Kaufman, catapulted to stardom previously marginal figures like Steve Martin, and even induced George Carlin and Lily Tomlin back to the medium for occasional hosting gigs.

The enormous "cult" success of *SNL* opened the way for a flood of not-conventional-enough-for-prime-time syndicated shows. All three networks passed up the aforementioned *Mary Hartman, Mary Hartman*, and Jim Henson was also unable to secure a network slot for his variety series starring The Muppets. Both of these shows were forced to go the syndicated route and wound up becoming the two most successful first-run comedy series to do so. As a by-product of *Mary Hartman*'s success, Martin Mull was given the opportunity to bring his facetiously third-rate smug and smarmy entertainer character to television. His shows, *Fernwood 2-Night* and *America 2-Night,* used the talk show format to satirize society's ever-increasing obsession with media celebrity. But the ultimate creative use of media analysis to satirize the values of the medium itself came from Toronto's Second City troupe whose *SCTV Network* invented so much of what 1980s/1990s television comedy is still vainly trying to imitate.

Through their constant exposure on the college circuit, the stand-up comedians gradually began to reach the iconic level of rock musicians. And, as rock continued to fragment into more and more stylistic camps, the comedians eventually came to be the consensus choice among young adults for live entertainment. Naturally, as the stature of stand-up comedians grew, so did the number of people entering the field aspiring to be (to the ironic astonishment of Paul Zimmerman and Martin Scorsese no doubt) "The King of Comedy." All told this led to the mushrooming of a nationwide network of "comedy clubs" which came along just in the nick of time for the development of cable television.

In many ways the marriage between the stand-up comedy nightclubs and the cable networks has resulted in programs that recreate much of the look and feel that network shows had in the medium's formative years. The cable networks needed good, cheap programs to fill up huge amounts of air time and setting up a single camera in a nightclub setting to photograph a huge parade of stand-up comics seemed made to order. On premium pay channels, like HBO, the up-and-coming and established stars of stand-up present their entire acts with half-hour or hour-concert specials, while the basic cable channels provide the less popular and unknown comics doing portions of their acts on anthology shows like *Caroline's Comedy Hour* and *Half-Hour Comedy Hour.*

But there are even more direct ways in which television and modern comedy are combining to offer reinterpretations of the medium's history. Paul Reubens' character creation Pee-Wee Herman is, to a large degree, an analytical reinterpretation of Pinky Lee. So when Reubens/Herman turned his energies to television, it was all but inevitable that he would create a simultaneously revisionist and reverential take on 1950s kids shows. *Pee-Wee's Playhouse* is, within its self-conscious transformation of the 1950s stylistics into an 1980s idiom, both more abstract and more literal-minded than its models. The slapdash burlesque settings of the black-and-white originals were transformed into a rainbow of painterly and sculptural surrealism, and the other-worldly interactions between the puppet characters and the new-age versions of the 1950s kid show icons, such as the cowboy hero and the Merry Mailman, became a Rainbow Coalition of harmonic diversity. *Pee-Wee's Playhouse* stands as the optimum example of how present-day modern comedy both plays off traditional forms and forms new traditions of its own, but it may ultimately be equally significant as the model for many future shows. Indeed, if Bill Cosby's recent venture, a new version of Groucho Marx's *You Bet Your Life*, is any indication, we may soon have to deal with yet another one of those clumsy critical terms, "revisionist modernism."

The difficulty in writing about modern comedy in a historical context is that the artists and the programs that they create tend to be individualistic responses to trends within comedy rather than the traditional mode's individualistic expressions within those trends. So while one can effectively discuss traditional comedy in groupings organized around genre forms, themes, and historical periods, it is usually more productive to discuss modern comedy as a series of separate entities. While this approach tends to inevitably reinforce a romanticized image of modern comedy, at some point one must put aside concerns about how the message will be received and concentrate on making certain that the message is accurately sent.

9
Visit from a Small Planet

The Comedy World
of Ernie Kovacs

During the five years prior to Ernie Kovacs' death in 1962, the television viewing public could be basically broken down into three distinct categories: a small group who thought Kovacs was the most original and creative figure in the medium, another small group who thought what Kovacs was doing was unadulterated garbage, and the majority who never watched Kovacs and barely acknowledged his existence.

Now, more than three decades after his death, the viewing public can be said to have whittled down to only two groups: a small legion which maintains that Kovacs was the only true genius to have worked in television, and the overwhelming majority who have never heard of him.

The romantic residue of early death having cut short a promising and innovative career has actually contributed to both perceptions, but the time is long overdue to rescue Kovacs from both the isolating deification of his admirers and his unjustifiable obscurity to the general public. It is time to return Kovacs to the continuum of television comedy history in order to take a good look at what this tremendously influential person really did accomplish.

Many of the major performers who established the foundations of television comedy in the 1950s were those who, like Jack Benny and George Burns, were already stars on network radio. Others among the television comedy pioneers were performers, such as Milton Berle and Jackie Gleason, who had had long careers as headliners on stage and in nightclubs. What is less commonly discussed is the process of how many of the fresher, younger personalities like Kovacs, Steve Allen, and Bob and Ray progressed from working for local radio stations, and then moving over to local television stations before finally becoming national network television performers.

In their individual ways, all of these newer voices were bringing a fresh perspective to television comedy. These newer perspectives came about not simply because the comedians came from a younger generation, but also because the different formats in which they had worked during their formative years had caused them to take very different approaches to the vital issues of relating to a studio audience and working within the already established television comedy genres.

For the most part, while performing on local radio these comics did not have a live audience to play against. They were left alone in the booth armed only with the records they played or the interviews they conducted to hold together the long, daily, mostly unscripted shows they hosted. So by necessity they had to develop a person-to-person rapport with each individual listener using marathon conversational projections of whatever was in their immediate improvisational imaginations.

With the almost instantaneous demand for round-the-clock television broadcasting in the early 1950s, local television stations were faced with huge blocks of time in the morning, mid-day, and late-night periods which could not immediately be filled with network or syndicated programming. Suddenly many of these radio personalities were being called on to use their fast-on-the-feet wits and person-to-person contact skills in order to hold together the hastily constructed television cooking, interview, and quiz shows that the stations came up with to fill those time gaps.

But, more than any other style of programming, these new local television stars were hired to handle the hosting duties on the long, early morning live children's shows. With Bugs Bunny and Popeye cartoons replacing pop records and interview guests as the loose glue that held their shows together, these celebrities now held forth for hours each day kibitzing with puppets, enacting skits that featured the comic adventures of their own character creations, inventing schtick with dimestore props, and exploring whatever meager studio equipment was used to broadcast their shows. Many of these kiddie show hosts never ventured beyond their individual local market. However, almost everybody who grew up watching television in the 1950s, including people like Andy Kaufman and Paul Reubens, fondly remember their own area's "Kansas City Star" (in New York it was Sandy Becker and, a bit later, Chuck McCann). Further, most of these kids shows' loyal audience realized, at least subconsciously, that the daily marathon of improvisation that their local bozo offered them was actually much more inventive than the high-priced pap being presented on the slicker network programs.

When Pat Weaver introduced the landmark NBC shows for the early morning, late night, and mid-day time slots (*Today*, *Tonight*, and *Home*, respectively), he was actually nationalizing local television concepts. And, in so doing, he struck the first blow in what would become the decade-long decline and fall of local programming. Further, by using two of the most creative people who had come up through the local route to anchor these shows (mellow, midwestern Dave Garroway for *Today* and musical, maniacal Steve Allen for *Tonight*), Weaver was able to retain the sense of individual person-to-person unpredictability while refining it with the force of network budgets and techniques. By the time Garroway had faded from the scene and Allen had been fully integrated into the mainstream with his own prime-time variety series, however, a rigid structure had engulfed both shows and their network power had all but crushed the possibility of any resurgent local competition.

And yet, contrary to all of the inevitable logic of history, along came Ernie Kovacs. From 1957 to 1962 Kovacs kept popping up on the networks in various unpredictable formats and guises, like a guerrilla insurgent. It was evident that there was something singularly out-of-step about the look, the feel, and the tone of his shows. And while that something was never baldly stated, the fact of the matter was that however the networks tried to present Kovacs they could never get him to abandon the philosophies and stylistics of local television.

Many of Kovacs' most famous character creations (e.g., the lisping, martini-sipping poet Percy Dovetonsils, lounging in his armchair, asiding about how manly the cameraman's legs are, and intoning doggerel such as "Leslie the Mean Animal Trainer"; or lederhosen-clad, pidgin-German-speaking disc jockey/pitchman Wolfgang Sauerbraten) were his personalized extentions of the kinds of eccentrics who had received forums through local television's desperate need for time fillers. Some of his most characteristic practices (e.g., inserting himself into old movie footage) came out of the experience of hosting local late night movie presentations. But the overriding reason why Kovacs stayed rooted in the mechanics of localism was that it allowed him to remain unfettered by a studio audience or the sketch and plot structures which had become defined as the rules for nationwide network television comedy. To Kovacs, rules were made to be examined, not followed.

Take, for instance, Kovacs' continual japes at the panel/quiz show format. Game show dynamics have changed considerably since Kovacs' time. The current mania has mutated the game show to the point where most of them now look very much like lotteries embedded in neon. Today the emphasis has shifted entirely towards pumping up hysteria about acquiring consumer goods and the winning of those prizes is almost entirely divorced from demonstrating any work or knowledge within the games themselves. Current shows have become both lunatic wallows in sleazy greed and carnivals of alienation as the fifth-rate stand-up comic hosts and the media-wise contestants debate each other about who is degrading whom along the road to fifteen-minute fame.

But in the 1950s, game shows were the networks' inexpensive way of filling holes in both their prime-time and daytime schedules, and with so much space opened up to them, the games took many different forms in order to fulfill many different functions. One of those forms was the panel/quiz show. Employing batteries of upper-class, witty, intellectual "expert" panelists, soothing, charming masters of ceremonies, and rigid rules of time and structure, the function of these shows was to make recognizably safe and regularized many of the more disturbing social questions that had come to dominate the news.

For example, one of the most dramatic television events of the early 1950s was the Kefauver Senate investigation hearings on organized crime. Day after day a parade of beefy, menacing-looking people took the stand in order to continually refuse to answer any of the Senate panel's questions about the nature of their work. Not long after the hearings, the long-running panel/quiz show *I've Got a Secret* was introduced. In this show ordinary citizens challenged the expert, celebrity panel to identify the one extraordinary aspect of their lives while they tried to reveal as little information about themselves as possible during the questioning.

Later in the decade the Army-McCarthy Senate hearings brought forth heated accusations of Communist connections or leanings by the Senate panel and equally heated denials or modifying explanations by the witnesses. Out of this came *To Tell the Truth*. On this game show three audience contestants appeared together, each insisting that they were the same person. The expert panel questioned them in hopes of figuring out which of the three was actually the person they all claimed to be.

Kovacs, a games-player and addicted gambler, must have appreciated the ingenuity necessary to turn these unsettling social issues into cheery parlor games. But Kovacs also found that the elimination of the horror in these problems through domesticating rules and formats superseded the creativity through the sheer force of its repression.

His best known, most anthologized panel/quiz parody, *Whom Dunnit*, had some poor yokel from the audience being hustled backstage in order to be fatally wounded by an absurdly obscure intellectual "celebrity" and then paraded in front of a smugly dim-witted panel who asked a set of inappropriate and formulaic catch-phrase questions in a half-hearted attempt to name his celebrity assailant before he expired. When Kovacs himself wound up fronting a panel/quiz show called *Take a Good Look*, the puzzle clues were staged as typical Kovacs blackout skits and became so poetically abstract that the panel (which included Kovacs' wife Edie Adams and his longtime friend Hans Conreid) spent most of its alloted time sputtering in complete mystification.

The homogenizing safety of television genre rules was the prison that Kovacs' free-form programs was trying to escape. Yet one of the lynchpins of his attack was to use a frightening, almost maniacal overkill of these mechanical repetitions so that the dehumanizing horror lurking beneath them came strongly into focus.

Kovacs would often introduce segments of his shows from a behind-the-camera, empty-studio setting in order to underline both the localized and deconstructive aspects of his work. On one memorable occasion, he sat aside the camera with his control-room headset on to inform the audience about the standard formula for success in the entertainment industry: "If it succeeds, beat it to death." Then, expounding on the then-current mania for westerns, Kovacs explained that while it was necessary for every episode of these shows to have the same totemic elements in them, the producers felt it was at least possible to vary the way that these elements were presented. What followed was a rapid-fire series of scenes showing the exact same white hat vs. black hat gunfight photographed from every conceivable camera angle. The spectacle of seeing the relentless repetition of the exact same human movements turning into queasy abstractions took the visceral violence out of the gunfight but replaced it with an even more violent dehumanization of the people being shown. As with much of Kovacs' work, it became impossible to separate the humor from the horror. But even more horrifying is the retrospective realization that today's hip "visual" culture has managed to unlearn all of Kovacs' analysis and now presents totally straight-faced informational versions of this technique, particularly in sports coverage.

The mechanistic nature of repetition was always central to Kovacs' work since he saw not only its dehumanizing, repressive aspects, but also its musically harmonious structural advantages as well. In his clusters of poetically interlocking blackout gags, he would always single out one of his favorite targets of baroque portentousness—such as the flowery entrances through French doors that Loretta Young used in the introduction to each episode of her anthology series—and use it as the home-base constant. At timed intervals within the cluster of blackout gags, the Loretta Young figure would pop up again and again walking through the same doors in the same way and the humor came as much from the exact sameness of the accompanying music, her physical movements, and her facial expressions as from the anticipation of which variation of trap door, exploding furniture, or pastry-in-the-puss would befall her this time. Further, the tension between the harmonious and mechanistic aspects of the repetitions within the blackout segments was underscored by the music that accompanied the entire cluster—old European language recordings of two songs that became pop hits after being anglicized as "Mack the Knife" and "Mona Lisa."

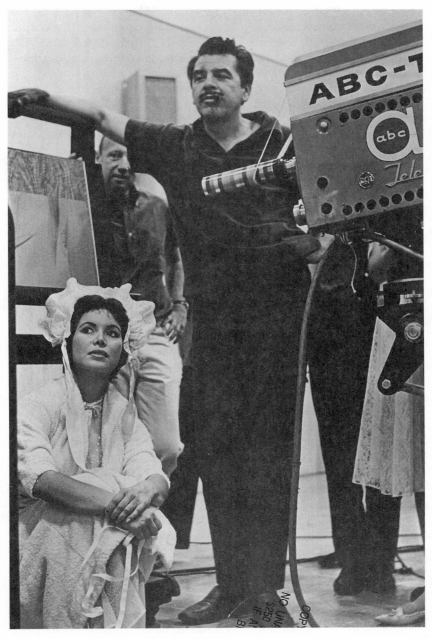

Ernie Kovacs standing next to his favorite collaborator, a television camera. Kovacs regular Jolene Brand sits in costume at left.

Indeed, for this most abstractly lyrical of comedy be-boppers, the way that pop and classical music each depended on repeating riff structures constituted the same mixed blessing. For while the relentless rhythm of the music joined isolated individuals into a harmonious whole, it also stripped them of their personal identities through having to conform to the hypnotic beat. This idea was probably most graphically displayed in the antics of Kovacs' best remembered creation, The Nairobi Trio. An inspired variation on Sid Caesar's classic Swiss belltower routine, the trio was a group of three actors in monkey costumes (Jack Lemmon and Edie Adams were among thoe who took occasional flings at Nairobidom)—one seated at an upright piano, one seated with a leader's baton in his hand, and one standing with drum mallets in both hands—who simulate the jerky, mechanical movements of wind-up dolls while playing to the beat of yet another recording which features a catchy pop melody with foreign language lyrics.

All goes well with the trio's visual reproduction of the song's click-clack rhythm, until the monkey with the mallets turns to hover over the monkey with the baton and proceeds to simulate the song's bongo drum break by hitting him over the head with his mallets. The surprise of the slapstick mayhem is funny in itself, but the actual gag is the long, contemplative pause by the baton monkey as he gradually realizes that what the mallet monkey is doing conforms to the rhythm of the music, but any action he could take to avoid being clobbered would force him to break out of his narrow path of prescribed movements. Even more affecting than the mayhem or the contemplation is the pathos of the baton monkey's inability to adequately express his anguish through the fixed expression on his rubber mask face.

Like the repeating gag within the blackout segments that keep coming back with different punchlines, such as the Loretta Young entrances, The Nairobi Trio spots depend on a recognized and familiar exact sameness to all of the movements leading up to the gag and the audience's anticipation of how the pattern will be broken this time. Using this format, which is actually a personalized restructuring of standard burlesque schtick procedure, Kovacs offered the comedy version of a jazz soloist who continually finds new interpretations of the same standard songs in performance after performance.

Most of Kovacs' shows included segments that were devoted to visual interpretations of pieces such as "The 1812 Overture" and "Sentimental Journey" through the actions of animated office furniture or food interacting with kitchen appliances. In many ways these segments were the apotheosis of Kovacs' localism, a democratic demonstration of do-it-yourself television using only a record, your imagination, and stuff you can find around the house. But it was also a more analytical and sophisticated version of a common kiddie show practice—interspersing the cartoons with similarly animated arts and crafts renditions of songs such as "The Happy Wanderer" and "A Lonely Little Petunia in an Onion Patch."

Doing such sequences on children's shows was logical because they were natural extentions of one of animation's major preoccupations: exploring ways to depict music visually. White elephant extravaganzas like *Fantasia* brought the idea to the general public's attention, but it has always been a constant theme in Hollywood animation, particularly for a director like Friz Freleng whose films, such as *Rhapsody in Rivets* and *Pigs in a Polka*, are mini-masterpieces of contemplation on the relationship between musical and comedic timing.

It is not surprising that Kovacs would share these animators' interest in visualizing music, since the positive alternative to the mechanical retrictions in genre forms and repetitions that Kovacs posits is a world of gags that shared the animator's vision of unshackling the literal constraints of physical law. Numerous Kovacs gags (e.g., a man boring a hole through a television set and having the drill entering the picture being shown on the screen, a sketched drawing of a cannon shown on one half of the screen firing on and destroying the solid objects pictured in the other half, people who are watching a film of a river suddenly being drenched by an outpouring of water from the screen) suggested, as possibilities for humans, physical experiences previously ghettoized as animation fantasy. But at the same time, he would also suggest these same consciousness-expanding possibilities to the art world, as with his gags that showed paintings which continued in human form beyond the frame. Just as in Kovacs' continuous fascination with combining animal and human behavior (The Nairobi Trio) and gags that depend both on repetition and surprise (the Loretta Young entrance spots), the idea of combining elements from both the concrete physical world and the abstract world of the visual arts serve to open broader, more inclusive ways of interpreting reality and therefore make Kovacs the most romantic and optimistic of television comedy's originators.

Kovacs' celebrated non-speaking narrative show *Eugene* was almost a compendium of his possibility-expanding concepts. As the mime-like title character wandered through a singularly peculiar kind of library, he stumbled over all kinds of typically Kovacsian comedy devices. Some were consciously reminiscent of particular animation concepts such as the "book-come-to-life" theme (when Eugene opens *Camille* he is greeted by the sound of a terrible coughing fit, or he gets the overwhelming sounds of either war or peace depending on which section of the Tolstoy novel he opens) or the mounted moosehead that is eventually revealed to be part of an entire moose, the rest of which had been hidden in the off-screen space. Others were live-action gags with underpinnings of animation philosophy created through Kovacs-invented camera trickery. Probably the best remembered sustained sequence of such pratfall expressionism came when Kovacs engineered a combination tilt of both the camera and the furniture so that the table at which Eugene sat while he tried to eat lunch looked perfectly level but everything solid he tried to set on it rolled off the end and everything liquid he tried to dispense poured at an angle.

Like many originators, Kovacs has proved to have a more profoundly influential effect on his artistic colleagues than on the general public. And as more and more television comedy now aspires to reshape established genre modes, the claims to Kovacs' mantle have grown louder and more defiant. Shows ranging from the network super-slickness of *Rowan and Martin's Laugh-In* to the localized super-sleazoid of *Gorgeous Ladies of Wrestling* have picked up on Kovacs' blackout segments containing the repeating gag with the varying punchline, and Jim Henson's Muppet shows, which proudly retain their roots in local children's programming, also retain a Kovacsian sense of visualizing music. The most creatively rigorous disciples of Kovacs have been the Second City Television troupe who invented their own local television station in mythical Melonville and used the structures of established local formats like "The Fishin' Musician" and "Monster Chiller Horror Theatre" as the launching pads for their deadly media analysis.

In recent years David Letterman has been hailed as the Ernie Kovacs of the 1980s. While many of Letterman's format-deflating pranks harken more to the equally important mode of Steve Allen, his tendency towards trying camera-tilt trickery and sight-and-sound synchronicity games are certainly creative forays into Kovacs' realm. Unfortunately, his smug, self-satisfied smirks and "us smart sophisticates vs. them dull squares" attitude also make him the Chatsworth Osborne, Jr. of the 1980s. Closer to the mark is Julie Brown's sharp-shooting *Just Say Julie* on MTV. Here Brown's frontal assaults on airhead bimbodom and pipsqueak macho posturing are presented through her own hyper-theatrical, pop-culture, fame-obsessed comic character. It is in how Brown uses her single-camera format, junk-cluttered localized set, and rinky-dink beach and street remote broadcasts to counterbalance the often over-produced music videos she presents and sometimes invades that the Kovacs spirit shines brightest.

In many ways, the burgeoning expansion of cable television systems has recreated the less corporatized world of 1950s local television. And, if more experimental comedy styles continue to be nurtured on cable, the spirit of Ernie Kovacs may continue to be nurtured as well. However, to expect anybody to duplicate Kovacs' ability to combine grace and force, both in his deadly assaults on confinement and his exuberant celebrations of possibility, may be asking for too much.

10

"It's *My* Show
So Who Cares"

Martin Mull, Julie Brown,
and the Stand-Ups

When writing for any length of time about television comedy, the point comes where you must start considering all of the comedy that has not been on television. The unspoken assumption built into every medium of communication is that its authority is absolute, that the newspaper gives you "all the news that's fit to print," the television newscast tells you "the way it is," and the rock radio station presents "all the hits all the time." While many are aware that alternative news outlets and underground music sources have no problem filling their time and space with material not found in the mainstream, it is difficult to overcome the cultural assumption that these outlets constitute the minor leagues, try-out venues where, if the material proves popular, it becomes validated for inclusion among all of the news and all the hits. History often offers its own correctives with material from the initially ignored minority sources eventually usurping what had first been considered both superior and wise. But even if you took an encyclopedic approach to the medium, your understanding of the past forty years in American comedy would include gaping holes if all you knew of it was what appeared on television. There have been many important artists whose work simply would not conform within the unspoken boundaries beyond which television simply would not venture.

One of these key figures is the "legendary" Lenny Bruce. In fact "legendary" has become attached so often to the front of Bruce's name that it has all but turned into a joke along the order of how SCTV turned "funnyman" into Bobby Bittman's first name. But Bruce came by this appellation honestly. He possessed all of the qualities that become a legend best: (1) a singular talent and original approach to his art which proved to be highly influential on later generations of practitioners, (2) a wild streak of self-destructive behavior that led to an early death, (3) an insistence on confronting social taboos and questioning received knowledge in his work, and (4) while optional, extremely helpful, a paucity of recorded material to document his work. In fact, were it not for the vogue of long-playing comedy albums in the 1950s, we would now rely on hearsay to appreciate Bruce's work as we do for many major figures of early twentieth-century vaudeville and musical comedy.

There are documented appearances by Bruce on television, primarily on *The Steve Allen Show*. Allen, a cool jazz musician as well as a writer and performer, was very sympathetic to the beat scene that nurtured Bruce. Allen was willing to risk some mainstream popularity in order to present some of these "dangerous" figures, and even went so far as to have Jack Kerouac read excerpts from *On the Road* on his show. But on television, the Lenny Bruce who relentlessly savaged all of our national repressions and intolerances, the Lenny Bruce who was indeed a "legend" to his fans, somehow got left back at the coffeehouse. The comedian on the *Allen Show* is a toned-down, almost neutered Bruce doing material that he could fit into the standards and practices of 1950s television. As visual evidence of Bruce's physical gestures and the stylistics of his timing, these shows are invaluable. But if television were all there was to comedy, Bruce would hardly seem legendary. In fact, he would barely register an impression at all.

Philosophically, Bruce was working on ideas that were in the same general range as many of the other rising young comedians of the late 1950s who were collectively called "the new breed." But the extremities of his language and the defiance in his attitudes scared the television establishment. For them Bruce represented a mortal threat to all of the shared beliefs that held the television-viewing community together. Bruce became a television outlaw by choice. He was naïve enough not to fully understand why television would not accommodate him, but he was dedicated enough to refuse any compromise when the "TV or not TV" gauntlet was cast. But concurrently with Bruce's legendary refusal to sell out there was an entire race of performers for whom Bruce's choices and opportunities were just so much academic theory. Indeed, for the television community, the mere appearance of a black person in front of the camera could be as threatening as Bruce at his most radical.

When the full story of comedy that did not appear on television is told, the still under-documented history of African-American comedy will finally come into deep focus. During the 1950s, Ed Sullivan's ecumenical approach to variety brought national attention to such popular mainstream black stand-ups as Timmie Rogers and George Kirby who were welcomed to join Sullivan's regular rotation of New York–based nightclub comedians on "the really big show." And during the heightened civil rights consciousness of the liberal 1960s, talk show hosts Merv Griffin's and Mike Douglas' reverence for the comedians of their youths not only offered historic opportunities to see such key live stage performers as Smith and Dale and Bert Wheeler, but also introduced contemporary equivalents from the black circuit like Moms Mabley and Pigmeat Markham. But irrespective of talent, the defining factor that made all of these African-American comedians ultimately acceptable to the television audience was that they spoke in the voice of the Depression/World War II generation whose collective approach to comedy was based on developing a universalized audience rapport which assumed that despite individual personalities and particular ethnic backgrounds, we all shared a consensus set of values and experiences.

Of course, to one degree or another, this assumption is a necessary prerequisite to *any* form of communication. But one of the distinguishing trademarks of the new breed comedians was that they no longer spoke in the voice of John Q. Public. They came across as highly personalized, sometimes extremely isolated individuals who attempted to connect with whatever part of the audience was willing to participate in their particular viewpoint on life. In effect, what these new comedians, such as Jonathan Winters and Bob Newhart, were asking for and receiving was an expanded definition of the range of behavior that would be permissible in the collective consensus audience. What Lenny Bruce was demanding and being denied was an end to consensus and the birth of an unstructured society of universal inclusion.

In the context of this expansion, Dick Gregory's sometimes acid, always ironic political commentaries were now considered artistically important enough to appear on Jack Paar's progressive late-night salon, but still too risky for prime-time where the idea of a black man directly challenging the political establishment remained a threat to consensus. So it was left to another black new breed comedian to make the mainstream breakthrough, a comedian whose approach proved to be the perfect conduit between the generations and the races, and whose impact remains enormous to this day—Bill Cosby.

Cosby's richly detailed child's-view stories about going to kindergarten or having tonsils removed were comfortably familiar for the older, mainstream audience in that they wonderfully brought out the universal comedy in shared experiences, and their urban enclave settings mirrored the milieu of that generation's own Depression-era childhood. At the same time Cosby's stories were heralding this audience into the spirit of the next generation by way of his deeper investment in the individual psychologies of the stories' characters and the new rhythms in comic timing and speech he pioneered out of his ethnic heritage. Cosby's popularity as a stand-up on television led to his becoming the co-star of the action-adventure (with comedy) series *I Spy* which, in turn, opened the doors for the stream of black-themed sitcoms (*Julia, Good Times, What's Happening!!*, etc.) and integrated action dramas (*The Outsiders, The Mod Squad*, and others) that followed during the next decade. All of which led up to what, at least on the surface, seemed like a logical decision by NBC to premiere a comedy/variety series starring Richard Pryor in 1977.

The evolutionary progression from Cosby's own variety series to the popular *Flip Wilson Show* to Pryor is consistent with the general pattern of developments in television history. And, disconnected from content, Pryor's performance style fits very comfortably into the new tradition that Cosby's work had established. In his early years, Pryor had appeared on television with routines so closely patterned on Cosby in both style and content that he almost left the impression of being Cosby's kid brother. While Pryor's artistic scope soon expanded and he found his own distinctive philosophic voice, he has never abandoned the techniques of storytelling and timing he learned from Cosby. One way of understanding Pryor's landmark innovations on the Cosby style is that he, a black man from Peoria, Illinois, has been able to infuse the urban storytelling patois with elements from the Gothic midwestern style, with a particular debt to Jonathan Winters' character sense for his depiction of flat-voiced white dullards. But no matter how well you can logically rationalize the attempt, the fact remains that anybody who was truly listening to Pryor understood that he was to hip 1970s comics what Lenny Bruce had been to hip 1950s comics. The interesting issue remains: why did network television attempt an alliance with Pryor in the first place?

In the late 1950s, television did not feel the need to accommodate somebody like Lenny Bruce. The cohesive mass audience felt that it was already getting all of the comedy fit to print and for the few who wanted something else—let them eat record albums. The new breed expansion of the behavioral consensus progressed through the 1960s, reaching its high point when two of their own, The Smothers Brothers, were given a comedy/variety series that strove weekly to push the limits of mass audience tolerance for social and political satire. One way of pinpointing the moment when the assumed resilience of American consensus began to disintegrate was CBS's decision to discontinue *The Smothers Brothers Comedy Hour* despite its enduring mass popularity. By the late 1970s all of the commonly recited litany of events which had combined to completely break down the consensus society (the generation gap, the Vietnam War, Watergate, et al.) had already occurred. And while network television was not yet ready to admit it, its cohesive mass audience had broken down with it.

In fact, all of those events which lead up to the logical attempt to integrate Richard Pryor can also be read as television's desperate measures to head off the impending collapse of consensus.

Again, disconnected from his considerable artistry, the basis of Bill Cosby's television popularity as a stand-up was that he invented new horizons for the Depression/World War II mindset after that era had been sociologically exhausted. As the consensus audience started drifting away, the subconscious decision was made to attempt its resurrection by pouring the old wine of genre forms into the new bottles of social groups formerly excluded from the consensus. Just as the terminally ill movie studios were then using black casts to revive pre–World War II genres so the recently diagnosed television networks turned to the idea of black families in traditional sitcoms and black comedians fronting variety shows in order to bring the mass audience back for "the same thing—only different."

And for a while this strategy worked. Unable to ignore the evidence of disintegration in their own communities, the mass white audience tuned in to see sitcoms about black nuclear families and white "families at the workplace" during the 1970s. Then the "over the rainbow" retro 1980s offered a general revival of family sitcoms led by none other than Bill Cosby himself. But by this time syndication, cable, and home video had made any claim to consensus ring hollow and the dazed giants of network television were sent scrambling after special demographic interests.

The breakdown in consensus can be understood as a public loss of faith in any shared national identity and the subsequent retreat into whatever tribe of ethnic heritage, sexual preference, religious sect, or political persuasion individuals felt best represented them. The bitter irony of finally being invited in through consensus' front door only to find that it was a futile desperation tactic to keep the roof from caving in was not lost on a black population that was well versed in every aspect of the experience of exclusion. As the social glue dried and crumbled and the collection of tribes stepped up their competition with each other for a share of what has been defined as a limited pool of legitimacy, each group (and by extension each individual) came to interpret their social situations, if not their emotional experiences, as being similar to that of African-Americans. And while most national institutions continued to lose credibility at the same time that this internecine competition intensified, television celebrityhood came more and more to represent the fastest and most tangible way to validate one's identity. So while the usual criticisms of television originating from the consensus era continued to be proclaimed, mainly variations on the distortion through homogenization theme, they were all now being superseded by the post-consensus charge that while television might misrepresent everybody and everything that it shows, a much greater problem is—*I'm* not on it.

Actually, the breakdown in consensus only accelerated America's obsession with self-validation through media celebrity. It has, in fact, been a constant theme in American twentieth-century art. The 1920s stage plays, such as Hecht and MacArthur's *The Front Page* and Maurine Watkins' *Chicago*, and 1930s/1940s screenplays, like Watkins' *Professional Sweetheart*, Claude Binyon's *The Gilded Lily* and *True Confession*, and almost everything by Preston Sturges and Billy Wilder can be pointed to as milestones along the road to television. While television was staking out the parameters for all of its genre forms in the 1950s, Jack Benny and George Burns brought their radio shows to the tube and demarcated the medium's basic principles of meditations on television celebrity. It was not until the 1960s that television's first home-grown philosopher of the celebrity/society conundrum appeared in the person of the hip, urban, Catholic, impressionist/comedian John Byner.

Although Byner has been an almost continuous television presence for thirty years, currently hosting A&E's *Comedy on the Road*, he has always been relegated to a kind of reliable utility infielder status that makes him a prime contender for the "Most Underrated Comedian" Lifetime Achievement Award. Primarily this is due to his inability to break out of a public perception of being the first runner-up to another comparable comedian in all of his endeavors, with Rich Little and Frank Gorshin considered to have more distinctive voices among impressionists and George Carlin considered hipper among urban, Catholic comedians. But through the very act of presenting comic interpretations of celebrities, impressionists must ponder the relationship between celebrity and society. And it is in his astonishingly creative forms of presentation that Byner has done work which is still light years ahead of everybody else in the field.

While the conventional impressionist's approach is basically a vicarious basking in the glory of celebrity both for himself and his audience, Byner set up a tension where celebrity represented a comically monstrous aberration from normal human behavior, almost a failure at being human itself. His general manner of presenting a series of impressions with the celebrities envisioned in inappropriate professions (Rod Steiger as a stand-up comic, John Wayne as an altar boy, etc.) set up the general principles on which his comedy worked. But his most memorable routines were early classics of the modernist sensibility in which he would add layer upon layer of self-implication both as being a failed celebrity (a person who can only imitate celebrity) and as a celebrity failure (a performer who cannot relate to the ordinary experiences of his audience).

In that regard there is nothing to top his routine about a mediocre impressionist bombing in front of a glum, dull, tank-town audience. Playing on the impressionist's device of turning his back on the audience in preparation for returning as the celebrity he is about to mimic, Byner set up a situation where the backdrop curtain represented his comedian character's unresponsive audience and the live audience got to hear his wild, panicky thoughts when he turned to gather himself together for the next impression.

> [Facing curtain] All right, so you didn't like that one. Well for my next impression I'm gonna do Walter Brennan and I know you're gonna like it folks because he's a farmer *just-like-you!* No! Please! Don't leave! I'm just kidding! Just kidding folks. Okay, Walter Brennan.
>
> [Turns to audience] Oh my God! Oh my God! I almost lost them there. What do they want from me!?! The guy with the toolbox is okay but that guy with the fishing rod is killing me! Okay, what am I doing—Walter Brennan. And if this doesn't work the only thing left is "request time."
>
> [Turns back to curtain] Aaaa, Luke, the barn! Luke, the barn! Luke—the—barn. Luke—the—. All right, you don't like Luke. You don't like the barn. It's "request time"!

In the late 1960s, Byner created a character called Lenny Jackie—The King of Mirth who was a compendium of every loud and untalented Vegas/Borscht–belt comic who ever lived and a living metaphor for an entire style of comedy that was artistically forgotten but not yet gone. Bounding onstage in nerdy specs, wearing a bad tuxedo and a worse haircut, Lenny Jackie would bombard the audience with a breathless barrage of the tiredest jokes imaginable propelled only by an unshakable confidence in his own talent. Byner would not even bother to do the punchlines for the grab-bag collection of public domain whizbangs that was supposed to be Jackie's act. Byner's words merely served as timed pauses between the shouted comic exclamations with accompanying rim shots and the aggressively buffoonish body gestures that was the actual core of the character. A typical Lenny Jackie routine would sound like:

> AH-OH! Good evening ladies and gentlemen. BOW! What is this an audience or an oil painting? BA-BOO! A funny thing happened to me on the way to the studio. A bum walked up to me and said he hadn't had a bite to eat in a week. TOOO! OOOHHH! Then there was the time, then there was the time when these two Armenians got off a streetcar in downtown Boston. Ha! Ha! Ha! Ha! Don't applaud folks just throw money. ZA-FOW! But seriously folks, moving right along here, how do you like me so far? JOO-BOO!

Byner later admitted that he finally dropped this character because his audience was simply baffled by it. In fact, he received many letters telling him that Lenny Jackie's jokes just weren't funny and therefore there was no reason to watch him. It took the general public another decade to figure out that the jokes not being funny was the point and make Eugene Levy's

Bobby Bittman character a cult figure. If Byner had been doing Lenny Jackie on the college campus and coffeehouse circuit instead of in nightclubs and on television, it probably would have been recognized and appreciated as the parody that it was. Indeed it might even have been recognized as the death knell for the Depression/World War II consensus comedy that it actually represented.

Part of the counterculture's oppositional stance rested on its delight in hip facetiousness and the vanguard of the television generation would have been enthusiastic about laughing across the cultural gap at all of the moldy fig comics they had grown up watching on *The Ed Sullivan Show*. But that did not mean that they were any quicker to recognize a parody of their own cultural mores, as Martin Mull was soon to find out.

Blond, blue-eyed, midwestern Martin Mull looked like the "all–American boy" although his cultural history reads closer to our image of the typical British youth with its concentration on a quality university education leading to the twin artistic pursuits of painting and rock/blues guitar. But somewhere along the line he became more interested in creating a parody version of the "sensitive" folkie balladeer. He came up with an act that was darn close to duplicating the original except that all of the crass, condescending self-absorption was stunningly presented as a matter-of-fact part of the performer's personality.

Lounging in an easy chair in an onstage living room set designed to produce a deceptive sense of intimacy, Mull would pour on the "jus' folks" smile and conversational voice of sincerity to promote such a shallowly blatant line of self-satisfaction (probably best summed up by his Kristoffersonesque song "I'm Everyone I've Ever Loved"). Even the most sensitive audience needed acclimation time to figure out what to make of this guy. But, unfortunately, the most sensitive audiences for a goof on folk/rock were in short supply in the early 1970s. While hippie put-on artists would be quick to spot the humor in a Lenny Jackie, the very idea that their own cultural foibles could be savaged never seemed to have entered their minds. In recounting his early struggling years, Mull later recalled what he fondly remembered as a magical shock of recognition when an individual member of a typically unresponsive audience suddenly shouted out, "Oh I get it! It's *supposed* to be bad!"

Later, after Mull's stage act and records won him a recognizable following, he branched out into acting and won the role of the smug, supercilious Antioch grad Garth Gimble on *Mary Hartman, Mary Hartman*. Reduced to working in the town's factory, Garth nevertheless imposed all of his wiseguy hipness and self-satisfied trendiness on the residents of Fernwood, Ohio. When it was revealed that he took out his frustrated delusions of grandeur in wife-beating, he was quickly dispatched via Christmas tree impalement. But as the series was winding down, Mull was re-introduced as Garth Gimble's twin brother Barth, a show-biz personality who had come to Fernwood in search of his brother after having to leave Miami Beach under a cloud of suspicion involving a payola scandal. And even though Garth's death came as a great shock to him—for a few minutes—he stayed on in town to become host of *Fernwood 2Night* ("thirty minutes of quality entertainment with your host—for tonight—Barth Gimble").

Hosting a fictionalized talk show gave Mull, as Barth, the opportunity to present the full range of his "in-one" stage persona. His opening monologue, presented from the same easy chair he used in his stage show, often featured songs and anecdotes culled from his live act. For example, he often prefaced a song by telling what key it would be in, explaining, "I always tell the audience what key I'll be playing in in case some hippie brought his harmonica and wants to stand up and make a complete jerk of himself." At other times the monologue would be used to chronicle ongoing narrative adventures in order to plumb the depths to which Barth's quick-buck sleaziness would sink. For instance, the saga of his whiplash suit developed out of an argument in the supermarket express line over whether Barth's six-pack constituted six items or the other guy's carton of eggs constituted twelve items. The ruckus culminated with Barth being hurled into the Tic Tac display.

After the monologue Barth would be joined by his announcer/sidekick, Fred Willard as the All-American airhead Jerry Hubbard. Just as *Mary Hartman, Mary Hartman* elaborated on the understated absurdity in Bob and Ray's soap opera spoofs, so *Fernwood 2Night* worked off of their equally matter-of-fact interview routines. While Barth Gimble would distance himself from his interview subjects, repressing any connection between their pathetic claims to public recognition and his own behavior with offhand zingers like "that was darn near close to being interesting," Jerry Hubbard's contribution was to pick out the least cogent point in any conversation and smother it to death through overattention. For instance, when a guest casually pointed out that in a hypothetical situation a particular response would be typical of nine out of ten people, Jerry immediately jumped in to earnestly ask how many that would be out of 12 people. Then, unwilling to give up this point, Jerry painstakingly worked it out to the conclusion that this would constitute 18 people out of 20 as Barth stared on in open-mouthed disbelief. Paired, they turned into the classic comedy team with Jerry taking the Stan Laurel/Ed Norton part of the innocent naif whose stupidity is actually superseded by the pretentions of his pseudo-sophisticate partner, Barth in the Oliver Hardy/Ralph Kramden role.

But the centripetal force that actually kept this team together was their unshakable, tunnel-ego conviction that their jobs constituted the very heart of the entertainment industry. And this attitude put them at a perfect vantage point to interface with their guests, a horrifyingly unstoppable parade of star-struck burghers who are devoting their life's blood to the proposition that the measure of all human achievement is self-validation through television celebrity.

This potpourri of celebrity manqués ranged from *Guinness Book of World Records* hopefuls such as the young Jim Varney playing a Podunk Evel Knievel who cycles over mobile homes, to conceptual non-acts like the Fernwood Synchronized Swim Team (including a *very* young Rosanna Arquette) performing sans water on wooden planks. In taking a contemporary revisit to this death march through the spotlight, the most astonishing revelation is that while the show is nostalgically dated by its satirical attachment to all of the cultural flapdoodle of the late 1970s, the incisive cultural insight of its central premise made it amazingly prophetic of where society was headed.

All of the pop cultural cheese of the Carter years takes its turn on the *Fernwood 2Night* stage. There's Dr. Richard Osgood (Craig Richard Nelson embodying haughty condescension as only he can) presenting his theory that leisure suits cause cancer—complete with fully outfitted lab mice for demonstration purposes. There was the then mushrooming mania for franchise restaurants represented in the ongoing feud between bandleader Happy Kyne's (Frank De Vol) "Bun 'n' Run" chain and frequent guest Susan Cloud's (Susan Elliot) new age "Butterfly Cafe" which favored such delicacies as falafel on a stick. And there was Barth's disco salute to Abe Lincoln backed up by the roller-skating Dunbar sisters.

But when Barth picked out a boast by Jimmy Carter's media consultant to the effect that the president was the nation's number one television celebrity, contended that anybody who gets simultaneous coverage on all three networks and still can't beat the ratings for the reruns on the UHF stations is not much of a draw, and challenged the president to a talent contest on the *Fernwood 2Night* stage, he couldn't have anticipated the three-ring circus that the presidency would soon become. And indeed many of the show's hopefuls who seemed improbable in the late 1970s turned out to be only slightly exaggerated harbingers of future events.

Long before instruction show hosts like Bob Vila used their PBS prestige to launch careers as product endorsers, *Fernwood 2Night*'s consumer advocate Lou Moffett's (Lou Felder) fast-shuffle caveat emptors transformed into blatant shills for specific products—all of which turned out to be from Gimbleco Enterprises. And long before the "G Spot" was foisted on us, Mickey Deems was portrayed as the discoverer of a new body organ (it is the organ that controls the sharp pains you feel whenever you eat something very cold too fast) which had heretofore avoided detection because it hides behind other organs in X-rays.

Fernwood 2Night was designed to be a short-run series, but the Hollywood community was so taken with it that requests from actual celebrities to appear brought it back as *America 2Night*. The show was relocated in a small California town where the inclusion of well-known actors on the guest list would seem more believable. While this version generated an equal amount of madness (Elke Sommer coming on directly from a kids' show guest stint in clown makeup and regalia, Jill St. John being interviewed via remote from her dentist's office while having emergency root canal work), it also stood as the hardest evidence of *Fernwood 2Night*'s social viewpoint prophecies. The changeover from *Fernwood 2Night* to *America 2Night* was another step along the trail for a culture that saw itself as increasingly divided into two classes: celebrities and losers.

This was the society that Julie Brown saw when she entered the stand-up scene in the early 1980s. The contrasts in time, space, form, and demeanor between Mull's and Brown's rise to prominence go a long way towards defining how the culture had shifted in the decade in-between.

Both Mull and Brown use popular music and the rock-n-roll mindset as the basis of their comedy. But whereas Mull is playing off of the self-enraptured sensitivity of the folk/rock "poets" who came in Bob Dylan's wake, Brown is responding to the over-inflated glitz and lip-synched posing of the hyper carnival rock that now tours under corporate banners bearing self-important titles. Stylistically then, it is not surprising that while the milestones along Mull's route included his comedy records like "Dueling Tubas," the comparable moments in Brown's career are her comedy music videos: "The Homecoming Queen's Got a Gun," "Trapped in the Body of a White Girl," and "Girl Fight Tonight."

Further, as Mull's own Ohio background gave credence to the look and rhythm of the fictionalized Fernwood and made him the perfect choice for the reassuring midwestern talk show catalyst (a tradition that has lasted from Dave Garroway to David Letterman), Julie Brown embodied the culture of her native southern California, a mindset thoroughly saturated with the vicissitudes of show business.

Hollywood, the land's end for all of the country's pop-culture mediums, was able to constantly renew itself in the first half of this century through the constant migrations and fresh influxes of talent from across the nation. Before Hollywood could settle into provincial complacency as the home of the silent film community, new crops of writers, actors, and directors were migrating to work on the talkies, and the same process continued when radio and the music recording industry later went west. However, after television production settled in southern California in the late 1950s, generation upon generation has grown into the same stagnant climate until the entire culture of the area is now engulfed by the single-track obsession of breaking into the entertainment industry. And as the national hunger for individual redemption through celebrityhood has reached such a frenzy that spectators at televised sporting events jump up and begin mugging furiously whenever they become aware that they are in the background of the game action shots, Hollywood has taken this to be a vindication of its Jukes family lifestyle. One need only survey the current crop of network sitcoms to see those shows that do not specifically locate their "family" in some area of show business usually exhaust their initial premise early on and relocate most of the plots in a show business background.

So while Mull/Gimble assumes that whatever act he offers the public will confirm his self-image as an important show-biz celebrity and never understands that the parade of wannabes he justifiably deflates on *Fernwood 2Night* are only trying to emulate him, Julie Brown's character assumes that she is a show-biz celebrity simply because she wants to be one and spends half of her time on her MTV series *Just Say Julie* bashing all of the popular stars whom she thinks have been unjustifiably rewarded with what she desires.

Just Say Julie is set in Julie's rat-trap condo which is designed as a post-hurricane mish-mash of pop-culture artifacts ranging from a *Julia* lunchbox to Julie's beloved "poodle phone," a telephone shaped and decorated to resemble a dog and which barks instead of rings. Like everybody else on MTV, Brown presents music videos. But the point of *Just Say Julie* is not the videos themselves but how Brown uses them to complement and comment on Julie's moods and viewpoints. If rock-and-roll songs are crystalizations of emotional states and their videos are visualizations of the songs, then Brown arranges the presentations to better dramatize the conflicts in Julie's personality—which basically comes down to a tug of war between her desperate need for the deification that is rock stardom and her bitter resentment towards the long list of bogus posers who have been granted Golden Calf status, a list that includes macho blowhards like Rod Stewart, airhead decorative models like Tawny Kitaen, and every woman who has blonde hair.

Julie herself is not a blonde but rather, in the words of her self-promotional theme songs, "the hottest little hennahead on MTV." And Brown is acutely aware of the history of hennahead comedy on television as she has borrowed from many key figures in building Julie's persona. As one might expect, the queen of television comedy, the original hennahead striving to crash show business, Lucille Ball as Lucy Ricardo, contributes heavily to the foundation of Brown's approach. But the specifics in Julie's tensions seem to derive from more localized sources. Her bubbly teenage enthusiasm for the emotional glitter of rock plays very much like a stylized goof on Patty Duke's Patty Lane character, sort of like Patty after she has had a very serious hot dog overdose. But the cynical, debunking counterforce in Julie's character seems heavily influenced by one of the most thoroughly overlooked heroines in television comedy history, Cara Williams.

Like many minor film figures of the 1940s, Cara Williams found salvation in the new opportunities offered by television as she carved out a niche for herself playing every conceivable variation of cheap dame and fly-by-night floozie that the new medium could propose. During the period between the ending of *I Love Lucy* and the beginning of *The Lucy Show*, Desilu wanted to keep their Monday night "wacky redhead" franchise intact. A spinoff of *December Bride* was conceived, centering around the unseen object of Pete Porter's (Harry Morgan) "take my wife please" anecdotes. Williams won the starring role opposite Morgan in *Pete and Gladys*. But while Williams' robust physical clowning instantly transformed her public image, the originality of her concept was to retain elements of the skeptical hand-on-hip attitude and caustic side-of-the-mouth delivery from her previous work. Thus, a bawdy, faintly sleazy undercurrent ripped through the domestic plots and suburban setting like a dagger. There is a strong facial resemblance between Brown and Williams and Williams seems to have provided Brown with the final tonal colors for that singular mixture of giddiness and grunge that is Julie.

The twin aspects of Brown's attack can be seen in comparing her "How to Be a Rock Star" instructional episode with the narrative show where Julie sells her soul (such as it is) to the Devil. She opens the former show with her best stiletto smile:

> Hi! Want to be rich and famous? Hang out with models? Ride in a limo and laugh at the poor? Well, sure you do! It's a lot easier than you think and today I'm gonna show you everything you need to know about how to be a rock 'n' roll megastar. Hey, if Rod Stewart can do it, anybody can.

Julie goes on to elaborate on the three aspects of rock stardom: talent, attitude, and look. Since talent is the least important of the three, she skips over to the proper rock star attitude which she sums up as: "I'm cooler than anybody.... Make that your mantra even if you know it's not true. It worked for the Bangles and it can work for you too."

In this instructional mode Brown uses the music videos as visual aids to punch up the points in Julie's monologue. So she now presents a montage of clips, featuring such luminaries as Mick Jagger and George Michael, that demonstrates the proper arrogance of the rock attitude. "Ooo, I feel so inferior," she chuckles on return.

Next Julie is joined by nirvanic model Lake Arrowhead, one of the many characters played by the remarkably versatile Stacey Travis who became the show's resident "blonde for all seasons." A character plumbed from the absolute depths of Julie's spite and envy, Lake Arrowhead is so blissfully stupid that her cheerful explanation for turning up late is that the pause at a stop sign took so long that she forgot how to drive and had to walk the rest of the way. Here she is brought on as an expert in the rock 'n' roll look, and together, she and Julie go about the task of deconstructing Guns n' Roses' "Patience," freezing the action to color in makeup effects for the band or to offer commentary on the images ("It's really just a video about room service," Julie coos).

In the narrative episode the videos are shown complete and rather than Julie offering commentary on them, they serve as commentary on her. While the instructional show opened with Julie at her most gleefully sardonic, here she is in one of her frequent snits of bad temper fuming about the undeserved popularity of Paula Abdul even though Abdul has swiped Julie's "fake leopard look" and presents an act that *anybody* could do. But then, up pops the Devil proposing to give Julie all of the fame, money, and attention she craves for the mere price of her soul.

Julie is skeptical, citing all of those *Twilight Zone* episodes where only the Devil profits from these agreements and her inner turmoil is played out to the tune of INXS's "Devil Inside."

> *Julie*: Now I'm a little confused. I mean they [INXS] actually have talent. Why did they have to make a deal with you?
> *Devil*: They had talent but no pull. I got their videos into heavy rotation on MTV.
> *Julie*: Wow! You mean you have *that* much pull with MTV!
> *Devil*: Are you kidding? I invented MTV! I *am* MTV!

The clincher turns out to be the Devil's assertion that Madonna is one of his clients. He tells the dubious Julie to think about it and she muses, "Let's see. Okay body, so-so voice, four years later she's the hottest act in show business! Where do I sign?!"

So we now move on to Julie's fantasy of being "Queen of the World" (actually, the entire series plays like her personalized elaborations on Rupert Pupkin's daydreams). As Peter Gabriel's "Big Time" is shown, we are treated to inserts of Julie making stars like Tom Cruise and Meryl Streep grovel before her power, and of her blithely murdering members of her entourage who displease her. She even goes so far as to liquidate her poodle phone ("That poodle phone is trying to destroy me!") and asides to the audience, "Elvis, I know how you felt," after shooting it.

Finally, the Devil returns to take Julie home with him but she stalls long enough for Lake Arrowhead to arrive by persuading him to sit through one last showing of the Bangles' "Eternal Flame" with her ("They could use the air play," he reasons). It seems that Julie can retain her soul if she is able to find somebody stupid enough to take her place in Hell and who better for the job than a blonde model. Indeed, all Julie has to tell

Lake is that she is going to a place where she can maintain a year-round tan and the easy-going nincompoop complies.

But while these two episodes covered most of *Just Say Julie*'s artistic strategies, it was on a third show that Brown perhaps best summed up the entire sociological movement she explores. Here she spoofs the entertainment industry's ever-mushrooming parade of self-congratulatory awards shows as she presents "Julie's Choice for the Julie Awards." And, as she points out, since all of these shows open with a cheesy production number, she begins hoofing her way *a cappella* through a self-composed ditty sung to the tune of (what else) "There's No Business Like Show Business" that climaxes with this powerful thought:

> So let's all make fun of Madonna and Cher
> Even if they don't deserve it anyhow
> It's *my* show so who cares

The philosophical underpinning of stand-up comedy is also predicated on the principle "It's *my* show so who cares." Therefore it really should be no surprise that it has grown to be the most popular form of entertainment during the past twenty years. The breakdown in consensus television has basically hollowed out the traditional forms of sitcoms and variety shows but at the same time it has expanded the structural possibilities for television comedy beyond those two formats. While many of these looser new shows are nothing more than strung-together highlights from everybody and his brother's stand-up acts, such previously inconceivable shows as *Fernwood 2Night* and *Just Say Julie* have used this new freedom to create formats where the self-contained attitudes of their stand-up stars could be expanded to make explicit all of the logical conclusions implied in their social worldviews.

Coming out of the experimental wing of Norman Lear's factory, *Fernwood 2Night* not only gave Martin Mull his most conducive setting for presenting the ego-inflated show-biz mediocrity he invented, but also created a world surrounding it which explained why this character was a significant emblem for the times. Besides Fred Willard, a host of wildly disparate people who have played important roles in television comedy history worked on this show including Jack Douglas, Rita Dillon, Judy Kahan, and Alan Thicke. But probably the most fruitful collaboration was between Mull and Harry Shearer, who was billed as the show's "creative consultant," and whose own style of exploring America's obsession with self-expression through show business is also evident in every aspect of the show. *Fernwood 2Night* may turn out to be the high point of both careers since Mull's unassuming self-mockery helped to cut Shearer's "more perceptive than thou" condescension, and Shearer's "take no prisoners" satirical ruthlessness anchored Mull's tendency to glide on the surface.

Just Say Julie was much more of a one-woman operation with Brown not only hosting, co-writing, and co-producing her show, but also serving as its "fabulosity consultant." But since even as a stand-up Brown's style is primarily one of self-dramatization, it is necessary to have Julie's personality run rampant for the full scope of her internal contradictions to be expressed. Since *Just Say Julie*, Brown has gone on to become the first among equals on the sketch comedy series *The Edge*. The show has its ups and downs but even at its best, such as the mock documentary on the shooting of the *Sports Illustrated* swimsuit issue, it can only convey Brown's dead perfect savaging of the fashion industry without even suggesting the counterforce ambiguity of how desperately Julie craves to have everything she despises in other people which informs each moment of *Just Say Julie*.

The good news about the breakdown of consensus is that everybody who had been artistically and sociologically left out of that cohesive "us" is now beginning to get access to the stage. The heirs of Richard Pryor can be seen on the Fox network (*In Living Color*), in syndication (*Uptown Comedy Club*), and on cable (*Russell Simmons' Def Comedy Jam*). Further, the integration of more offbeat voices from stand-up also constitutes the few signs of life remaining in mainstream sitcoms as Roseanne Arnold has been able to incorporate such figures as Mull and Sandra Bernhard into her show and Jerry Seinfeld experiments with a hybrid series fusing the narrative techniques of monologue and situation comedy.

The bad news is that the social disintegration documented by *Fernwood 2Night* and *Just Say Julie* is not an internal show business phenomenon. And if the fundamentalist attitudes of our warring tribes continue to harden into "it's *not* my show—so who cares?" it will no longer matter whether everybody gets to be on television since nobody will be out there watching except the immediate family. At this point it remains to be seen whether the state of affairs that Martin Mull and Julie Brown are describing is a harbinger of imminent social collapse or the necessary prelude to the formation of a more inclusive consensus. But as one recent occupant of our *circus maximus* presidency was fond of saying, it would be wise to "stay tuned."

11
Ernie Kovacs' Nastiest Whelps

The Comic Strip and British "Alternative Comedy"

MTV stands for music television, a combination that immediately places it at the crossroad of a conflicting media pull. The fragmented and factional world of rock keeps forcing this mass market television system into the middle of the musical road where it accents the universally popular and segregates the experimental and innovative. On the other hand, its rock music audience also draws MTV towards a search for series programming which is so far out in front of the smug safety of its network and cable competition that it is becoming the natural locus for creative television.

Indeed, almost by demographic design, MTV gravitated to a wildly surreal and cartoony British sitcom called *The Young Ones*. It proved so popular that MTV later began to program the television work of *The Young Ones'* parent organization The Comic Strip—the most creative band of comedy writer/performers to come along since the Toronto Second City troupe defined this form of media as metaphor humor.

Both the autonomous, mini-feature *Comic Strip Presents* films and *The Young Ones*, as well as other Comic Strip projects, the "breaking the fourth wall" *French and Saunders* variety series on Arts & Entertainment and Peter Richardson's recent features *Eat the Rich*, *The Supergrass*, and *The Pope Must Die* are the flowering of what, in England, came to be called "the alternative comedy movement."

Alternative comedy defines a collection of fledgling stand-ups who invaded London's comedy clubs in the late 1970s. Using *Monty Python's*

Flying Circus as their initial point of reference, the constant factor in their varied styles was a revolt against the unctuous and comforting qualities of the television sitcoms and variety shows they had grown up watching. These newcomers thought of Monty Python as the antithesis of middle-of-the-road stylization, but, in retrospect, alternative comedy can be seen to be a much larger break with Monty Python than Monty Python was from its continuum with *The Goon Show* or even The Crazy Gang.

Society uses comedy to purge its citizens' aggressions by first putting them in contact with these aggressions and then reassuring them by tying them to an ennobling self-image. It is thus up to the comedian to be "likable," to join with the citizenry in a sympathetic conspiracy by becoming the mirror image of how they want to justify their disgust with how society treats them. For the establishment, it is usually some form of "we are kind, decent people who are constantly being preyed on by vipers so it is right that we loathe our relatives and peers and cheat the government" (i.e. your basic Rodney Dangerfield). For the insurgency, it is some form of "we are hipper and more artistically sensitive and aware than anybody else so it is right that we scorn the mainstream and cheat the government" (your basic David Letterman). Alternative comedy was trying to loosen the bond between performer and audience (did someone mutter "Brechtian?") and hold the mirror closer to the aggressions than the self-image.

Much of what passed itself off as alternative comedy, during its exciting ferment of self-definition, was pretty awful. But, unlike the people in the United States who were working on similar impulses and wound up either "succeeding" in television sitcoms and John Landis movies or never being offered a chance at a wider audience, their British counterparts fell in with sympathetic producers who banded together some of the movement's leading lights and gave them the chance to do television on their own terms.

The Comic Strip, like The Crazy Gang, had itself banded together from three separate comedy duos: The Outer Limits (Peter Richardson and Nigel Planer), 20th Century Coyote (Adrian Edmondson and Rik Mayall), and French and Saunders (Dawn and Jennifer). One of the earliest alternative comedy shows brought together Dawn French, Jennifer Saunders, Peter Richardson, and Adrian Edmondson with a dog in a send-up of a popular series of British children's adventure books, *The Famous 5*. Later, Rik Mayall and Nigel Planer joined them, the dog was given its walking papers, and *The Comic Strip Presents*, 30-minute self-contained story-films written by various combinations within the group, began.

The Comic Strip films can best be understood in relation to their Canadian contemporaries, the Second City Television shows. Both are satiric reactions to the 1980s culture taking shape when the phenomenal acceptance of *Rocky* and *Star Wars* indicated that we were preparing to extract artistic and cultural assumptions indigenous to earlier eras and graft them onto contemporary situations. Sleeked out in high-tech argot and self-conscious joviality, these notions reached their logical fulfillment in the arts with Steven Spielberg and in politics with Ronald Reagan. Together, they combine to cover all of the various meanings of the era's theme song, "When You Wish Upon a Star."

Another logical conclusion to 1980s culture is what is politely called "The TV generation." That is, a generation of television creators who, along with their audience, grew up with television at the center of their lives and whose understanding of the world is limited to what they have previously seen on television.

SCTV embraced the "TV generation" concept but then turned this whole "life is a television show" mindset inside out by creating short sketches that weaved and spliced the styles and assumptions of differing movies and television shows over, under, and around each other. Their viewpoint, like those they were satirizing, was totally within a show-biz consciousness, but by Eisensteining these ideas into unexpected combinations (John Candy's Lou Grant as a pre-teen bully running the school paper, Joe Flaherty, Catherine O'Hara and Rick Moranis as the *Ordinary People* cast doing a James Garner-Mariette Hartley camera commercial) they were able to analyze what these artifacts were really telling us, as well as suggesting states of being that went beyond what the media prescribed for us.

The Comic Strip uses a common world intellectuality in relation to the "life is a television show" mentality to produce their effects, as did their mentors Monty Python. But the Pythons blended the intellectuality and the show-biz mentality into a single level of burlesque that turned every manner of thought into some aspect of an all-consuming vaudeville show. The Comic Strip uses the tensions between an intellectual revulsion at what the media expresses about society and their artistic and emotional gratification in being part of its forms and rewards as the basis of its humor, and keeps pushing until something or other has to explode.

This can be seen in the way the four *Comic Strip Presents* films, which aired on New York's PBS station prior to their MTV slotting, operate:

• *Dirty Movie* (written by Adrian Edmondson and Rik Mayall). A movie house manager's attempt to privately screen a porn film turning into an all too Monty Pythonesque exercise in quirky obsession born of social and sexual repression which saved itself by having all of the characters' peccadilloes continually colliding with each other so that the whole thing winds up playing like Monty Feydeau.

• *Consuela* (written by Dawn French and Jennifer Saunders). An elaborately surreal spoof of *Rebecca* that draws its female antagonists into a convoluted death struggle of alienation through symbiosis.

• *Bad News Tour* (written by Adrian Edmondson). A mock documentary covering the vérité exploitation of a nincompoop heavy-metal band during its out-of-town engagement that was everything somebody told you *This Is Spinal Tap* was going to be. This became MTV's natural choice for its premise show.

• *The Beat Generation* (written by Peter Richardson and non-player Peter Richens). A group of 1960 "crazy poets" collectively trapped for the weekend in the individual ether of their exterminating egos.

Andrew Sarris has commented that most comedy teams have an internal cohesion that unites them against the outside world. This is basically because in most comedy-team films, the conditions of the unimaginative outside world are presented as a previously defined given and the behavior of the teams' members, both individually and towards each other, as a reactive rebellion the audience is invited to join in against society's bland conventions. The Comic Strip has an abundance of internal cohesion, but they use it to inhabit and define a much more malignant outside world. A world from which there is no possible inside rebellion. A world that contains no romantic elements at all.

The key to their strategy is their resurrection of the two-reeler format. This gives them the room to build the world of each film so that their viewpoint emerges naturally from the collected details. It is the kind of world where a pretentious rock musician can reject the suggestion that his music is futuristic by saying, "But we're more modern than futurism" (*Bad News Tour*), or an upper crust party guest can protest that he found none of the alleged lack of freedom in South Africa except "You can't ride on a black bus" (*Consuela*). And while these are gag lines to be sure, they are not presented as punchline climaxes, but the logical extension of all we have heard and seen previously. This will, in turn, lead to the next level of world-view definition through character development as the film becomes darker, richer, more jagged-edged as it goes along.

The juvenilia and heavy touches bite deeper into your kidneys here because it is all being plowed into the same furrow. But the group is also able to doggedly persist with what seem to be dead-end ideas until they become integral to some startling larger concept. If *Bad News Tour* relies too insistently on gags where the band members are unable to fake the conventions of documentary reality ("Oh, I get it. . . . Can we cut this bit as well?"), the repetitions ultimately add resonance to the band's finally getting fed up with their exploiters and seizing the camera equipment at the end. If *Rebecca* seems a pathetically soft target for surrealistic spoof, when the *Suspicion* and *Birds* and *Vertigo* quotes start kicking into the plot, you come to realize how savvy French and Saunders have been in recognizing *Rebecca* not as the commonly understood commercial aberration in Hitchcock's career, but as his vision of a "normalized" social and sexual world for which all of his nightmare art is a threat. Ultimately, even their klunk-iest ideas somehow become indispensable to the total effect.

Working in a thirty-minute format, the writers put quite a strain on themselves as actors. Like the SCTV people, they all have powerfully in-dividual comic styles. Indeed, the basic personas of Dawn French (a kind of sexually aggressive Alice Brady whose every appetite and emotion is ex-pressed expansively across her round, open face) and Rik Mayall (a wild-eyed artiste constantly on the verge of paranoid frenzy) come at you with such force that you initially wonder how they will manage to sustain their pace. But, unlike the quick-take skits that SCTV did (with the exception of John Candy and Eugene Levy's beautifully sustained Schmenge Brothers featurette *The Last Polka*, the closest American television has come to the tone of a Comic Strip film) that allowed them each to swoop in like Goose Gossage, blow you away with some high hard ones, and march off in triumph, The Comic Strippers have to be out there for all nine innings and keep constantly adjusting their game to support whoever is currently on the mound. As such, you can almost think of them as the comedy equiva-lent to the Duke Ellington Orchestra, a group of highly distinct soloists who have learned to combine their sounds, with Peter Richardson acting as the Ellington figure, the mainspring of creative organization and sup-port.

Just like the films themselves, the performers keep surprising you in what they can accomplish over the long haul. Perhaps in compensation for his natural affinity to John Lennon sardonicism, when playing nerds Adrian Edmondson has a tendency to indulge himself with too many "silly ass" mannerisms. But, as Bad News' leader, Vim ne Alan, he tones down and perfectly captures the character's half-smart self-absorption ("I could play 'Stairway to Heaven' when I was 12. Jimmy Page didn't actually write it until he was 22. I think that says quite a lot."). Nigel Planer seems limited to spaced-out dunderheads until his startling turn as the cynical, emotionally constipated literary agent in *The Beat Generation*. He is so quietly and precisely self-contained that you begin to wonder what he might have borrowed from Jennifer Saunders for the occasion. But with Saunders we are dealing with a different level of accomplishment.

When you think of the major female artists in caricature, as opposed to romantic, comedy from Mabel Normand to Sandra Bernhard, the one constant is that they are all strongly projecting outward, all using their voices, faces, and bodies in their individual ways to stretch beyond the con-ventionally accepted limits of "feminine" behavior in order to reveal inter-nalized emotional and psychological states. What is so stunningly original about Saunders is that she seems to be reaching these ends by working as much as possible in the opposite direction. There is no knowing what she has seen or how she has understood what she has seen, but it is difficult to even think of something to relate this to, except perhaps some sort of inspired reinterpretation of Mae West. Watching her is like suddenly encountering Count Basie after a lifetime of listening exclusively to Art Tatum.

Saunders speaks in quick bursts of verbiage within a small tonal range, conveying moods by changes in cadence and inflection. She looks like a British cousin to Julia Duffy and rarely distorts her facial beauty to reveal her character, expressing thought mostly with darting eye movements, and emotion with head flicks and furtive mouth gestures. Watching her quietly coming unglued on marijuana in *Bad News Tour* or haltingly understanding that she will be given free run of the candy counter in *Dirty Movie* is the pleasure of seeing something done in a way you could not have previously imagined. It is almost like a movie star version of broad comedy, completely expressing the character while the actress herself remains a mystery. Like Rik Mayall's character in *The Beat Generation*, you do not even know if she wants to ban the bomb.

These films will surely click with their target audience and become a major influence on a new generation of American comedy. However, if there is anything that might halt a popular groundswell for The Comic Strip it would be America's insistence on cuddling up to its television. There is very little that is endearing in these films and the actors never really ask you to be their friends. They steadfastly refuse to sentimentalize themselves or anything they do but neither do they pass judgment on the "dog eat cat" world they present. Each film soars with the most graceful deadpan ambivalence. However, when they really drop the hammer on their collective concerns—the yin-yang of repression and liberation, the coming of age in the mid–1960s consciousness (things like *The Sound of Music* and *Georgy Girl* seem permanently lodged in their craw and Cliff Richard is their iconographic obsession), the Bunuel and Hitchcock influences—their stuff actually begins to resemble punched-up excerpts from Freddie Francis horror films. And this might be the highest compliment paid to them.

Once out of the comedy clubs, alternative comedy became basically a television response to television. The Comic Strip films speak most closely to a cinematic sensibility, but the group's genre format shows are more in line with the movement's other television work in being examinations of and assaults on the forms and functions of television comedy itself. What distinguishes their work from the scratch-and-tease school of jolly self-reference humor is their hard-edged understanding of the forms they are working with.

It is not too outrageous an oversimplification to say that practically every form of television comedy as we know it in the United States was invented by Jack Benny, Lucille Ball, Jackie Gleason, and Ernie Kovacs.

Benny's contribution was so enormous that hardly anybody could build a format that completely ignored his legacy. It is not surprising, given alternative comedy's concerns, that The Comic Strip crowd would take the least traveled road and become Ernie Kovacs' nastiest whelps.

Kovacs has had so few progeny and he himself never found a regular niche on television because of the difficulty in finding a continuous vehicle for a form that is itself an analysis of form. To a large extent, The Comic Strip's continuous format shows succeed in doing just that—as a variety show with *French and Saunders*, and as, of all things, a sitcom with *The Young Ones*.

French and Saunders fashioned a show that is totally inside show biz but in a completely analytical way since show business is their metaphor for an almost Hobbesian world view of an eternal life-and-death struggle for survival and domination. The norm in British television is for most shows to run for only six episodes per season and *French and Saunders* is no exception. However, they use this condition advantageously as a structuring principle that all but turns the show into a continuous narrative mini-series.

The six episodes work in succession like a super Comic Strip film. Initially, they define the format which is sort of like "Laverne and Shirley Do the Muppet Show" with Dawn and Jennifer struggling to present their variety program amid crepe paper sets, clodhopping support, and their own interpersonal demons, to a scattered and indifferent studio audience. Then, each week they develop the various thematic strands as the central metaphor expands out further and further.

By week three they are wandering the corridors of the BBC offices, swiping British Emmys from the trophy cases to convince head programmer Michael Grade, who has them listed on his chart as "*French and Saunders*—very light entertainment," to pick up their show despite ratings which indicate that only twelve people are watching. This sequence ends with perhaps the series' most stunning moment: Dawn waiting outside Grade's office with her finger up her nose while Jennifer is inside pleading that Dawn is a borderline psychotic and doing this show is her only form of therapy.

By week four BBC has padlocked their studio, draped the door with a sign saying "closed, cancelled, never again," and French and Saunders have to sneak onto a popular kiddie show's permanent set to smuggle out their broadcast, as Jennifer runs rampant in the control booth and Dawn mucks up the camera.

Within the variety show format, French and Saunders' most successful gambit is in codifying Kovacs' impulse to superimpose himself onto preexisting material in sketches featuring their characters of ambitious, Lucy-like extras who are liable to pop up in anything from the filming of an airline commercial to a production of *Carmen*. Constantly chattering about the improvements they have made in their costumes and commenting on the means of the production they are in, they invert your understanding of each form by focusing attention on their position in the background as they attempt to shove their way into the foreground.

Educated guesses can be made as to what their stand-up acts were like from the way they present themselves here: French, a cornucopia of maniacal glee and two-bit celebrity impersonations designed to seduce the audience into identifying with more eccentricity then they had bargained for; and Saunders with an eerie, deadening anti-performance of hoary hokum that could possibly be approximated by having Steven Wright do Red Skelton's act.

Their basic incompatibility acts as just another spoke in the wheel for these performers who even seen symbiosis as a form of power struggle. Within the show they most creatively use this to fashion what might have been the most bizarre opening stand-up routine ever seen on a variety show. Decked out in costumes that even Milton Berle would find asinine and are probably parodies of popular male British comics, they isolate themselves in their individual styles and patter back and forth, pelting the audience with pilfered music hall–style gags. It plays just as cacophonously as it sounds.

French and Saunders are not only incompatible on stage, they are also extremely hostile backstage. This was the thematic thread that had dominating the final programs. By week six they are back in the studio for a farewell show of such bile that Dawn winds up locking Jennifer in the toilet to preclude her total takeover of the show. And the musical guest, this time Joan Armatrading, is given directions to her dressing room that lead to an airplane ride out of the country. When they troop out for the final goodbyes in tattered costumes after having finally slugged it out backstage, you get the feeling that the only way they could sustain this concept in a second series would be as a variety version of *Whatever Happened to Baby Jane?* But compared to *The Young Ones*, French and Saunders still have a lot of room to maneuver in terms of interpersonal hostility.

The Young Ones starts off with a pretty standard sitcom premise: four mismatched college students sharing a house. However, you know that you're in for it when you see that the four are Adrian Edmondson as a terminally violent punker, Rik Mayall as the ultimate effete twit, Nigel Planer as a soft-all-over hippie, and Christopher Ryan as Zeppo with wisecracks. Ironically, this show plays more like a comic strip than all of their other work. It resembles Max Fleischer cartoons that have been written and directed by Screwy Squirrel.

As written by Mayall, Ben Elton (another key alternative comedy writer/performer), and Lise Mayer, each episode is a tightly wound top that spins out like a gyroscopic tornado. Chance remarks lead into full-blown send-ups of other sitcoms, camera glances at wall posters turn into filmed promos for fictitious television events, walk-on character players (usually Alexei Sayle) walk out of character and address the audience or walk toward the camera crew explaining their acting philosophies, inanimate household objects spring to life, and subliminal visual metaphors flash by. As Joe Bob Briggs so incisively points out, the first rule of a good spam-in-a-cabin slasher movie is that anybody can die at any moment. So it is that the first rule of *The Young Ones* is that any idea can be transformed into any other idea even before you reach the moment.

Of course, there are antecedents for what is going on here. *The Monkees*, particularly in their "psychedelic" second season, experimented with most of the same strategies. It is the very different ways in which the strategies are presented and thus perceived, however, that make *The Young Ones* the breakthrough show. It goes to the heart of what alternative comedy is all about.

On *The Monkees* all of the wonderfully enjoyable and creative playing with form is presented as an extension of the liberating impulses of the characters, the satisfactions and rewards to be had from opening yourself to the greater possibilities of life. *The Monkees* is as much an expression of the 1960s as *The Young Ones* is of the 1980s, and there are quite a number of people who would sooner be back in the 1960s. By unlinking the techniques from the characters, *The Young Ones* deromanticizes the process and allows you to see how the ideas work on people rather than dreaming about how they could work through people. And the less you have to identify with these characters the better off you are.

With its bleak world view and forceful attack, alternative comedy sheds much of the ingratiating baggage of electronic-era stylization but links up strongly to the knockabout immigrant and regional comedy that dominated early century burlesque. In fact, when they really push it, French and Saunders begin to resemble an intellectualized Abbott and Costello and *The Young Ones*, who continually push it, a deconstructive Three Stooges. These comedians are consciously aware that they are the smartest kids on the block. But one of the major reasons why comics softened their acts for radio and television was that they were aware they had to sustain the same audience every week.

It is amazing to see how Edmondson can turn his usual geek from Comic Strip wimpy to *Young Ones* menacing with so few changes in mannerisms, and Mayall seems to be daring us to accept a character who comes at you like William F. Buckley on rat poison. It is a tribute to their imagination and skill that they can hold this stuff together at all. But the pacing is so relentless and the characters so locked into the edges of their outlines that they come out on the other end as doppelgangers of what they are reacting against. Their behavior becomes so predictable that ultimately they might as well be alternative Norman Lear characters.

This full-circle abstraction also turns Nigel Planer, who is already set up to be the audience sympathy character (much like Opus the penguin in "Bloom County"), into such a sentimental figure that you wind up with a new version of the standard sitcom balance. Planer is essentially playing the same character he did in *Bad News Tour*, but there, where they were all working with a multitude of ideas, he came off just as ambivalently as everybody else.

To a lesser extent this is also at work in *French and Saunders* with Jennifer's ever-increasing backstage Daffy Duckery designed to take over the whole show. Edmondson, Mayall, and Saunders are such paragons of alienation to begin with that it might have been more interesting to see the process being reversed. On the other hand, when you combine rebellion with sentimentality you get rock 'n' roll (rock music performances are also part of *The Young Ones*'s mix). This brings us right back to why we are seeing these shows in the first place. The spirit of comedy has always been closely connected to its era's music. You can hear the grace and drive of swing in Bob Hope's rhythms, the unshackled rampage of bop in Lenny Bruce's outbursts, and the intricacies of acid rock in George Carlin's musings. Alternative comedy will probably be the most lasting artistic legacy of the punk sensibility.

Other dynamics relate to this situation as well, particularly the different ways we perceive performers on film and on videotape, an issue whose complexity has yet to be fully explored. The Comic Strip films are far more ambitious in terms of character construction than the two continuing video series, but their mere presence on film seemed to automatically give Edmondson and Mayall more dimension. Further, while Jennifer Saunders is just fine in everything, whenever she and Dawn French did a bit on film, particularly their devastating *Chorus Line* parody, the magical modulation of her cold fire inner mystery immediately snapped into place.

The Comic Strip shows have not exactly created a groundswell mania for alternative comedy, but over the last few years quite a few series which could be said to participate in the movement to one degree or another have been quietly infiltrating the ranks of "quality" British imports on cable and PBS. Without prior notice, slipping in among the mainstream sitcoms that always seem to feature Richard Briers and/or Penelope Keith and the inevitable reruns of *Are You Being Served?* have been such shows as the four series of *Blackadder* historical satires, the sci-fi sitcom *Red Dwarf*, Dawn French's cuisine show *Scoff, A Bit of Fry & Laurie, This Is David Lander, Alexei Sayle's Stuff,* and *Wax-on-Wheels*. Further, if one loosens the membership standards a bit, you could also include Rik Mayall in the political satire *The New Statesman* and narrating *Grim Tales* for children,

Emma Thompson's *Thompson,* and the more traditional but alternative friendly *Lenny Henry Show.* While this list of programs covers a wide range of comedy stylistics, it contains one common link: an enthusiasm for projecting comedic rebellion through formal experimentation.

American expatriate Ruby Wax has probably found the most completely realized strategy for expressing her multi-faceted alienation. With an in-your-face style suggesting a counter-culture version of Joan Rivers she is well-established in England as a stand-up and comic actress (she co-starred with French and Saunders in the as-yet-unseen-in-America *Girls on Top*), but she finds her most perfect milieu in her own productions of what might be called "stand-up documentaries with buttinsky interviews."

Separated from her own culture but totally unassimilated into any other, Wax presents herself as the perpetual outsider plowing her way through the natives insistent on finding out why all of these people are so exasperatingly different from her. *Wax-on-Wheels* puts her and her beleaguered production crew on a bus which wanders all over the British Isles and plops down each week in a different location for Wax to examine. Punctuated with stand-up observations and expository camera pans, the main portion of each show features Ruby cornering local celebrities and everyday people and prodding, poking, puncturing into every private part of their lives with her blunt instrument interview techniques. Some of the interviews are pre-arranged and some are taken on the run; some of the subjects join in the spirit of her style while others are offended by her approach; some of the segments are clearly scripted while others seem improvised; and it is sometimes difficult to make concise sense of it all. However, if you view this series in relation to her three hour-long efforts, *East Meets Wax, Class of '69,* and *Miami Memoirs,* you'll see what Wax is up to.

East Meets Wax takes her into a much more alien territory as it chronicles her semi-disastrous stand-up tour of the U.S.S.R. Her ironic commentaries on American mores and tongue-in-cheek costumes seem to lose just about everything in the translation for the stolid Russian audiences. And she has even more trouble than usual dealing with the morose citizens who seem fatalistically adjusted to the conditions imposed by their omnipresent government. But the center of the film is dominated by Wax's relationship with her government assigned guide/translator. The guide is quietly determined to fulfill her professional obligation of remaining emotionally neutral while offering Wax all of the information and advice she will need. But Ruby is just as noisily determined to break her down and make her respond just as spontaneously as Ruby does to their adventures. Wax badgers the guide all through the film as if she were a comic stooge, bouncing all kinds of remarks off her in hopes of eliciting an unprogrammed response. The film climaxes after Wax explodes, explaining to the translator that she seems so angry with her because her government treats its own people with such little respect for their humanity. Wax cannot understand how the translator can live with these never-ending affronts to her emotional self-respect. What follows is a long, painful sequence in which the camera rivets on the translator as she struggles in her awkwardly non-professional language to retain her composure and inner dignity while acknowledging all of the pain she lives with and still affirming her love of her culture and her people.

Class of '69 and Miami Memoirs bring Wax back to America and, especially in the latter, fundamentally turn the camera's fire back onto her. In Class of '69 Wax attends the twentieth reunion of her suburban Chicago high school class and in Miami Memoirs visits her parents in their new Florida retirement home. In these two films you can see the origins of her sense of displacement. Indeed she ends Class of '69 with the observation that she now remembers why she left America in the first place: "Life here for me feels like there's always a parade going on and I can't get in on it." Wax is first generation American and it is in the Chicago home where she grew up that we first meet her old-world, self-made parents who still retain their native country attitudes and thick immigrant accents. But it isn't until we see the family behaving in Miami with scenes of the elder Waxes constantly condescending to and quietly shaming their daughter into being their version of a good little girl, and Wax swallowing her usual big-mouthed rebellion in raging impotence, that her sense of being culturally dysfunctional becomes apparent. What is most disquieting about these sequences is how hard it is to judge what within the formal staging is happening spontaneously and what has been pre-arranged for the camera—on what level do Wax and her parents mean us to understand them?

However, within another continuous story in Miami Memoirs, Wax's developing relationship with a loquacious middle-aged smoothie named Marty, the presentation crosses the line into fictional recreation. This story climaxes for Wax with a humiliating restaurant dinner date where it eventually becomes clear that Marty is a professional gigolo who expects to be compensated for his time entertaining Wax with his stories by her picking up the dinner tab. Clearly, even if Marty was somehow unaware that he was being filmed in the restaurant, nobody in their right mind would give clearance for scenes showing this kind of behavior.

Wax's films consist of scenes which have her spontaneously interacting with new environments, totemic scenes that are formally staged but contain both ritualized and improvised elements (e.g., those with her parents), and scenes that are completely recreated experiences (e.g., with Marty in the restaurant). Wax is able to present these forms as if they had equal weight because, for her, the documentary mode mirrors the process through which she reinterprets her life experiences into her comedic art. These three forms simply represent the before, during, and after stages of the same process.

Once this is accepted, you can look back and see how her interview technique is actually her way of demonstrating for her guests how they too can convert their own lives into comedy routines. Her blunt insistence on hearing people's authentic responses to the world's treatment of them and then offering them editorialized, ironic interpretations in exchange for their own views, is simply the conversational equivalent of how she goes about making her documentary of self.

As such, Wax does not care if she comes off looking like an insensitive bully or a pathetic fool. She does not care whether her interview guests appreciate her efforts or have their self-esteem damaged in the process. All that is important is the process itself; that the process be allowed to function and that whatever results from it be reinterpreted for comedy. The only strategy that foils her approach is an interview subject who presents him/herself as an already fully formed, seamless work of comic art. These interviews can be interesting insofar as the subject presents an entertaining self-portrait, but they eliminate all of the creative tension, leaving Wax nodding mutely on the sidelines.

Dawn French's *Scoff* is structured along the same lines as *Wax-on-Wheels*. French and her crew span the countryside investigating matters concerning all things edible. However, her show is not nearly as successful because, of all things, she turns out to be far too nice a person to be doing this sort of format. Like all good Comic Strippers, French is not only willing, but eager to embody unflattering personality traits, but she also has a highly cultivated empathy with other people's need for self-respect. She lacks Wax's ruthless devotion to the process and allows her guests as much space as they require to define themselves on their own terms. Unfortunately, that makes for a less-interesting show in this case. The brilliant results of French's approach are evident, however, when applied to her completely fictional Comic Strip film *Summer School*.

The documentary tradition is much stronger in Britain than in the United States both in terms of motion pictures and television. Shows such as *Wax-on-Wheels* and *Scoff* would be inconceivable on American network television. And a show like *This Is David Lander* could only be imagined with all kinds of warning disclaimers built into the presentation. In *David Lander*, Stephen Fry is the title character. Fry is a doggedly literal-minded, none-too-bright television journalist who presents his in-depth investigative reports on hot social issues like health care and art world fraud.

Fry completely nails down the somber voice of authority and blank stare of objectivity used by real television news reporters. What is so stunning about the show is how accurately they have duplicated every aspect of the form from the grainy, revelatory paparazzi photographs to the soft-toned, conversational casualness of the actors playing the people being interviewed. All of the players have the form down so well (e.g., the pausing between thoughts, the personal digressions amid the testimony, etc.) that when such accomplished and distinctive actors as Juliet Stevenson and Frances Barber turn up among the witnesses, it actually takes a few beats before you can recognize them. As you watch the show you begin to realize that it is necessary for the form to be perfectly captured because the content is fundamentally a demonstration of an encyclopedia of ways in which people will obfuscate or somehow miss the points of events.

Perhaps the best episode has Lander investigating malfeasance in the munitions industry. "The Rocketing Cost of Defense" begins with him asking the fundamental question, "Isn't there something badly wrong with a business that panders to the darkest, most cruel side of human nature and still makes a loss?" The focus of the investigation is on the Sea Demon missile which has been regularly landing in residential neighborhoods after test launches. One couple tells Lander that a missile recently got tangled up in a neighbor's clothesline, which is not a problem for them because they own a dryer. However, the missiles' constant low buzzing over the house has been playing havoc with the electrical appliances, such as programming the VCR to record the Spanish language channel and always cutting off the last five minutes of the shows.

The admiral in charge of the Sea Demon project dismisses allegations of waste by flatly stating that the missile is the product of state-of-the-art-technology. The fact that the missile is defective does not faze him in the least since, "Unfortunately that is the state of the art at the moment. But we're working on it and we hope to have it operational very shortly," he reports.

When Lander suggests that having a missile which is as likely to shoot down one of our own aircraft as one of the enemy's could be a disadvantage in battle, the admiral proves with geometric logic just how superficial that argument is:

> One, the Russians have far more aircraft than us so clearly it is far more likely to shoot down one of theirs than one of ours.
> Two, uncertainty is a crucial element in any battle. If you can keep the enemy guessing, you've a far greater chance against him. So obviously, if we have no idea what the Sea Demon is going to do, neither do they.

This Is David Lander is just one of many shows in which Fry and or his partner Hugh Laurie have had continuing roles. Laurie supported Rowan Atkinson through most of the *Blackadder* series and Fry did so as well in the most recent installment, *Blackadder Goes Forth*. Fry and Laurie also played Jeeves and Wooster in a series of P. G. Wodehouse adaptions that recently aired on PBS. However, it is as a comedy team that they are best known, and as a team they might be termed the new generation Peter Cook and Dudley Moore. Stylistically, Fry matches up to Cook and Laurie to Moore and both teams' work basically explores the insanity of express- ing absurd viewpoints through well-mannered behavior.

A Bit of Fry & Laurie, their sketch comedy series, has absorbed the kind of dadaist presentational devices that *Monty Python's Flying Circus* pioneered but its influence is not nearly as prevalent with them as it is in *Alexei Sayle's Stuff.* For Sayle, the stream of consciousness turnabouts and blendings of one idea into another are not merely a strategy to produce comic surprise, but an extension of his all-encompassing satiric vision, probably the most complex sensibility of all of the comedians in this dis- cussion.

To many, Sayle is the most significant of alternative comedy's found- ers. He toiled for years in obscurity waiting for a new generation of both comedian and audience to catch up to what he was doing. In part, Sayle's material and viewpoint were so different because he himself was so differ- ent. Born to a Jewish, Marxist, working-class family, Sayle could never quite picture himself as part of "this happy breed." But whereas Ruby Wax uses her sense of otherness as a jumping-off point for outsider observations on community customs, Sayle has completely internalized his sense of differentness and now gleefully goes about the business of shoving it down our throats.

A self-billed "fat ugly bastard," Sayle's trademark look is a shaved head, a three-day stubble beard, and ill-fitting, unfashionable suits much on the order of Arte Johnson's Mr. Rozmenko character from *Laugh-In*. His work then proceeds to demolish just about every form of sociological, political, and moral certitude. Sayle's approach has often been called "sur- real" because his comic metaphors range so far from the concrete premises he sets up. But this is really more a function of his almost frighteningly facile technical and intellectual ability to switch unexpectedly from one divergent mood, attitude, or idea to another to demonstrate how all of them feed us equal doses of manure. For example:

> Young comedians really admire me. Occasionally, I'll see a young comedian in a club or somewhere who is fast, funny, has interesting things to say, and in that case I always make it a point to go backstage, talk to him, and tell him he's completely crap. "Give up comedy and become a carpentry teacher in Norway." I don't want the competition.
> But one piece of free advice I will give young comedians: It's not what you say [switches to the guise of a spastic moron]. It's the way that you say it!

Alexei Sayle in one of his friendlier moods.

[Stares disgustedly at the camera] Oh honestly, you piss me off, you audiences. We spend hours coming up with exquisitely honed gags, we spend millions coming up with elaborate visual effects and we get the biggest laugh from me saying [back to spastic moron] "It's the way that you say it!" Ooo, you really annoy me you audiences. You sit there at home, you pay sixty-eight quid for your television license, and you expect us to entertain you! [turns reflective] Sounds fair enough actually.

Sayle's almost nihilistic capacity to see the inadaquacy of all viewpoints pervades every aspect of his show. On an elementary gag level he uses those glaringly artificial cuts where the speaker turns his body to switch from facing one camera to another as the basis of a bit illustrating a Jekyll/Hyde personality split. Within the larger comedy picture it allows him to follow a sketch that depicts England's complacence about the practices of predatory real estate agents by portraying it as a light-hearted game show, with a mock-documentary exposé of slum conditions in which the ad agency documentarian decries the injustice of the priest who is running the neighborhood soup kitchen not being able to afford fashionable slashes in his jeans. In fact, while Sayle is a committed left-winger, many of his best monologues are about the shallowness and superficiality of the left.

I do a lot of left-wing benefits and one of the really weird things about left-wing audiences is that you do a joke and then there's a five-second delay while the joke is politically vetted and then they laugh. Like you say "Stalin was a bit of a looney wasn't he?" and they say "Stalin was a bit of a looney? Umm, yes, I have definite disagreements with him over the collectivization of the Kulacks. Yes. Haw! Haw! Haw!"

And they're really worried, you know, in case you say something suspect. Like you say "Two women go into a shop" and they go "Oh my God he's mentioned women! He's mentioned women! He's gonna say they're lesbians in a minute and we're gonna be laughing at lesbians! He's gonna say that they're black and we're gonna be laughing at black lesbians! Oh my God! No! No! No!"

Over the years Sayle has frequently found himself being linked with Ben Elton in critical appraisals. Both are particularly noted for their political material, both have expanded their literary horizons through writing books, and both have been described as the most talented stand-up single acts of the alternative comedy movement. But while Sayle's career actually predates the movement, the much younger Elton came to prominence towards the end of its initial surge. And, more significantly, neither man appreciates being compared to the other.

Elton has more than made up for having come late to the party by turning out a staggeringly large body of work in his career to date. In addition to being one of the most ubiquitous stand-up performers in England, he has written, either singly or with colleagues, a huge number of television series, including *The Young Ones* and *Blackadder*. He is currently turning out full-length stage plays and novels. Despite his enormous popularity in England, there have been very few opportunities to see him in America. *A South Bank Show* profile of him ran on Bravo, but America's only real chance to see him in stand-up performance came when he hosted HBO's *Live from London* special.

While it is difficult, and perhaps foolhardy, to judge a performer based on only one appearance, this show presented Elton as a rarity in the comedy world, someone who has complete mastery over his material and seemingly little over his physical presentation. Elton more than lives up to his knickname "Motormouth" with a delivery that rivals any street vendor for speed and intensity. He augments this with a collection of herky-jerky body gestures that seem to be anticipating a hook coming after him from any possible direction. Indeed, five minutes of Elton's natural behavior communicates more anxiety than an entire hour of Richard Lewis' manufactured gestures.

But if his style can have the effect of jangling your nerves, his material systematically goes about the task of measuring, probing, attacking, and most often striking whatever vulnerable spots your nerves may have. In *Live from London* he introduces himself to his new friends in America by lobbing a barrage of observational grenades about U.S. culture and history.

He begins by telling how he now wants to come to America to perform because Americans are making the country safer—by outlawing smoking.

> I mean they're banning cigarettes in New York City. They're doing it for safety reasons. This is in a country where you can buy a handgun over the counter. "Watch out, he's got a cigarette! AGGH!
> —"What's that bulge in your pocket, kid?"
> —"It's a magnum! It's a magnum!"
> —"All right, I thought it was a packet of cigarettes."

He then goes on to give an astonishingly succinct summation of U.S. political parties:

> Apparently the big trouble for the Democrats is that they're trying to get their liberal angst together. They're trying to adjust to the idea of a black man in the White House. They're trying to adjust to that problem see. Now Republicans don't have that problem. "No, no, that's no problem. A black man in the White House. I mean, after all, who is going to polish the silver and serve the coffee, right?"

Paradoxically, while Sayle and Elton cite different reasons why they reject the comparison between them, they are both actually making the same point. Elton rejects the comparison by citing stylistic differences saying that, unlike Sayle, he does not do "surreal" material. Sayle is simply not very fond of Elton's work, claiming that he preaches to the audience. In their own ways they are pointing out their fundamental philosophical differences.

In fact, Sayle's "surrealism" is mostly a question of how you choose to define the word and Elton does not actually preach to the audience. Far from being surreal, Elton sees an extremely concrete world filled with basic moral choices. Underlying his humor is a hopeful optimism that tells us that if we can only face the realities of our follies we can accept them and then go on about the business of creating a better world. Sayle does not preach because he can find nothing valuable enough to preach about. Underlying his humor is a despairing anarchism that tells us that all systemizations of thought are simply contrasting ways of denying differing aspects of the overall truth to ourselves.

Just like beat or counterculture, alternative comedy is an essentially meaningless term used as a shortcut to indicate a general philosophic solidarity among a large group of contemporaneous artists without having to indicate exactly what that philosophy is. As we move further away from the term's inception and each artist herded under this collective title takes his or her own distinct path, each will be blessed by the individual attention that his or her work deserves and cursed by having that work continually judged for fidelity to a movement that the artists never announced and the critics never satisfactorily defined.

While it is possible for Americans to approach the work of these British comedians without all of the complicated cultural baggage, the fact that they are steadfastly committed to a minority viewpoint makes it unlikely that they will gain any kind of mass following in the United States. Still, Joaquin Andujar once said that you could sum up baseball in one word, "you never know." And that same common sense principle applies to the arts. After all, Nigel Planer recently turned up as the star of a Bud Light commerical.

12
French and Saunders
Anatomy of a Comedy Team

In one of the promo spots for their comedy/variety series on the Arts & Entertainment network, French and Saunders introduced themselves to their new American audience:

> *Jennifer*: Hello, I'm Dawn French and Jennifer Saunders.
> *Dawn*: And so am I.

A clever gag. And, as anybody who has watched them with any degree of comprehension would expect, a gag that tantalizingly touches on a number of philosophic and aesthetic questions, not the least of which being: How does one identify the members of a comedy team?

The internal chemistry of any kind of teamwork has always been difficult to dissect since, almost by definition, successful teammates will blend their talents to create a coherent team voice. In terms of comedy duos the situation becomes somewhat simplified in that they traditionally take the form of one "straight man" and one "funny man" and the style of comedy they do will be dictated by the rhythm of their interaction. Sometimes the material will come from pre-existing sources (Abbott and Costello), sometimes it is shaped by the creative head of the team (Laurel of Laurel and Hardy, Burns of Burns and Allen). But the general principle has been to develop one indivisible comic viewpoint from the combined effort of two comic performers.

Consider French and Saunders. While the other members of The Comic Strip have since developed their careers in various other forms of writing, acting, and directing, they have steadfastly continued to function almost exclusively as a comedy team. Yet, in the traditional sense, they would seem to be the least likely to have stayed together. Both are comedy writers with differing styles and concerns. Yet neither's material dominates the other's nor, as performers, do they conveniently break down into one straight and one funny. Their chemistry is derived from their incompatibility and yet their teamwork is so logically blended that it is almost impossible to consider them apart from each other even if one cannot quite figure out why.

They are certainly not alone among current performers in breaking down the traditional functions of comedy duos, but their interaction is so quirky that just watching their teamwork in action gives few clues as to how it is put together. As members of The Comic Strip, both wrote separate films. In watching French's *Summer School* and Saunders' *Slags* (also referred to as Dawn's *Prehistoric* and Jennifer's *Futuristic*) their individual contributions can be isolated, thus allowing for an inductive reconstruction of how they operate as a team.

Saunders is a genre analyst who seems to have spent half of her life at the movies. Unlike The Comic Strip's other film culturist Peter Richardson, who air-pumps hyperbole into familiar melodrama situations in order to bas-relief the social and political assumption embedded in them, Saunders works along the lines of SCTV style. She montages moments from different media sources to create new metaphoric interpretations, but with an eerie, dreamlike Beckettesque orientation that is similar only to Rick Moranis from the Second City Television group.

Slags, along with another Comic Strip film, *A Fistful of Travelers Cheques*, is part of a relatively recent sub-genre that might be termed "punk proto-noir." This is a playful, self-conscious New Wave adaption of the thick romantic fatalism of film noir mixed with the strain of dark-humored nihilism in the post-war western (which can be traced from *The Treasure of the Sierra Madre* through *One-Eyed Jacks* to the Italian westerns made by Sergio Leone and others that constitutes the hardest edge of 1960s counterculture). This approach turns up in such movies as *The Blue Iguana* and *Straight to Hell*, but also in most of the other arts under the amorphous rubric of post-modernism, such as science fiction's "cyberpunk" movement.

Most of what has come out of this movement in film has been inconsequential, mainly due to the filmmakers' smug "We're too hip to take any of this seriously" swagger, the freshness of which wears off after about ten minutes. Saunders however enjoys and respects genre film structures even while savaging the manure that the individual works shove at us. Thus her satires explore why these forms attract us emotionally despite their cynical and corrupt applications.

Slags is a through-the-looking-glass retelling of film's only successful adaption of cyberpunk, Ridley Scott's *Blade Runner*. As narrated by the Rutger Hauer character (Adrian Edmondson with white hair and a German accent), *Slags* takes the cyborgs' viewpoint, turning them into juvenile delinquents for the *Mad Max* version of *West Side Story*, where the hooligan, rebel, "alien" Slags battle the blandly mellow and entrepreneurial Hawaiians for control of the turf, values, and soundtrack music of some vaguely futuristic colony.

Saunders fills your eyes and ears with all of the plethora of film history references we have lately come to expect, including sequences from *Psycho*, characters from *The Deer Hunter*, imagery from *Quatermass and the Pit*, and a thirty-second recap of Marlon Brando's career in which *The Wild One* meets *The Godfather*. But her manner of presentation is what separates her from the television generation pop culture jovials, a stunningly abrupt style that demonstrates for her lightweight contemporaries the actual meaning of the term "remote control." Her film references come whizzing into and out of the story with what appears to be an arbitrarily surreal randomness. But this first impression is only so striking because we have become dependent on having these references couched in all kinds of safety cushions. By pointedly eliminating all of the friendly context build-up and pause-for-laughs falling action, her montaged film allusions become quantum-leap recognition shocks, the disorienting effect of which destroys the self-satisfied pop culturist illusion that we are in control of this avalanche of images continuously being hurled at us.

Saunders' dwarfed, lonely figured amid forbidding, irregular landscapes, courtesy of director Sandy Johnson, become pawns for the story-telling devices that genre filmmakers try to make mythically totemic and enjoyably readable. But she turns these devices just enough so that you can continue to recognize what their functions are supposed to be even while they fail to take hold in ordinary, almost anti-climactic ways. So it is that the supposedly transcendental "Romeo and Juliet" lovers, Slags second-in-command and comic sidekick Little Sister (Saunders) and head Hawaiian Ricki (Anthony Head) are pictured in Saunders' version of romanticism as dewy-eyed chowderheads blathering at each other slightly misremembered pulp fiction cliches that they do not quite understand.

Similarly, Saunders' sense of highly structured dialogue, particularly her favorite trope of oddly rhythmed rhyming speech that sounds like jump-rope songs turned into prose, make dangerously discombobulated that which you once thought familiar.

> You're going to have real trouble walking all the way home in those shoes. In those high heely hikey spikey shoes. In those stiletto wetto high heely winkle picker licker shoes.

> They thought I didn't know—thought I wouldn't know and never would. But I did and I told everybody. And I laughed—and I really really

laughed. And they thought "He's not laughing at anything." And I wouldn't tell them what I was laughing at. And they would never know.

French is a culture clasher with a particular interest in behavioral detail. *Summer School* is a Chinese box of interlocking character relationships all ultimately exploring the gap between the conflicting demands of individual appetite and socializing restraints. Using a group of college students attempting to recreate and inhabit an iron age community in the middle of their university campus, French pictures her constant concerns, the ever primal needs for food and sex, slamming up against all of the many layers of organization we have created under the general heading of civilization.

Language becomes the centerpoint around which all of the myriad conflicts are played out. A pair of stripped-down lovers, referred to as Tarzan and Jane, who remain totally silent throughout the film, are played off against Peter Richardson's motormouthed make-out artist. The cultural disharmony between intellectual, verbal rationalization and elemental, physical action is all but summarized as Jane listens impassively to Richardson's ridiculous come-on pitch ("That's amazing. I had a twin sister named Jane. She died when her pram was run over") until Tarzan reappears brandishing the food he has captured for the day, causing Richardson to retreat in defeat. In another variation on the same clash, the quiet, thoughtful Liz (Saunders) wants the group to reduce its level of communication to what the iron age people would have known, while the pushy, paranoid Tark (Rik Mayall) wants to justify and codify rules that will allow the group to kill civilian students who wander into their village.

Nobody can ever strike the necessary balance between the two impulses for, as the other women in the group remind Liz, we cannot pretend that we do not understand about language. The group keeps sliding into the chasm between their instincts and their habits as they slink along the university's massive architecture, stalk their puny village stream for fish (spearing used condoms for their efforts), and finally, in desperation, raid the animal husbandry lab to satisfy their craving for meat. Their assumptions and rationalizations about what is primitive and what is sophisticated keep dancing around each other without ever merging. Ultimately, their night of "cave man" sleep-around mate swapping results in what appears to be a fatality stemming from implied homosexual sodomy and ends with a climactic panicky, giddy *Lord of the Flies* ritual sacrifice where the group's confusion between solemn recreation and high-spirited games-playing ("Yes, I can make fertility symbols from his teeth!") finally collapses into chaos.

French's approach to the material is very similar to the story she sets up. Like the students in the iron age village, the actors seem to have been

told what they are basically there to accomplish and then left on their own
to figure out how to get there. The actors are given a lot of space with many
of them, including French, doing variations on characters they have
previously created. Much of the dialogue has the unhurried spontaneity of
improvisation and is supported by Sandy Johnson, the chameleonlike
director of much of The Comic Strip's best work, shooting in a kind of
Warhol/Morrissey long-take style to capture the documentary developments. French is alone among the Comic Strippers in her willingness to
sacrifice tight structure and narrative drive in order to capture unexpected
character detail. A scene featuring Jennifer and Adrian Edmondson, who
are in fact married in private life, sharing their feelings the morning after
the mate swapping is lyrical by any standard and positively startling in a
Comic Strip film.

In *A Fistful of Travelers Cheques* the Sergio Leone heroes are challenged
in their macho posturings by the question: "Are you guys kidding?" They
respond. "Do we look like comedians?" Every person whose career is
writing and performing comedy sooner or later confronts this question for
it goes to the heart of their central dynamic—how will they express their
ideas through the medium of their personality? As performers, French and
Saunders are almost perfect embodiments of what they are communicating as writers.

French looks like a comedian. Short, plump, and robust, with a full,
generous mouth, big devilishly pixie eyes, and jaunty dancelike speech
cadence, she attracts instant audience rapport and has to go a yard further
than anyone else in The Comic Strip to make something snap back at us.

Saunders does not look like a comedian and, to make credible the
dim-witted Little Sister in *Slags*, wisely gravitates to a Mortimer Snerdlike
facial disguise. She looks rather like a slightly jaded ingenue, the sort of actress Hitchcock might have used as his "cool blonde" were he in his prime
in the 1980s. With her penetrating stares, minimalist gestures, and queasy,
toneless inversions of show-biz mendacities, Saunders is constantly striving to distance herself from the audience.

If you were only to see their individual writing and ensemble performances in The Comic Strip, it would never occur to you that French and
Saunders were primarily known as a comedy team. French's touchstones
are all sensual and tangible, Saunders' are all abstract and analytical.
French's expansive performance style grows to its full height only in the
presence of an audience, while Saunders' internalized style is best captured
by the camera. Yet when viewing their writing and acting teamwork in
their tandem Comic Strip film *Consuela* and the first block of episodes in
their BBC/A&E variety series, what had looked initially irreconcilable suddenly fits together like the dissimilar pieces of a jigsaw puzzle joining to
form a larger picture.

Given their contrasting methods, in cowriting *Consuela* it would naturally fall to Saunders to construct the plot and she would structure it as a movie parody, returning to her favored Hitchcock, the classical filmmaker who most closely reflects her own interests in self-analysis through film form and the sadistic expression of emotional retardation. *Rebecca* is the logical choice for the specific target, not only because it zeros in on a pair of female antagonists, but also because the gooey, gothic nature of the narrative allows Saunders, playing the second wife, to expound and expand on her "dumbbells enraptured" anti-romanticism.

Taking charge of the Mrs. Danvers character, French instinctively reinterprets Consuela's "strangeness" to be a reflection of her belonging to an opposing culture. Applying her incisive gift for accents, French's family retainer becomes the standard bearer of a clandestine clan from some non-specific Mediterranean country whose rivalry and hatred of Jessica, "the second Mrs. Saunders," is an extension of her vendetta against British/Western cultural arrogance.

All the way down the line French and Saunders' concerns weave in and around each other, widening the tapestry as the horror described by both the Gothic and Hitchcockian fear of a commanding id is defined as anxiety over being controlled by an alien race embodying incomprehensible values.

Jessica's dread and disorientation in confronting Consuela's way of life, expressed in typical Saundersian style by a flock of birds swooping down on her from out of a clear blue sky, is fed by such incidents as her capturing disjointed glimpses of Consuela and family's flamenco dance party in the manor pantry. Further, what is supposed to be the comforting control represented by the white male characters turns out to be Adrian Edmondson as the upper-class twit of a husband and Rik Mayall as his densely noble overseer, offering nothing more than infantile versions of social regression and repression. And these western values find their mirror-opposite reflection in Peter Richardson's portrayal of Consuela's manically lewd and pointedly silent brother (a character who resurfaces as the goony, Elvisesque guitar player Eduardo on the variety series) whose only function in life is to roll his tongue and eyes while unrestrainably groping every available female, like Harpo Marx overdosing on Love Potion #9.

French and Saunders are constantly finding ways to have their opposing styles play off each other. Ironically, the wellspring of these incorporations is that they both structure their visions in terms of a melodramatic and often fatal conflict: rebels vs. mainstreamers, nature vs. culture, Mediterranean vs. British. With their expansive understanding of theatrical form and individual psychology they are constantly merging, flip-flopping, and reversing these oppositions. For instance, the opposition between the characters in *Consuela* takes the form of a sinister and scary symbiosis which reaches a hyperbolically ridiculous level. For example, after announcing to Consuela a number of household duties she intends to accomplish only to discover that Consuela has already completed them, a frustrated Jessica says that she will go down to the lake to sketch some ducks, whereupon Consuela shows her some completed sketches and tonelessly explains, "I took the liberty, madame."

This push and pull of opposites is not only how they think individually and intersect their ideas, but also how they play with each other's performance styles in what almost amounts to practical joke inversions of each other's personas.

In *Slags*, Jennifer casts lovable Dawn as the gang's foul-tempered leader Passion. Scowling as if from a permanent migraine, with eyes rimmed in burnt cork and hair piled up like a cross between a Gibson girl and Kate Pierson of the B-52s, she looks like somebody transplanted into the future from a 1910 Griffith Biograph film.

In *Summer School*, French casts cold Saunders as the only member of the group anxious to engage in communal experimentation, as she remains endearingly good-humored and enthusiastic amid continuous rejection and miscomprehension of her desire to have the group invent their own prehistoric language.

This practice continues in *Consuela*, with Saunders playing the ever-increasingly hysterical second wife and French the mysteriously enigmatic housekeeper. But their presentation of the backstage "real life" French and Saunders in the variety series constitutes a double reversal since what they are doing here is reversing the roles they created in *Slags* with Saunders now playing the power-mad Passion and French doing the dopey tag-along Little Sister. As such, French now gets to do the punchlines in the patter versions of Saunders' jump-rope song dialogue:

> [after being released from prison and waiting outside the gate for the rest of the gang in *Slags*]
> *Passion*: Where are they?
> *Little Sister*: They're not here.
> *Passion*: They're supposed to meet us here.
> *Little Sister*: They didn't know we were getting out—probably because it was a secret. Did you know it was a secret?
> *Passion*: Yes, I knew.
> *Little Sister*: I knew it was a secret so you must have known that—
> *Passion*: —it was a secret, yeah. God, you're giving me a real buzzing pain in my head.
> [standing outside Michael Grade's office preparing to get hold of his ratings list to doctor their numbers upon entering in *French and Saunders*]
> *Dawn*: Jenn, should I do it carefully and secretly?
> *Jennifer*: Yes, good idea.

Dawn: Or quietly and stealthfully?
Jennifer: Whichever you prefer.
Dawn: I prefer carefully and secretly.
Jennifer: Yes.
Dawn: Jenn, quietly and stealth—
Jennifer: —I'm knocking on the door!

Their orientation towards reversals and oppositions also leads them to an almost perverse insistence on creating foreground/background tensions in what is usually the relentlessly flat-spaced world of the videotaped variety show. *French and Saunders* is one of the few examples in television variety history where you could use frame enlargements to illustrate the program's philosophic underpinnings. Not only do they offer sketches featuring their "background artists" characters desperately trying to attract the camera's attention (such as when pounding their prop typewriters behind the sportscaster's foregrounded desk), but will also pop up as themselves failing pathetically to blend in as background singer/dancers during Alison Moyet's musical number. (This sequence forms a fascinating cross-reference to Moyet's appearance on *The Lenny Henry Show* where her rendition of Marvin Gaye's "Hitchhike" was staged as a communal cast sing-along. Henry is, not coincidentally, French's husband and both shows are overseen by producer/director Geoff Posner.)

Even more to the point, they will set up unexpected, slightly unnerving developments like Saunders deconstructing an unctuous intro into the wrong camera leaving her standing off center in medium distance while French looms up, almost bursting into 3D, directly in front of the right camera to stage whisper to her partner about the goof. The whole shebang is probably best summed up by a similar intro segment where they come out on stage and the boom mike fails to pick up Saunders' umpteenth "ladies and gentlemen, we've got to stop meeting like this" in the foreground but stays on French who is busy calculating the days leading up to her period in the background.

In their second group of six episodes, French and Saunders abandoned the show-within-a-show backstage structure for a looser series of sketches, songs, and blackouts. This allowed the material to become more far ranging, but most of their work can still be broadly broken down into two categories: behavioral studies (e.g., their sly depiction of mischievous schoolgirls on a class field trip) and media parodies (e.g., their deadly impalement of morning news/talk shows).

Unfortunately we don't have enough tragedy for you this morning but luckily our own Dawn has informed us that her pet rabbit Thumper died this morning. So we'll be discussing that tragedy and trauma with Dawn, and asking experts whose fault they think it was and who is entirely to blame.

You can see French's domination in segments like the mock documentary profiles where they play ridiculously inappropriate characters like ballerinas or fashion models and exchange, muttered, trailing off comments about starving themselves on their latest diets. You can see Saunders' domination in most of the media spoofs as well as a sketch where they play a pair of furniture movers both named Jim, which contains stretches of her signature dialogue and turns mounds of styrofoam into science fiction landscapes.

But if you persist in following this line of reasoning too insistently you run the risk of trivializing French and Saunders' art and turning them into a parlor game. Ultimately, Jennifer *is* Dawn French and Jennifer Saunders and so is Dawn. And I, for one, wouldn't have it any other way.

13
"I'm Not Sure What Motivates Them"

The Gorgeous Ladies of Wrestling

The GLOW We Should Know

What in the entire wide world of television coverage ticks sports fans off the most? Is it 15 "heartbeat of America" ads during the first period? Commentators whose pithiest comment is "He's some kind of player?" Statistical breakdowns and career projections based on three previous appearances? The answer, according to "informed sources," is none of the above. It is television wrestling shows.

I have always shared that resentment against television wrestling until I stumbled over what looks like the results of a back alley mating between Charles Dickens and Sandra Bernhard—*The Gorgeous Ladies of Wrestling* (*GLOW*).

Why do most sports fans disdain wrestling? To many, wrestling is an inversion of competitive sports. Most sports begin as games that the press and public then overlay with their own wish-fulfillment fantasies in order to turn the games into melodrama. Wrestling begins with the situations and characters of melodrama and then, through its own devices, turns them into a game.

Melodrama in this context means a setup where one group of characters, representing the positive social values, are pitted against another set of characters who are out to destroy the fabric of the good society. Politically conservative melodrama usually has good guys who are law enforcers (e.g., cops, lawyers, etc.) who must subdue all kinds of challengers to the currently existing social order.

Television wrestling is melodrama at its most conservative and, when it is good, at the same time a spoof of the form itself. It is not surprising that wrestling has been at its most popular in the 1950s and 1980s, the two decades when the American society and its elected officials have tended to a world view of almost pure conservative melodrama.

Indeed, *GLOW* displays a stunningly expansive understanding of American melodrama. Its gallery of "bad girls" encompasses all of the culture's most repressive and xenophobic fears: Russians, ghetto blacks, Arab terrorists, uncivilized Africans, violent rock-'n'-rollers. But it is in its satiric countercurrent that *GLOW* truly distinguishes itself. Unlike other television wrestling shows, where the lack of variety in the nonstop blowhard posturing quickly wears you down, *GLOW* assaults you with a battery of media concepts, burlesque schticks, and musical comedy extravaganzas that manage to combine all of the best and worst aspects of MTV, *The Three Stooges*, and *Hee Haw* while imploding your existing understanding of television wrestling.

The matches follow the standard rules of America's melodramatic self-image. The "good girls" are brave and tough but fair; they play by the rules and rely on the referee to maintain order. The bad girls bring their favorite weapons into the ring (everything from billy clubs and nunchaku to spears and buzzsaws), backbite, rabbit punch, throw sand, and use black magic. Victory is the only form of honor for the bad girls and the infliction of pain is its own reward. But the way that all of this is played out constitutes one of the most complex and subversive expressions of good vs. bad morality portrayed in popular culture for quite some time.

The breakdown of moral certitude begins immediately with the depiction of the two male authority figures: *GLOW*'s promoter/commissioner/ring announcer David McLane, a sleazeball yuppie hustler directing his wrestling empire from a downtown Las Vegas phone booth, and the hangdog schlep of a referee (played by the show's head writer Stephen Blance) who looks like he is moonlighting from the croupier job he picked up after his lounge act doo-wop group broke up.

Each week's card of matches is preceded by the *GLOW* rap video featuring the entire cast bopping in and around the ring singing the praises of wrestling in general and *GLOW* girls in particular. Then, as the women are introduced for their matches, their solo stanzas intercut into their ring entrances.

Some of the cards are called by Howard Cosell–imitator Motormouth Mike Morgan; "monitoring moves and maneuvers." This is an inspired choice. Morgan has Cosell's mannerisms down perfectly (the weak attempts to impose personalized nicknames on already colorful figures [Dementia becomes "The Demented One"], the corny, out-dated sports lingo ["a fired-up Doll returns to the fray"]). But the use of Morgan as

Cosell also allows for full, straight-faced descriptions of what is actually happening in the ring ("Did she go for the bite? It was hard to tell") and places Cosell where he always belonged—on the side of melodrama rather than sports.

The other agendas are handled by *GLOW*'s gossip columnist, alleged hologram Sir Miles Headlock with color commentary by a guest good girl who is not on the current card. Tara the Southern Belle, a kind of Blanche DuBois with biceps, did her stint while on the disabled list. On an earlier show Tara was carried from the ring after Manna the Headhunter tried to remove her drumstick for a cannibal ritual. However, Tara cheerfully assured the crowd that the Headhunters had only sprained her leg and with therapy she would soon be back in action. These sessions tend to be less effective than Morgan's, relying heavily on pain pun patter. But they also have their moments of wacky metaphysics. For example, while watching the three most psychotic bad girls kick the bejabbers out of their opponents, Susie Spirit idly mused, "I'm not sure what motivates them."

Between bouts we are peppered with a steady stream of sideline schtick including one-liner insult locker room banter picturing the good girls schmoozing while applying their makeup or the bad girls cackling while swilling their ale, episodes of running comedy features such as "Angel's Hell's Kitchen" (a series of "waitress, there's a fly in my soup" gags), and even an occasional musical number. In one musical number go-go cheerleader Susie Spirit and regal Russian Colonel Ninotchka did an all-singing, all-dancing, all-body slamming version of "S'Wonderful" that demonstrated just how graceful these women are.

The locker room scenes present the good girls and the bad girls on the same moral and social level and the rap video pictures them as all part of the same family. Like the lyrics say, they're *all* champions in the ring.

The running comedy vignettes actually give a slight advantage to the bad girls. The good girls are generally pictured as a group of friendly airheads whose collective model would be the Goldie Hawn of *Laugh-In*. The best example is surfer-girl California Doll's idiotic philosophical "points to ponder" (her signature logo is a pasteboard cap adorned with a smiley face sticker). In contrast, the bad girls are shown mainly as a collection of world-weary cynics. Their model would be Nicole Hollander's "Sylvia," as best demonstrated by Colonel Ninotchka's "Easy as KGB," where she is continually frustrated by her dum-dum assistant Vladimir's inability to understand American culture.

Like most melodrama heroes, the good girls are disadvantaged by being primarily defined negatively, by what they do not do: break the rules. They have to contend with the limited number of images that society will tolerate as good girl behavior. Thus, only a few of them are allowed to show intelligence; the combination of beauty, brawn, and brains would be just too intimidating for the current culture. Most of the good girls are Southern Californian and or blonde, joined by a small variety of Miss America types and an occasional mother figure.

Some good girls are distinguished by their ability to absorb enormous amounts of punishment. Champs include the gallant Little Fiji (constantly being beaten to a pulp to counterbalance the invulnerability of her sister/partner, the 350-lb. Mountain Fiji) and Amy the Farmer's Daughter (a too-dumb-to-die superhick who continually invites justifiable pummelings with her innocently egregious pre-match chatter).

There was a movement to project a more aggressive aura onto the good girls. The main prong in the strategy was having the top ranking among the good girls shift from midwestern superpatriot Americana to Beverly Hills' Tina Ferrari, a hard-edged, glittery version of Doris Day in her "spunky" period. Ferrari's "Tips from Tina," sensible, pep-talk dating advice for low self-esteem women, was the only element of the entire show that was played straight.

Like most melodrama villains, the bad girls are larger than life, and they dive into their characterizations with gleeful gusto.

The liveliest presences are the Soul Patrol, a pair of raucous home girls from the Chicago projects named Adore and Envy. They handle the "Soul Patrol Hip Dictionary," a series of word-play gags based on street usage, with a barrage of expressive body gestures and expert verbal timing, and carry their powerful exuberance over into everything they do in the ring.

Envy and Adore are masters of the big, swift movements. They entertain the audience with their early power slams and kicks and, as they inevitably begin losing, with ending death staggers and agony screams (they specialize in winding up piled on top of each other for a double pin). Envy and Adore are gymnasts who bring the passion of a battalion of opera divas into each match. Their titanic struggle teamed with Angel against the Fiji sisters rivals anything in Moe Howard's oeuvre.

But, as forceful as the Soul Patrol is, the fact remains that there is not a single weak sister among the bad girls. Your particular favorites will no doubt relate to your own individual style and taste—from the mercenary marine Attaché, a kind of mean-spirited Bette Midler; to the playfully ghoulish Heavy Metal Sisters, Spike and Chainsaw, who maniacally shriek death threats while brandishing their namesake hardware; to top-ranked bad girl Colonel Ninotchka who handles her Natasha Fatale material with the haughty imperiousness associated with the classic "other women" of screwball comedy; and to the child-like psycho ax-murderess Dementia.

Dementia's talents, in particular, help point out the show's main failing. A silent character whose white-face make-up is often initially obscured by a *Friday the 13th* hockey mask, Dementia is an expert mime who in kinder, gentler times would probably be touring in *Godspell*. Her locker-room time is spent blowing bubbles (occasionally splitting them with her ax) and tending her dollie. But in the ring Dementia is able to more fully define her character with her deft bent-legged, small step walking, flailing forearms, and goggly-eye gestures.

The match plot lines can become wonderfully baroque. For example, in one episode Americana and Susie Spirit dedicated their bout to the inalienable American rights of free-will and individualism only to be turned into competing she-devils under the spell of the Princess of Darkness's magic mojo bone. In another instance, the Heavy Metal Sisters were carried into the ring directly from shock therapy, manacled together at the wrists and in hospital gowns. Chainsaw was still biting down on the rubber mouth block. But, with the exceptions of Dementia and the Headhunters (who do not speak English), little effort is made to combine the women's talent for movement and the particulars of their characters, and no effort is made to integrate both elements into the plot lines.

Still, you can't have everything. One season's cliffhanger ending had Colonel Ninotchka being awarded the *GLOW* crown after what looked like a draw with Tina Ferrari. A voice-over during the bad girls' celebration reported that after being named "announcer of the year," McLane had skipped to South America with his girlfriend Matilda the Hun and the *GLOW* treasury.

Every year is a new ballgame both for television shows and sports teams, and next season will no doubt bring changes in personnel and emphasis. Being based at the Riviera Hotel in Las Vegas opens all kinds of show-biz angles that *GLOW* has yet to explore.

The Games of Summer

Perhaps the most exciting aspect of watching *GLOW* is the early realization that everyone connected with the show has no shame. There is no concept too obvious or hokey for them to embrace, and, consequently, no flight of brilliance beyond their capabilities. Thus, inserted in some of the reruns is *GLOW*'s version of the trash sports "superstars" competitions—the "*GLOW* Summer Games."

Part of *GLOW*'s appeal is the stylistic tension between the choreographed wrestling and the documentary camera coverage that usually cannot quite capture all of the action, particularly in multiple women tag team bouts. The "Summer Games" reverses these tensions as the action takes prescribed camera routes and the women struggle to maintain their characterizations amid instinctive athletic competition.

In one summer season's first episode, the players were splashing around in the pool trying to push rubber rafts past their opponents, across to the opposite end, and out of the water. Pool activities are expected in something called "Summer Games." And, since the women wear even scantier outfits than their wrestling costumes, it is obviously very appealing for part of the core audience.

The audience, however, was not prepared for the next round of action. Since the teams' big women, Mountain Fiji and Matilda the Hun, are not exactly built for water sports, they were pitted in a pizza pie eating contest at the Riviera's in-house parlor. The challenge was to see who could wolf down five complete pies faster (Fiji competed with pineapple pizza and Matilda with sausage pizza).

Watching large people eat quickly is not exactly the most stimulating television event. In this instance, the viewer's anxiety builds—wondering what wackiness will develop, and, as time wears on, beginning to fear that nothing ever will.

As Matilda began to fall a bit behind, the goofy, hambone terrorist Palestina (who practically swallows the camera during her ring entrances) tried to register protests into McLane's microphone. The mike was not working properly and the audience caught snatches of what she was saying (for followers of the show this was not disconcerting since Palestina is constantly blathering on about something or other and at the best of times is only moderately coherent). But when Spike, and then Chainsaw, took up the argument we gradually understood that they were claiming Matilda had been cheated out of her choice of topping (she requested mushroom but was given sausage instead). Then, when Matilda threw a tantrum about being forced to eat dog food, the contest quickly degenerated into a shouting match and collapsed into a food fight.

The tough demeanors and implied violence in the wrestling matches can mask the fact of what is actually being presented here—a world of unending schoolyard arguments between characters who are simultaneously representing interpersonal, national, and international attitudes.

The pizza pie eating contest brought everybody down to their most primal level. Angered and disappointed by having her victory turned into a farce, the normally tolerant and jovial Mountain Fiji stooped to maliciously taunting her opponent by charging Matilda (who was busy demanding a rematch in which both contestants would use pineapple pizza), facing her eyeball to eyeball, and defiantly continuing to munch pizza and sip cherry cola. Even the commanding Colonel Ninotchka was reduced to making whiny complaints about how her hat had been damaged in the fracas.

Not surprisingly, *GLOW* is popular with children. They see their own world accurately reflected on the show every week. What they are not sophisticated enough to tell us is that they are also seeing the adult world accurately reflected as well.

AfterGLOW

The manner in which *GLOW* ended its second season hinted at major changes for the following year. *GLOW* and McLane parted company. McLane signed on with the American Wrestling Association and opened a mainstream women's wrestling unit, the Powerful Women of Wrestling. He brought with him a gaggle of *GLOW* girls, including Tina Ferrari, California Doll, Amy the Farmer's Daughter, Matilda the Hun, Attaché, Palestina, and Little Egypt (now known as Nina; Malibu; Brandi Mae; Queen Kong; Jeanne Beret, the Terrorist; and Yosmine Yurick, respectively).

This switchover constituted a major setback for *GLOW*'s producers, who then compounded the problem by failing to retain almost all of the rest of the practically perfect cast. Returning for the third season as "all new *GLOW*" were: Colonel Ninotchka, Mountain Fiji, and Hollywood of the bad girl street kid team Hollywood and Vine (Vine, who was still visible in some of the rap segments during which Hollywood was continually reaffirming their partnership, was one of the show's most sensual figures), writer/referee Stephen Blance, announcer Motormouth Mike Morgan, and bad girl team manager Aunt Kitty.

The show became a collection of blander, depoliticized versions of their original concepts played by an enthusiastic but decidedly second-string cast. As many of the new good girls tended to blend into the canvas, one gained a retrospective appreciation of just how compelling Tina, her flighty partner Ashley Cartier, Susie, and the rest had been to hold their own against such flamboyant opposition. McLane, who exuded the bubbly rancidness of a game show host infected by a diseased chipmunk, was replaced by a soft-voiced lounge singer-type who bore an eerie resemblance to Morton Downey, Jr. The new, homogenized bad girls did not carry weapons or drink alcohol in the locker room. And everybody was made to shill endlessly for the show's corporate sponsor, Fabergé.

The all new *GLOW* was not a total loss. A few of the newcomers (the gentle, Stan Laurel–faced giantess Daisy; rambunctious rock-'n'-roller Melody Trouble Vixen (MTV); and Pee Wee Hermanesque Zelda the Brain) brought life to the party, but even they could not compensate for the loss of their predecessors. While MTV was a lot of fun in her own right, she couldn't hold a blowtorch to Spike, let alone Chainsaw, and she pretty much embodied the mood changeover from hard-edged heavy metal to candy-assed disco.

The all new *GLOW* related to McLane's *GLOW* pretty much the way Shaun Cassidy's version of "Da Doo Ron Ron" related to the Crystals' version. But even in its middle of the road incarnation, *GLOW* was just about the most astonishing thing you are likely to see on non-cable television. The show still had its share of jaw-dropping moments although they now came almost exclusively when the matches became bizarre enough (Zelda and Major Tanya playing chess in the ring or the counterfeit Dementia and new rich girl Roxy Astor exchanging personalities under Big Bad Mama's voodoo spell) to carry the lightweight cast.

In the end all of these changes went for nought. *GLOW* completed its four year run and drifted off into the abyss populated by the formerly fashionable. Meanwhile its actual accomplishments have since become credited to its cult status successor, *American Gladiators*. It is now left to us lost Soul Patrollers to hold high the banner of the original *GLOW* and hope that the show, and all that it represented, will eventually be rediscovered. After all, as Scarlett O'Hara tells us, tomorrow is another day.

Afterword

Subjects for Further Research

The essays presented in this book have attempted to delve far beneath the surface of their selected topics on television comedy. The problem with the surface of television comedy is not scratching it, it is getting the chalk around its outline in order to determine its shape.

Our insatiable appetite for television has produced a nonstop avalanche of programming that continually adds to and reconfigures the dynamics of its history. Already some of the "current" programs discussed in this book are now securely lodged in television's historical past. It would be futile to attempt an up-to-date book about television. Even if such a project were continuously revised right up to publication date, so much would happen between the time that the last word was written and the first word was read as to render the book dated nonetheless.

Of more significant concern is how much of television's past is locked up in network and production company vaults or has disappeared completely. Nothing can be done about the bulk of live shows which were either never preserved on kinescope or whose kinescopes have been subsequently destroyed. There is, however, a huge backlog of filmed shows which have gone unexamined for decades. And until television history can get past its current "greatest hits" mentality the story of American television will not progress beyond the superficial generalizations that presently prevail.

I recently came across some episodes of an early 1950s sitcom version of the popular radio and stage property *The Bickersons*. This series, which starred Lew Parker and Virginia Grey as the ever-battling couple, ran counter to all of the accepted bromides about the bland and complacent family shows of the 1950s. The Bickersons are constantly arguing with each other and one of their formalized verbal routines culled from the stage or radio versions appears in each episode. But the narrative context created to explain their hostility pictures them as a couple of financial and social washouts who are desperately trying to maintain their marginal status within a suburban community that is constantly passing judgment on their standing. They are barely managing to hold on to their rinky-dink house (the ironing board doubles as their dining room table): he is in constant fear of losing the door-to-door salesman job at which he is a flop, and she is committed to spending as she pleases regardless of their financial situation. What's more, everybody else in the community is driving them further towards the edge with their callous disregard for anything that does not conform to the group's social status. Even the handsome young town doctor—the perennial symbol of community wisdom and tolerance—turns out to be a pompous, preening quack.

The Bickersons was produced by Bernard L. Shubert, who also gave us Topper and Mr. and Mrs. North. It was a syndicated series, meaning it never appeared on any network's schedule. That is pretty much the sum total of information available on this show since it is not listed in any of the standard television reference works, not even Vincent Terrace's excellent three-volume Encyclopedia of Television.

That the work of Terrace and other serious television researchers is available at all is only due to recent fashion trends in American culture studies that have elevated television to a level where it is now considered worthy of analytical examination. Unfortunately, the study of television has come almost exclusively from sociologists peering through their microscopes to decipher what the little people are inadvertently revealing about society through their taste in mass folk culture, or from polemicists who like the idea of a populist, vulgarian art to use as a club against the arid academic abstractionists. The main problem is that neither group has any interest in expanding the knowledge of television history since the more familiar a television show is to the majority, the better it fits into the schematics of their methodologies. This is not to say that both groups do not have valuable contributions to make to our understanding of television, but merely to suggest that the foot soldiers be allowed to finish digging the trenches before the generalists are brought out to survey the battlefield.

Even if control could be wrested from these groups, major philosophic changes in our approach to television history would have to occur before substantial progress could be made. If that old saw about history being written by the winners is true, then, in terms of pop culture, we still have not gotten over the Civil War. There is absolutely no excuse for the first chapter in television history to be so totally dominated by Milton Berle with Arthur Godfrey and Dave Garroway thrown in as footnotes. Nor is there any rationale for The Andy Griffith Show not to be given equal space with The Dick Van Dyke Show when discussing seminal 1960s sitcoms.

What is one to say in defense of assuming this attitude towards network television shows all of which were beamed into everybody's home regardless of sex, race, or regional origin?

But that is really just symptomatic of the much larger issue which, as Yogi Berra might have expressed it, is that history is written by the kind of sensibility that writes history. In terms of television comedy, this has always translated into the unexamined assumption that social issue comedy is *a priori* more profound than behavioral comedy and that verbal comedy is just as naturally more sophisticated than physical comedy. Again, while it is neither necessary nor even advisable to exorcize any of these attitudes, the fact remains that the examination of television history will not progress until other voices with alternative viewpoints are added to the chorus.

Specifically, the primary need is for a study that will have the kind of impact on television criticism that Andrew Sarris' *The American Cinema* had on film criticism. That is, a study that will present an entirely different prism through which television history can be interpreted. And, most importantly, a study that will elevate genre forms from their current status as formulaic hack work into respected traditions which need to be studied in order to define their formal properties and therefore make understandable the artists who worked within them. At the same time it is important that an analogous book on television avoid the kind of hierarchical groupings of shows' creators that Sarris built into his book. (Film directors were placed under such headings as "The Far Side of Paradise" or "Less Than Meets the Eye.") Sarris pointed out that the groupings were provisional and that no one's reputation should be set in critical concrete, but the stature of his book was such that these rankings came to be regarded as gospel—and further inclusions, rearrangements, or other revisions as heresy.

It was after Sarris and auteurism were added to the dialogue of film criticism that serious studies of the western, the musical, the gangster film, and the other staples of Hollywood filmmaking began emerging. It was then that the films of Ford, Hawks, Walsh, and all of the other directors lionized by auteurists began turning up in revival houses for public appraisal. And it was only then that elite venues such as the Museum of Modern Art put together sweeping retrospectives of film studios and filmic genres which finally provided the opportunity to see and evaluate the full scope of the American cinema without the dead weight of those predetermined status labels the films were assigned on their original release.

Unfortunately, it will be a far more complicated task to turn this trick in terms of television. There is no such thing as a revival house for television series. Even if we acknowledge the enormous expansion of opportunity that cable television has afforded the television historian, we must also acknowledge the limitations of its capabilities. Certain essays in this book might not have been conceivable without Comedy Central and Nickelodeon's Nick at Nite to help in the research. But even if a book such as this one piqued some interest in *I'm Dickens . . . He's Fenster* or *He & She*, the financial gamble for one of those networks to program the full cycle of their episode runs would be far riskier than for a company like Cinemax to drop two or three showings of Gerd Oswald's *Screaming Mimi* into its movie mix. And even if a cable network were willing to program a now obscure show such as *Valentine's Day* or *The Bickersons*, would the distribution rights holders be willing to look for the episodes in their vaults? And would they find them if they did look?

The best hope would be to generate academic interest in television history and thereby stimulate complacent institutions such as the Museum of Television and Radio (formerly the Museum of Broadcasting) to spearhead a movement to make the programs more accessible and thus more understandable. It is not simply a matter of collecting and projecting as many episodes of as many series as possible. Interviews, oral histories, and production records need to be gathered while the participants who created television history are still alive. The commentary of somebody like Leonard Stern who contributed in practically every era and to practically every form and style of television comedy would be invaluable. So would the views of somebody like Ruth Brooks Flippen whose work was more concentrated in a single era—the 1960s—and in a single form—the female dominated sitcom (*Bewitched, That Girl, Gidget*).

There is an underground network of individuals who sell, trade, and collect copies of television episodes on film and on videotape. There are certain sections of this book which could not have been written without this cadre of television enthusiasts. Unfortunately, these feisty individual entrepreneurs and the high-toned world of museums and universities tend to view each other with equal disdain. If television history is ever going to become a vital and expansive subject for scholars and public alike, these groups must join forces.

This book was designed to convey critical viewpoints as clearly and as forcefully as possible in order to help expand the ongoing dialogue between artists and audience. One section in Andrew Sarris' book was titled "Subjects for Further Research," and as an astute colleague of Sarris pointed out, *everybody* should be included under that heading. The same is true in the field of television. My fondest hope is that this book will stir further examination of the topics covered, other topics in the field of comedy, and other areas of television history.

Index

Boldface page numbers denote illustrations